Business Studies
A Level Workbook

Business Studies
A Level Workbook

DAVID NEEDHAM

ROBERT DRANSFIELD

McGRAW-HILL BOOK COMPANY

London · New York · St Louis · San Francisco · Auckland
Bogotá · Caracas · Hamburg · Lisbon · Madrid
Mexico · Milan · Montreal · New Delhi · Panama
Paris · San Juan · São Paulo · Singapore
Sydney · Tokyo · Toronto

Published by
McGRAW-HILL Book Company Europe
Shoppenhangers Road, Maidenhead, Berkshire SL6 2QL, England
Telephone 0628 23432
Fax 0628 770224

British Library Cataloguing in Publication Data
Needham, David
  Business Studies A Level Workbook
  I. Title II. Dransfield, Robert
  658

  ISBN 0-07-707607-9

Library of Congress Cataloging-in-Publication Data
Needham, David
  Business studies A level workbook / David Needham, Robert
Dransfield.
      p.   cm.
  Companion vol. to: Business studies.
  Includes index.
  ISBN 0-07-707607-9
  1. Business – Problems, exercises, etc. 2. Industrial management
– Problems, exercises, etc. I. Dransfield, Robert. II. Title.
  HF5351.N39 1993
  650'.076 – dc20   92-43624
                                                                 CIP

1234 TL 9543

Typeset by Wyvern Typesetting Ltd, Bristol
and printed and bound at Thomson Litho,
East Kilbride, Scotland

Contents

Introduction

The *Business Studies A Level Workbook* has been written to support *Business Studies*, our comprehensive A level text. In all of our books we have been keen to emphasize the practical nature of business education by making a wide variety of experiences available for both students and teachers that are designed to improve the value of the learning experience by making them both more interesting and memorable. This book has been written as a practical students' guide to business studies activities. It is mainly designed for A level courses but may also provide a useful source of ideas, experiences and materials for teachers delivering BTEC National courses in business and finance, post A level business courses, NVQ and GNVQ level 3 business courses and any other courses at a similar level.

The text contains 18 chapters. The first two provide advice for students on developing case study techniques and writing essays for business studies. Chapters 3 to 16 cover a wide variety of business studies areas and disciplines that roughly follow the order of those presented in business studies courses. Each of these chapters include:

- a brief introduction to each area;
- five case studies with supporting questions;
- three suggestions for practical activities;
- three essay titles with suggested answers;
- twenty essay titles;
- twenty short-answer questions;
- advice on project work;
- suggestions for further reading.

To determine the emphasis, needs, order and content of the above, we talked to many teachers and students and asked them about the sort of resource they felt would be both necessary and useful for the classroom and that could be used by students as a practical revision guide. Their ideas have been incorporated into this text.

Chapter 17 is concerned with integrated case analysis. There are two lengthy case studies in this chapter, both of which indicate a mark allocation, as well as a third integrated study. Chapter 18 provides answers to short-answer questions as well as marking schemes for the two long case studies appearing in Chapter 17.

This book has been designed to provide a range of materials that students can use both in and out of the classroom and during each stage of a course. Our aim has been to provide a text that supports business studies and which students and teachers alike will use regularly to reinforce the learning experience. It has been extensively researched and provides a range of materials from a vast array of sources. We hope that such experiences will provide users with a valuable insight into the world of business studies.

David Needham
Robert Dransfield

Acknowledgements

British Coal Corporation
British Gas PLC
British Standards Institution
British Steel PLC
Darlington College of Technology
Director
Family Expenditure Survey
Marketing
Martin Coles
Nottingham Trent University
Pegasus Group
Shell UK
The Independent
The Independent on Sunday
The Nestlé Company Limited
Unilever PLC
United Biscuits

1

Developing case study techniques

Why use case studies?

Business studies is concerned with the dynamic world in which all organizations have to exist and in which most of you will have to work. By its very nature it is an area of constant change—we hear daily of events that have taken place in the business environment.

Case analysis is a device that can be used both in and out of the classroom to accurately analyse how organizations respond to such constantly changing circumstances. It will help you to realize that business studies is not just theory; it also involves application.

A case study is a description of an actual organization's situation or of a specific event affecting the business environment. Analysing the case therefore involves an element of realism that bridges the gap between the classroom and the commercial world and enables you to apply your understanding to a practical situation. The purpose of such analysis is to:

- enable you to understand the forces underlying business activities;
- appreciate the various factors that govern decision making;
- provide a means by which you can develop problem-solving skills;
- enable you to apply quantitative tools;
- encourage you to recognize the significance of information;
- provide an opportunity to work in groups;
- encourage you to think about values, generate ideas and make practical suggestions.

Applying background theory to a case study will help you to become an active rather than a passive participant in the learning experience. It will help to make business studies more practical, generate greater realism and, ultimately, develop a genuine interest in the area. All of this should lead to a greater depth of understanding and improved examination successes.

Real people, real problems

It has often been said that case studies are an effective learning mechanism because they encourage *an inductive approach*. That is to say, the reader acquires the knowledge of, and need for, theoretical concepts by means of example, rather than by the more traditional method of being given a theory that is then supported, or 'proved', by example. Though a lot of business studies involves the use of common sense, like any subject you might study, it possesses its own unique language. By using case studies, you might see the common sense first, which can then be reinforced with theory afterwards (see Fig. 1.1 opposite).

The example shown in Fig. 1.1 was used with a group of A level students to introduce competition theory. Having presented them with the materials, they were asked to consider the following questions:

- Why did RoadCar move into Barrowby?
- What were the company's short- and long-term objectives?
- What about Reliance? Explain their reaction.
- What advantage might each company have?
- What factors would determine the likely outcome?

The students were then asked to write a newspaper report looking six months into the future and to comment upon the likely changes. They had to relate what they had learned about competition to other products and other sectors. Having looked at examples of competition, theory was then built into the course and students could immediately identify with its importance.

By observing events in the media and others affecting your everyday lives, you should find that business studies will help you to think about why things happen and become a medium through which you can find out more to improve your understanding of events and rationalize their causes.

Developing your case study techniques

Case studies can be taken from a variety of sources: they may be extracted from newspapers, magazines and professional journals; they may relate to international events, nationally recognized organizations; they may even be fictitious. Another feature of case studies is that they can vary quite a lot in terms of ease of comprehension. Some are fairly straightforward, only requiring a cursory analysis, while others will be highly complex and require considerable thought.

Always *read through the study carefully* before you attempt to answer any questions. If necessary, read it several times to make sure that you understand it. It might also be useful to *make brief notes* of the key elements in the study to serve as a reminder of what has taken place and help you analyse the evolution of the events.

When reading through the study, *try to think about the sorts of questions you may be asked*. Consider the areas the study covers, the work you have covered in these

Battle on the buses

A bus war has broken out around Grantham, giving villagers a super-service of six buses an hour.

Lincolnshire RoadCar has moved into Reliance's patch in Barrowby (a village on the edge of Grantham), slashed fares and given residents in the village a service they can hardly believe.

The long-established Reliance operation gave Barrowby people four buses an hour into town. Now Lincolnshire RoadCar has introduced a Road Runner service, upping the numbers by two an hour between Barrowby and Grantham.

It has set the scene for a battle between the established operator and the newcomer. In the Reliance corner is owner Joe Simmons, with 20 buses, while in the RoadCar corner, the company, which is part of Yorkshire traction, has more than 600 buses.

Joe Simmons has delivered 1000 leaflets to Barrowby homes stating that his service is reliable and well-known. RoadCar has chopped 5p off the 40p fare into town and Mr Simmons has matched the price cut. Mr Simmons is furious that the RoadCar schedule sees its Road Runner at bus stops just five minutes ahead of his service.

RoadCar is unrepentant and a spokesperson said, 'These changes are another step in the steady increase of our bus services. The introduction of the Barrowby route is just an extension of our success in other areas of the town.'

'If you think for one moment that will scare me, you've got another think coming!'

Figure 1.1 Battle on the buses. (*Source*: Reproduced courtesy of the *Grantham Journal*.)

areas, how the study relates to topical issues of the day, other examples of the same issue and so on.

Think, too, about *the integrated nature* of the study. To what extent has the study you have read pulled together elements from different parts of your course?

Read each question carefully. Ask yourself, what does this question require? If necessary, briefly *plan out* your response in rough, but, if you do this, remember to show the rough notes, particularly if a series of arithmetical calculations are involved in response to an accounting question.

If *mark allocations are indicated, look at them and use them.* For example, if a question asks you to make a series of points and is allocated eight marks, you can expect the mark allocation to be four marks for points made—one mark each point—and then one mark for describing each point made. Similarly, if two marks are allocated for a definition, you must try to identify the two elements of the definition that will gain you the two marks, one each.

Try to *answer questions fully.* Do not just list points, think about how you can expand your answer. Providing lengthy descriptions will add substance to your answer and enable you to pick up extra marks.

Use examples and analogies to support your case analysis wherever it is practical or feasible to do so. Such examples will serve to convince the marker that you have understood the area of analysis.

Wherever necessary, *refer to the text.* Questions will vary in level of difficulty and some might require you to refer to specific parts of the case in order to assess your comprehension of it.

When answering each question try to think about *the theory necessary* to enhance your answer. It would be a dreadful mistake to assume that all of the answers are in the study. Though this might happen if the study is being used as an inductive device to introduce a specific area in the classroom, in general, in a test you will be required to support your answer by showing a greater understanding of what you have been taught as a whole and how you can apply it to particular situations.

Do not be frightened to use *common sense, ideas and practical suggestions* in your answers. The case study is intended to put you in a realistic situation and so a realistic and practical response is perfectly acceptable, as long as it does not contradict established theories (unless you can logically support your assertions).

Always *read through your answer* at the end of each question and try to assess the value of your contribution. If you want to think further about your response and come back to it at a later stage, leave a space.

Case studies have become an exciting vehicle for learning and, in examinations, a creative means of assessment. In the real world, we rarely deal with business problems cold—we go and talk to the people concerned, we look at the problems with which they are faced and start with the details of their particular situation. Case analysis enables us to replicate the real world in this way in both the class and examination room.

2

Writing essays for business studies

The importance of essay writing

In recent years we have seen the introduction of an increasing variety of assessment techniques, including coursework, objective questions and case analysis. Though such changes of approach have led to less emphasis being put on essay techniques, being able to write good essays is still a crucial skill for A level students as they provide an invaluable guide to each candidate's ability to tackle complex issues in an effective way.

Few people would ever claim that essays are easy. They are not and, indeed, would lose their value as an assessment device if they were. Essays are designed to find out how you have responded to learning experiences. They allow you to describe something fully, show a depth of understanding and analysis and express your ideas clearly, logically, realistically and relevantly.

We will all come across situations in our professional or personal lives where we will be asked to make a statement, write a reference, send an article, make an assessment, write an appraisal, write a report or whatever. All these situations will require us to use written skills based upon our own knowledge, understanding and experiences of an issue or some research, a belief or maybe something we have witnessed. Sound writing techniques are useful, if not imperative, in all these instances. Though essay techniques are extremely useful in the school or college environment, their usefulness is not limited to this context. The skills developed can be transferred to any situation that requires a degree of written analysis.

Developing your essay technique

Before writing an essay you must ask yourself 'Do I fully understand this question?' Different types of question will require different degrees of thought and different types of response. Try to identify what it is that the question requires and remember to respond specifically to these requirements in your answer. Some essay titles are a little like a puzzle and so working out a solution might involve reading between the lines.

5

Look at the title. What are the key words in the title? (See Fig. 2.1.) Make sure that your answer responds specifically to these key words.

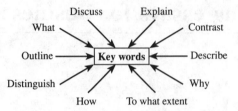

Figure 2.1 Possible key words in essay titles.

Plan your answer before you start to write your essay. Though you might think that planning may take up valuable time that could otherwise be spent writing, it will, in fact, help you to improve the structure, and therefore the quality, of your answer. For example, how many times have you written an essay and then, towards the end of the answer remembered something that you should have put in at an earlier stage in your response? Planning:

- helps you to structure your answer so that it is presented in a logical sequence;
- gives you a little time to think and rationalize before writing your response—it is sometimes easier to take a breathing space and think about the essay beforehand, than to try to think about your answer while you are actually writing;
- can be used to make brief notes that you can then follow in your answer;
- can be used as a revision device—looking at a series of essay titles, such as those that appear in this book, and writing plans for them is a useful way of revising for an examination.

Always *introduce your answer*. Try to show the marker that you fully understand the requirements of the question in your introduction. Respond directly to the question and, if necessary, make appropriate definitions at this stage.

When writing your answer, think carefully about how it is likely to be interpreted. *Try to make it interesting.* One way in which you can do this is to constantly refer to examples or analogies. There are usually marks for such examples as well and, by using them, you are showing the marker that you take notice of the business media and have an interest in the area. You can collect such examples during the course by cutting articles out of newspapers, filing them under different chapter headings or putting them in with your notes, then use them to support your revision programme.

Do not be frightened to use your own thoughts and ideas in your answer. An essay is an opportunity to show the marker that you can think, so it is perfectly acceptable to include your own ideas to support your response, as long as they are realistic. It is also acceptable to philosophise about such ideas. Be careful, however, not to stray away from the question and not to spend too much time putting forward your own viewpoint at the expense of generally accepted theories.

Make sure that your answer is relevant. Too often students spot a key word in an essay title and then fill the essay with *everything* they associate with that word. It is a bit like using a blunderbuss to shoot a rabbit! Be specific in your answer and target it at the question. Do not put in irrelevant material as it just wastes time and does not win you any marks.

Try not to make lists in your answer. When you do this you are not explaining the points you make fully. Marking schemes usually have one mark for making a point and then at least another mark for expanding on it. The only time it is acceptable to list is if you are running out of time.

Learning to write an essay in a given period of time is an important skill to develop. Many students, particularly those who have always written slowly, can find this extremely difficult. As all teachers will confirm, the announcement that there will be a timed essay next week will elicit the biggest groan from students. However, having to practise this will prove invaluable. As part of your revision programme, *undertake a series of timed essay responses* and ask your teacher to mark them.

Try to evidence *wide-ranging knowledge in your answer.* Remember that revision from just *one* source—either your notes or your text—is a little bit narrow. Try to use a variety of sources and then evidence the uses of these sources in your essays. During your course, you should, ideally, support your classroom notes with notes taken from background reading. It is also sometimes useful to learn a few short but key quotes that you may have a variety of opportunities to apply. If you cannot remember them exactly, then paraphrase them rather than leave them out if they are particularly relevant.

Many essays will require you to *integrate* business disciplines that you will have been taught separately. Be prepared to amalgamate information and use skills from a variety of different areas in your essays. For example, if an essay asks you to assess a particular change, you might be required to mention the process of decision making, investment appraisal, market research, current external factors, such as the economy, and so on.

Always *conclude your answer* with a rational summary of the response you have developed in your essay. It is sometimes useful to relate your conclusion to the question to show how you have answered it.

If you have missed points out of your answer, put them underneath your essay and key them into the appropriate place with asterisks.

Always *read through your answer* after you have finished it and make corrections and amendments where necessary. Checking does not take long and it may provide you with the opportunity to gain extra valuable marks.

Even if you remember all this and put it into practice, writing essays will never be easy, but developing and using sound techniques such as these, after some or practice, should help you produce an end result of which you can be proud.

3
Background to business studies

A business is a decision-making unit that sets out to produce a product in the form of a good or service (see Fig. 3.1).

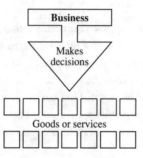

Figure 3.1 The function of a business.

Any business that we study operates in a complex environment of changing forces that are interdependent. A summary of some of these environmental factors is diagrammatically represented in Fig. 3.2.

The economic system is particularly influential in either inhibiting or enabling

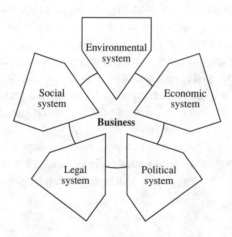

Figure 3.2 The business environment.

businesses to operate in certain ways. In a free market, consumers make their own decisions about what they will buy or how much they will sell at given prices.

Business units will have different aims and priorities, but making a profit is a prerequisite for survival and development in the long term.

Today most people in industrialized countries are engaged in the service sector of the economy. Manufacturing has been revolutionized by new technology and is capable of producing high outputs at low unit costs. People generally have a much higher standard of living than ever before, but a sizeable minority live in poverty: income and wealth are still poorly distributed.

Business can be seen as a power house, generating new wealth in an economy. Business studies is concerned with exploring the decision-making processes in which individuals, groups, enterprises, communities and nations engage.

Case Study—The fall of Communism

Slavenka Draculic, the Yugoslavian writer tells how she finally realized that there was no future for Communism in her book *Forward to the Past*. She argues that Communism foundered in a soggy mire of scratchy brown lavatory paper. She describes the coarse, dark sheets of 'Golub' she used in her childhood, then the soft, pink rolls eventually achieved by 'socialism with a human face' of the 1970s, then the day, in 1985, when she stood with her 17-year-old daughter in a chemist's shop, arguing bitterly because the recent price rises meant that they had had to go back to Golub. Her daughter refused point blank to adopt this symbol of poverty and Draculic knew then that it was all over: 'This was how the Communists lost: when the first free elections came in May 1990, the entire younger generation voted against Golub, against shortages, deprivation, double standards and false promises'.

The collapse of Communist regimes in Eastern Europe in the early 1990s had, according to historians, many complex causes.

In looking for political causes, they point out that Mikhail Gorbachev, who became leader of the Soviet Communist Party in 1985, allowed criticism of the state after 50 years of repression. The process of *glasnost* (openness) made the workings of the government less secretive. This allowed new political parties to set themselves up. New nationalist groups, such as those in the Baltic republics, began to demand independence. This *glasnost* spread through Eastern Europe like a wildfire.

However, perhaps the most important factor behind the fall of Communism has been the failure of the economic system. Communist parties failed to achieve one of their central objectives—to improve living standards.

For 60 years the Soviet Union had a highly centralized economy: most of the important decisions were taken by the central planners in Moscow;

prices were set by government rather than by the actions of consumers and producers.

It was Stalin who originally introduced the policy of centralization. During the 1920s and 1930s, Stalin rapidly expanded industrial production and brought most firms under state ownership. He also introduced a system of 'collectivized' farming. Land owned by better-off peasants was confiscated and turned into large holdings owned by the state or collectives of peasants so that eventually 99 per cent of all land was eventually collectively or state owned.

At first the system was successful in industrializing the Soviet Union, providing full employment and boosting food production. In the long term, however, it stifled enterprise because all decisions were taken centrally. Bureaucrats began to build their own empires and lose touch with the needs of consumers.

Industries tended to become concentrated so that, for example, the Ukraine produced much of the iron, steel and coal, while the Baltic republics specialized in producing electrical goods.

Raw materials produced in one part of the country had to be transported thousands of kilometres to be processed in another, which wasted time and energy. Agriculture suffered from shortages of machinery parts and difficulties in transporting produce. Energy resources were wasted recklessly. For example, in many towns, central heating systems were switched on and off from a central point so that individual householders had no control over the temperature in their own flats.

Emphasis was placed on military expenditure and scarce resources were channelled into this area. Levels of productivity in industry were low compared to those in the West, so Eastern bloc countries began to run up large trading deficits.

Although everyone was employed, underemployment was rife so that people were spending many unproductive hours at work. Prices rose faster than wages and living standards were relatively low. People had to queue for basic goods such as bread, butter and meat. Many goods had to be bought on the black market at inflated prices.

In the summer of 1991, the Communist system in the Soviet Union was overthrown, to be replaced by a Commonwealth of Independent States. Mikhail Gorbachev was replaced by the more radical reformer Boris Yeltsin.

On 2 January 1992, Yeltsin introduced a radical programme of free market reforms. In the first few weeks, observers were able to watch the literal collapse of Russian society as the reforms hastened a process of change. Prices of most goods surged as much as 300 per cent as price controls were swept away. Millions of Russians were condemned to poverty overnight. Controls over on milk, bread, oil and gas and transport were initially left in place and then raised by 300 per cent to bring prices in line with supply and demand.

The aim of this sweeping price liberalization programme was to eliminate inflation and introduce the market at every level of Russian economic life.

Based on the Polish model, the theory runs that, if prices are left to find their own level and the money supply is held broadly constant, then inflation will be crushed. Prices will soar, attracting goods into the stores,

MONTHLY INCOMES	Roubles	
Russian pensioner	342	$2.73
Teacher	500	$4.00
Space mission controller	600	$4.80
Retired KGB agent	750	$6.00
Surgeon	1,200	$9.60
Government minister	4,000	$32
Private music teacher	25,000	$200
Miner	30,000	$240
Russian entrepreneur	100,000	$800
Landlord	125,000	$1,000
Foreign correspondent	750,000	$6,000
ON THE MARKET		
Meat	250	$2.00
Potatoes	25	$0.20
Sour cream	100	$0.80
Green salad	10	$0.08
Mandarin oranges	80	$0.64
Narcissus	35	$0.28
IN THE STATE SHOPS		
Bread	5	$0.04
Milk	8	$0.06
Eggs	20	$0.16
Child's bicycle	800	$6.40
Coat	1,900	$15.20
Suitcase	20	$0.16
IN A COMMERCIAL SHOP		
Cigarettes	100	$0.80
Liqueur	500	$4.00
Perfume	600	$4.80
Leather jacket	15,000	$120.00
TRANSPORT		
Flight to Kazakhstan	784	$6.27
Train to St Petersburg	160	$1.28
Ride on a Moscow metro	0.5	$0.04

Figure 3.3 The relationship between incomes and prices in April 1992 in Moscow. (*Source: The Independent on Sunday.*)

but demand will collapse, eliminating long queues because the prices of many goods will simply be too high for ordinary Russians.

Eventually (according to the theory) demand will recover in response to the shock administered to the supply side of the economy. Prices will stabilize and inflation will subside.

The programme of reform has been coupled with extensive privatization: handing over to private hands small and medium enterprises, housing, local transport, shops, trading companies and construction. Large enterprises, however, and the energy sector, defence, communications, tobacco and alcohol production have remained in state hands. The ultimate aim is to privatize large tracts of the economy.

Figure 3.3 on page 11 shows the relationship between incomes and prices in April 1992 in Moscow.

A survey by the International Labour Organization has predicted that 45 million workers in the CIS, a third of the entire labour force, are facing unemployment in 1992 because of the switch to a market economy. According to the ILO, 15 million will formally lose their jobs and 30 million in the state sector will be so chronically underemployed that they will, to all intents and purposes, be jobless.

The difficult thing about the changes in Eastern Europe is that there is no charted path to the creation of a market economy. Poland experimented with drastic reforms in its 'Big Bang' of 1990. Although inflation was firmly subdued, the country continued in a state of recession and still remains depressed in mid 1992. The government has had to revert to state subsidies. It is argued that it is very difficult to develop a market economy where there is no previous background of private enterprise. The ordinary people of Poland had no concept of competition or profit.

(*Source*: *The Independent on Sunday*)

Questions

1. What do you understand by the terms:

    * market economy
    * underemployment
    * *glasnost*
    * centralized economy
    * competition
    * price controls
    * subsidies
    * price liberalization?

2. What do you consider to be the strengths and weaknesses of the Russian economy in its journey along the path of market reform?

What are the main external opportunities and threats? How could the strengths be used to good effect and the weaknesses minimized?

3. How successful has the Russian economy been in moving along the path to market reform? (Study press reports.)
4. How effective is the 'Big Bang' method of creating market reform? Is there an alternative?
5. Does the decline of central planning indicate that free enterprise is the most effective way of making economic decisions?
6. If the availability of soft toilet paper was to be used as the judge and jury of market reforms, what would be the verdict to date?

Case Study — The breakup of a central planning system

The burdens of the free market are weighing heavily on the director of the Minsk motor bike factory, Konstantin Ustymchuk.

'Business is very bad', he said with a long sigh. 'The economic ties that held the old union together are broken and the commonwealth is not working.' Supplies of metal and other components from Russia (Minsk is in Belorus) for his motor bikes and bicycles are running at 65 per cent of what he needs and from the Ukraine only 10 per cent is available. Republics are not trading raw materials as before.

The freeing of prices has forced Konstantin to put up the cost of the 125 Minsk motor bike — one of three in large-scale production in the former Soviet Union. It now costs 11 000 roubles instead of the previous year's 900:

'Can a human being afford that on a salary of 2000 roubles or even 4000 a month?', he asked. Sales are down, so the bicycle production line is being expanded and the motor bikes cut back. Konstantin has sent 'scouts' in trucks roaming the republics for spares and components being hoarded by manufacturers with little luck because they want to be paid in dollars.

(Adapted from an article by Peter Pringle in *The Independent*, March 1992.)

Questions

1. What barriers to a free market are highlighted in this report?
2. How is the motor bike factory responding to new market forces?
3. What further changes might the factory need to make if it is to survive?
4. What changes are required in the wider economy if firms like this are to survive?

Case Study—Environmental care and the creation of jobs

In January 1992, the Department of Employment's *Employment Gazette* reported that the maintenance of stricter environmental standards in industry will be an important source of new jobs and skills in the 1990s. This sector of the economy will rise by 8.5 per cent per year.

Stricter pollution controls are also likely to cause job losses because the adoption of stringent production standards will increase industry's costs. However, studies in other countries show that there will be a net positive effect on employment.

Almost half the companies in the UK's pollution control industry are involved in dealing with water pollution, 27 per cent with air pollution, 18 per cent with waste management and 7 per cent with restoring contaminated sites (see Fig. 3.4).

Figure 3.4 Industrial pollution—dereliction.

Pressure for higher environmental standards comes indirectly from consumers and directly from legislation. Britain's Environmental Protection Act (1991) puts the responsibility for waste not only on the producer but on everyone who handles it. Companies have to be able to demonstrate that they use the 'best available techniques not entailing excessive cost' to minimize pollution.

Questions

1. How can the growth of the environmental sector of the economy improve living standards for different individuals and groups in the economy?
2. In which major sector of the economy would you place the environment?
3. What do you understand by the terms:

    *   direct pressure
    *   indirect pressure
    *   net positive effect on employment
    *   pollution control industry?

4. Describe ways of implementing 'best available techniques not entailing excessive cost' that could be (or are being) used in your school or college.

Case Study—Does an economy need a manufacturing base?

'In the long run, an economy which has lost its manufacturing base has lost its vital centre. This is because it is only manufacturing that creates something new, which takes raw materials and fashions them into products that are of more value than the raw materials that they are made from. Services depend on manufacturing. When manufacturing prospers, all industries connected with it prosper—not only are more components, parts and salesmen needed, but also more accountants, more dentists, more petrol stations, more supermarkets and more schools.

When the manufacturing engine of an economy stalls, all these things are in less demand. You do not build dentists' offices or department stores unless you have a population with the resources to take advantage of them—and these resources can only come from jobs that add real value to goods—that is, manufacturing jobs.'

(Address to Institute of Directors, 1989, Akio Morita, Chairman of Sony.)

Questions

1. Do you agree with Akio Morita that manufacturing is the engine of the economy? Explain.
2. Do you agree with Akio Morita that 'these resources can only come from jobs that add real value to goods—that is, manufacturing jobs'?
3. Can you rewrite the article to argue that *services* are the engine of the economy?

4. What dangers are there from having too large a service sector?
5. What dangers are there in having too small a service sector?

Case Study—Employment by industry

Study the chart shown in Fig. 3.5.

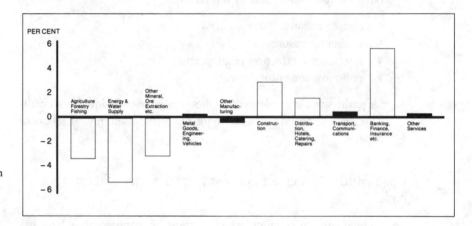

Figure 3.5 Employees in employment by industry (standard industrial classification) Great Britain percentage change September 1988–September 1989. (*Source*: Department of Employment.)

Questions

1. Can you classify the job sectors shown into the primary, secondary and tertiary sectors of the economy.
2. What underlying trends in the changing distribution of occupations is shown.
3. Have these trends continued into the mid 1990s? What has caused changes?

Activity

Carry out a study of a company to examine interdependence from a number of angles:

- How are individuals within the organization dependent on each other?
- How are processes within the organization interdependent?
- How are departments within the organization interdependent?
- How is the organization dependent on other external organizations?

Activity

Study a system that operates within an organization:

- What are the inputs into the system?
- What are the outputs that the system produces?
- Is the system controlled or regulated (for example, a central heating system is regulated by a thermostat to keep temperature at a required level, stock may be automatically re-ordered by a firm's computerized stock control system and so on)?
- What quality control mechanisms are used by the system?
- Is the system part of a larger system? Explain.

Try to illustrate your answers by drawing the systems you observe in diagrammatic form.

Activity

Try to find out from a small local company what its major objectives are:

- Are these objectives published anywhere?
- Are there some unwritten objectives?
- How does the organization go about meeting these objectives?
- How does the organization review its performance in meeting these objectives?
- What does the organization do if it fails to meet (or exceeds) its targets?

Essay title 1—Why has the service sector of the economy become so important in advanced industrial societies?

You may want to start off by explaining what is meant by:

- advanced industrial societies, such as using measures, say national income per head, output per head, size of service sector and so on; and
- service sector, which is the sector of the economy concerned with providing services to industry—insurance, banking and so on—and to people—health and education, for example.

You should then go on in the body of the essay to explore the growth of services in relation to manufacturing.

As manufacturing has become better (not just in improving quality and efficiency but also in responding to environmental concerns and other challenges), it has also become smaller. In every advanced nation, industry employed a smaller proportion of the work-force in 1990 than it did in 1980; in virtually every nation, it also contributed a smaller proportion of their gross national product (GNP). Everywhere, the slack has been taken up by services. It was in 1959 in the United States that, for the first time, the service sector of a nation became larger in terms of GNP than the industrial sector, but, in 1992, the service sector in every country is much bigger, contributing 69 per cent of the GNP in the United States, Britain and France, 63 per cent in Italy, 59 per cent in Germany and 56 per cent in Japan.

There are three broad reasons for this shift. One is that as societies become richer, they choose to spend a higher proportion of their income on buying services rather than things.

The second is that it has so far proved very much harder to wring additional productivity out of services than out of manufacturing. Greater productivity in a car plant means more robots on the production line: the product does not suffer, indeed, probably the reverse. However, if greater productivity in a school means fewer teachers in the classroom, quality of education suffers immediately.

The third is that, as countries become richer, they are able to 'export' their profits in the form of investments in other countries. It is evident that a number of countries have invested in manufacturing in new developing industrial countries. In turn, the rewards are returned in profits, interest and dividends that can be spent on leisure and services.

There is no sign at all that shift of demand towards services will cease. Indeed, there is a powerful reason to expect it to accelerate, namely the ageing population in industrial societies. The proportion of people over 60 will continue to rise in every developed country for at least a generation. By 2020, more than 30 per cent of the population of Germany and Italy will be over 60. Older people are most likely to spend their income on health care, holidays and domestic services.

The countries that increase living standards most quickly in the future will be those that can improve the way they run service societies. Services can be divided into four main groups: financial services and distribution tend to be in the *private sector*; health and education tend to be in the *public sector* and technology can be used to transform each of these areas. In financial services we will see, more than ever before, the development of paperless money. Financial services are becoming increasingly tailored to the needs of individual customers. In distribution, the benefits of bulk retailing are likely to be grafted on to much wider swathes of the industry with resultant cost-cutting. In health, technological advances have led to people living longer. The focus of health care will now shift to raising the quality of care and fitness throughout people's lives. Education, too, will become a continuous process, involving people of *all* ages. Workers can expect to be retrained to take on completely different skills several times during their careers.

In conclusion, you can then show that the service sector has become particularly vital today and that it is a state of revolutionary progress. The progress of manufacturing technology has been a tremendous achievement this century. Every year, manufacturers have found ways of designing, producing and selling better and better products, allowing us to enjoy a higher standard of living, better leisure opportunities, and a wider array of services than ever before. As we move into the twenty-first century, it is the service sector that is most likely to experience revolutionary change. Improvements in services will improve our standard of living.

Essay title 2—The collapse of centrally planned economies in the Eastern bloc proves conclusively that production takes place most effectively in the free market. Discuss.

This essay needs to be handled with caution. Many commentators have found fault with the old bureaucratic-style systems that prevailed in the Eastern bloc. However, it is unlikely that market forces will provide a quick-fix for the situation that arose once these systems were dissolved. Indeed, economies actually operating a freer market system, such as the United Kingdom, plummeted into the vortex of a world recession. It is all too easy to provide solutions to other people's problems; it is not so easy to find them for your own.

A useful starting point to the essay could be to chart some of the failures of centrally planned systems:

- heavy-handed planning and control stifles individual enterprise;
- the process of planning itself uses up scarce resources in administration and supervision;
- the absence of the profit motive removes the spur to individual effort and enterprise;
- in command economies, the process of communication between consumers and producers can become distorted so that goods do not meet consumer requirements;
- price controls lead to the emergence of black markets;
- factory managers hog scarce resources in order to meet production quotas, often wasting inputs.

All of these criticisms have been widespread during the 60 years that central planning operated in Eastern Europe. Poor-quality goods arrived at the wrong places and where the goods were wanted, there were long queues and many potential consumers were turned away empty-handed.

At the end of the day, these economies failed to meet the rising tide of expectation among consumers and were overthrown by a tide of dissatisfaction.

However, the transition to a free market has not been a smooth one. It will take a long time (a decade or more) before the new republics can achieve even halfway stable conditions in which a market economy can operate. A number of commentators argue that countries like Poland and the Commonwealth of Independent States have tried to move too quickly to reform. It is perhaps a mistake to forge ahead with the things that *can* be done quickly—freeing prices and introducing the right to conduct private businesses and trade, for example—without preparing those that take more time, such as privatization and the breakup of state monopolies to create vital competition, banking reforms, company law and administrative reforms.

After two years of Draconian reform, the new Polish Prime Minister Jan Olszewski stated that Poland was close to a catastrophe and moved back to *some* price controls and state subsidies. A survey carried out by the International Labour Organization in Geneva predicted that 15 million workers would lose their jobs in the first year of reforms in the Commonwealth of Independent States and 30 million others would be seriously underemployed. The liberalization of prices caused most pain to pensioners, the low-paid and people on fixed incomes. For those who could afford it, the free markets, where peasants sell their produce, offered an abundant supply of fruit, meat and vegetables. Those Russians with access to dollars, such as employees of foreign companies, private business people, taxi drivers and corrupt police officers and criminals hardly felt the price rises.

Clearly, there are many benefits to be gleaned from a centrally planned economy and these should be looked at in the essay:

- effective long-term strategies can be developed for the system as a whole;
- planning can be carried out to meet collective and individual needs;
- duplication can be cut out;
- resources and products can be shared out more equitably;
- a safety net can be provided for all citizens, including guaranteed employment and subsidized food (cheap bread for everyone);
- the system can be shaped in such a way as to reflect the social and political wishes of a collective of people.

Having established some of the main strengths and weaknesses of central planning, you should briefly explore the alternative forms: the free market economy and the mixed economy.

You could set out some of the key advantages of a free market:

- production reflects consumer choice;
- the system responds to changes in demand and supply;
- individuals have freedom to make demand and supply choices;
- resources are not wasted on administering the system.

However, it should be pointed out that so-called market economies have been dogged by periods of boom and recession. The economist John Maynard Keynes argued convincingly that there is no 'invisible hand' at work to ensure investment in an economy. Keynes, and many subsequent thinkers, have accepted the necessity for *some* kind of planning if unemployment is to be controlled. It is essential for government to act as a make-weight in an economy that lacks self-righting properties. Governments throughout this century in so-called market economies have intervened decisively in economic affairs. This is nowhere more noticeable than in times of recession. It seems inevitable that if Eastern bloc countries are to move towards an economy of market forces, they will still need to lean heavily on government interference in the economy.

Essay title 3—A company needs to look to its bottom line? Discuss.

Most people would agree that business organizations need to carefully consider the relationship between costs and revenues in order to make profits. Clearly, companies in the private sector need to perform for a number of interested parties.

Shareholders are the owners of companies. The Board of Directors and managers need to constantly have the shareholder at the back of their minds because, when shareholders are worried about the immediate or long-term future of their investment in an enterprise, they may withdraw their funds, leading to a crisis of confidence.

Managers are also important. The success of a company will be reflected in the managers' salaries and the prestige attached to their positions. Employees are a crucial part of the team. Most employees will want job security, recognition, rising pay over time and many other benefits.

Consumers are another vital link. Only companies that make profits can plough back investment into research and development. Companies that meet consumer needs best will need to keep ahead of the field.

Businesses will also gain credibility if they are able to contribute to the community by sponsoring charitable events and by paying taxes to the government. Profit is, therefore, highly desirable on a number of counts.

At this stage of the essay, you could briefly show what is meant by the bottom line by sketching out a simple profit and loss account and indicating the importance of published financial information and how it is reported in the press.

In the central section of the essay, you can refer to different aims that businesses may have, such as:

- profit maximization;
- sales maximization;
- prestige;
- survival;

- as a hobby or interest;
- satisfying needs and so on.

It is important to stress, however, that, in the long term, if a business is unable to make profits, then it is difficult for it to pursue other objectives. In competitive markets where there are only a few firms operating (oligopoly structures), it may be highly important to strive for maximum profits that can be ploughed back into market leadership strategies. If a firm fails to do this, it can suffer severe damage as a result of competitors' strategies.

Profit maximization must be explained in terms of the context of external factors. For example, maximum profit must be coupled with tight health and safety and other government criteria. If a firm tried to ignore these external criteria it would very soon find that its short-term profits were translated into heavy fines, which would cut into margins.

The bottom line is, therefore, highly significant, but consideration also needs to be given to how profits can be sustained over a longer period, rather than merely maximized over the short period.

In addition, most business structures can be seen as being based on a coalition of interested groups. There are a number of internal groups within a business whose interests might be widely divergent—employees, managers and shareholders, for example. External interests will include consumers, governments, pressure groups and other producers. Goal formation will involve a balance of interests. Profit maximization is likely to mean different things to each of these groups. Establishing objectives, therefore, involves compromising some interests for the sake of others that are more important.

Essays

1. Is a relative or absolute weakening of the manufacturing sector a problem for the British economy?
2. The free market system is best for everyone. Discuss this assertion.
3. Is profitability the best indicator of business success?
4. Do businesses need to operate in an environment based on consensus?
5. There is no clearly charted route to the market economy. Discuss.
6. What is the purpose of a company?
7. 'The business of business is business!' Discuss.
8. Why might a business *not* seek to maximize profits?
9. What are the major structural changes taking place in the British economy during the 1990s?
10. How is an ageing population likely to affect the business sector of the economy?

11. How does the economic system turn inputs into finished outputs?
12. Discuss the view that interdependence is a fundamental feature of business life.
13. Why does the government intervene in the economy? Illustrate your answer by examples.
14. 'Resources should be concentrated where they are most effective.' Discuss.
15. 'Scarcity requires choice.' Discuss.
16. Can governments spend money on the behalf of individuals more wisely than if individuals were to spend that money for themselves?
17. Why is structural change important in modern societies?
18. What is the most effective way of allocating scarce resources?
19. How does specialization benefit 'third wave' societies?
20. Who do businesses serve?

Short-answer questions

1. What are needs and wants?
2. What is meant by opportunity cost?
3. Define money.
4. What properties should money have?
5. List three command economies.
6. Define production.
7. What is meant by de-industrialization?
8. List three primary, secondary and tertiary occupations.
9. Distinguish between relative and absolute poverty.
10. Why are resources 'scarce'?
11. What is 'teleworking'?
12. What is meant by 'structural changes' in the economy?
13. What is a 'third wave' society?
14. What is the fundamental difference between conflict and consensus theories?
15. What is meant by ideology?
16. What are the three basic economic problems facing all societies?
17. What are the three main types of economic systems?
18. What do consumers vote for in a free market economy?
19. What is the 'goods sector' of the economy?
20. What is meant by sales maximization and profit maximization?

Projects

Some projects you might like to do are:

- study the Standard Industrial Classification and carry out a survey of people in your area to find out how they fit into the classifications, then analyse your results and draw up charts, graphs, tables and so on;

- study newspaper reports over a period of time to examine the development of a particular country towards a market economy;
- talk to a small group of managers about the objectives of their companies, make comparisons and draw out common threads.

Suggested reading

Draculic, Slavenka, *Forward to the Past*. Chatto and Windus, 1990.

Edwards, Ann, *Filling in the Background to Business*. McGraw-Hill, 1991.

Jones, Ken, and David Taylor, *Directory of Business Studies Resources—National Educational Resource Information Service*. Pitman, 1989.

Needham, David, and Robert Dransfield, *Business Studies in Practice* (2nd edn). McGraw-Hill, 1992.

Stefanou, Rosemarie, *Understanding Industry Now* (2nd edn). Heinemann Educational, 1991.

Whitehead, Geoff, *Business and Enterprise Studies*. Butterworth Heinemann, 1990.

4

Businesses in the private and public sectors

Fundamentally, a business is a formally constituted body that is set up to achieve particular *objectives*.

Any one business will be an example of a particular type of organization and will need to have an organizational structure. In the United Kingdom, the most common forms in the private sector are sole traders, partnerships and companies. In the public sector there are still a number of public corporations that are owned by the government on behalf of the people.

When a private-sector organization is taken over by the government, the process is known as *nationalization*. When a public-sector organization is turned over to private ownership, the process is known as *privatization*.

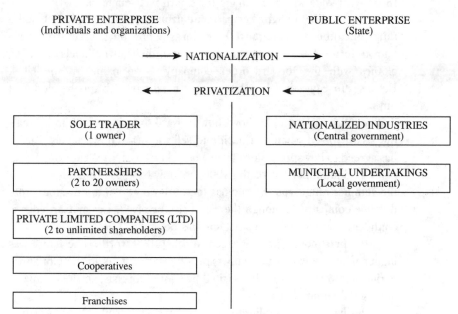

Figure 4.1 Types of business in the private and public sectors.

Case Study—Should I continue as a sole trader if I wish to expand?

Lesley Cartledge and her friends always found it frustrating not being able to buy fashion clothes in their home town of Bakewell. Lesley says that young people in Bakewell are quite 'with it' and resent having to travel 20 miles into Sheffield to find shops that sell the kind of fashionable clothes they like.

After leaving school, Lesley went to college where she became very interested in bookkeeping. As her experience in this field grew, she started her own bookkeeping business and provided a service that was especially valuable for small firms. However, with her interest in clothes and her business knowledge, it seemed a natural step to set up a boutique in Bakewell at the end of 1987.

Lesley's knowledge of the market was based on her own and others' experience in trying to buy fashionable clothes in Bakewell. With this knowledge and using her bookkeeping skills, she put together her business plan. This showed that she could do well with her own shop. She was fortunate enough to be able to lease one of the most attractive shop sites in Bakewell, in a cobblestone courtyard close to the town centre.

She calls her business 'In-Style Clothing' to project the modern image of her clothes. Lesley herself is 21 and In-Style's target market is those 18–35-year-olds who are looking for smart, well-made clothes.

At first, Lesley bought her garments from stock houses (which sell a range of clothes to boutiques). However, she now buys direct from well-known forward-order companies that sell their own 'labels', that is, clothes with the forward-order company's own name on the label. Because 'In-Style' is a new business, it must pay cash for the clothes it buys.

The following example shows how forward ordering works and reveals the risk involved when you decide to sell the best-known labels. Lesley has agreed to buy spring stock from a label known as 'In Wear'. She has to place a minimum order worth £4000, not only for the spring range but for the summer range, too. So she has to put down £8000 to buy stock from this one company. Although there is a risk involved, Lesley Cartledge is confident that she can sell what she has bought.

In the first month, she managed to sell £1000 worth. The figure was higher than she would normally expect because it took in the Christmas period. However, Bakewell is visited by a lot of tourists, so she is expecting a good summer season.

Lesley has worked out her forecast and expects to sell £60 000 worth of goods in her first year. She is able to do this because of the style of the clothes she sells and the lack of competition.

The main costs of setting up in business were:

- stock—clothing at £8000;
- rent and rates (quarterly outlay) of £1300;
- solicitor's fees, decoration and other starting costs of £1000;
- on top of this she has to pay electricity and phone bills each quarter, as well as other minor expenses, such as window cleaning.

Provided that Lesley can keep up a steady turnover, she could make a healthy profit.

Questions

1. Make a list of what you consider to be the advantages to Lesley of operating as a sole trader rather than taking on an alternative form of business.
2. What are the main risks that Lesley runs?
3. Lesley is now thinking of starting up a young man's fashion shop in Bakewell (18–35-year-old age group). Such a shop does not exist at present. By opening one—and so buying more clothes from suppliers like 'In Wear'—Lesley will be given much bigger discounts. Which of the following recommendations would you make to Lesley (give detailed reasons):

   - employ someone to manage the men's shop on a day-to-day basis while continuing to do all the administration herself;
   - employ a manager with full responsibility for running all aspects of the men's shop;
   - take on a partner and together become joint owners of the two shops, sharing all the responsibilities and the profits;
   - continue with her existing shop and put all her efforts into the women's clothes side;
   - another alternative?

Explain why you think that the alternatives that you have rejected are unsuitable.

Case Study—Nationwide consumer cooperative

In the summer of 1992, the first nationwide consumer cooperative since the nineteenth century was set up. The cooperative is designed to cut out supermarkets and deliver cheap, organic produce to consumers' doorsteps.

The initiative was modelled on Japan's Seikatsu Club, which provides 'environmentally friendly' products to more than half a million people and preaches 'Political Reform from the Kitchen'.

Among the supporters of the new cooperative are a number of organic farming organizations and agricultural research associations. A register of organic growers has been set up. The new cooperative aims to cut out wasteful packaging and distribution costs and deliver organic food at no more than the price of conventional food. (At the time it was up to 50 per cent more expensive.)

The cooperative raised £50 000 on interest-bearing shares, each valued at £50 or more.

Consumers have been organized into groups of at least six households who submit regular bulk orders and maintain regular contact with suppliers.

The Seikatsu Club was founded in Japan in 1965, buys food, 'real milk' and phosphate-free washing powders and has a growing influence in local politics.

Questions

1. In what ways can the development of the Creative Consumers' Cooperative be seen as a reaction against modern industrial society?
2. What benefits will be gained by members of the organization?
3. Is a cooperative likely to be the most effective form of organization for such a venture?
4. What factors are likely to influence the success of the cooperative? Relate your answer to both external and internal influences on the business.
5. To what extent could it be argued that this enterprise has found a gap in the market that cannot be met by existing forms of distribution?

Case Study—Grouping by function

A modern food processing plant is organized along functional lines. Most of the employees work on production tasks in the factory itself under the direction of the Factory Manager.

The plant is responsible for the manufacture of food products that are retailed throughout the United Kingdom by a major High Street food retailer. Many of the jobs carried out in the plant are: Accounts Assistant, Laboratory Manager, Quality Assurance Manager, Engineering Manager, Maintenance Manager, Packaging Buyer, Development Technologists, Technical Manager, Factory Manager, Production Manager, Production Planner, Hygiene Manager, Financial Accountant, Senior Accounts Clerk, Payroll Clerk, Purchase and Sales Ledger Clerks,

Management Accountant, Personnel Manager, Personnel Officer, Personnel Assistant, Nurse, Laboratory Manager, Laboratory Technicians, Product Development Manager, Development Chef, Kitchen Assistants, Buying Manager, General Manager, Shift Supervisors, Hygiene Supervisors, Production Line Employees.

Question

1. Try to set out a management structure (organization chart) to show how employees performing the tasks could be organized along functional lines.

Case Study—Docks deregulation 'detrimental to efficiency'

The abolition of the 'jobs for life' Dock Labour Scheme in 1989 may have taken the industry 'back rather than forward', according to the first independent report on the subject by Cardiff Business School. The School surveyed 200 organizations handling 70 per cent of UK traffic.

The report pointed out that the reintroduction of casual labour and the 'fragmentation' of the industry could lead to instability because there are too many ports and operators, overcapacity and underuse of capital. (At the time of deregulation the government had promised that there would be no return to casual labour.)

Abolition has also cost the taxpayer far more than the original estimate. Around 6600 registered dockworkers out of the original 9319 had each taken up to £35 000 in redundancy money by April 1992. Half of this money comes from the government. The government had originally said that the scheme would cost £25 million; so far it has cost £141 million.

The report concluded that, 'Deregulation and more intense competition in the industry has generated greater instability and, in many respects, made it more difficult for management to cultivate employee loyalty and commitment, other than through the fear of losing traffic and consequently jobs'. Industrial unrest has now become commonplace in the industry.

At the time of deregulation, the Conservative government had stated that the new freedoms for employment would stimulate investment. The authors of the report found, however, that no new appreciable investment had been thus prompted. Further, because new investment was largely undertaken by larger organizations, the proliferation of smaller companies may actually have had a detrimental impact.

Abolition of the Dock Labour Scheme has led to far greater flexibility in the work-force, where a core work-force can be supplemented by temporary workers. Working hours are flexible and employees are also expected to do any work ordered by management.

Questions

1. Who stands to benefit from the abolition of the Dock Labour Scheme? How would they benefit?
2. Who stands to lose out from the abolition of the Dock Labour Scheme? How would they lose out?
3. How could the government calculate whether the abolition of the scheme has been good for the country or not?
4. What evidence is given in the article that the government had originally underestimated the costs and overestimated the benefits of the abolition of the scheme?
5. What evidence is provided in the article that having many small ports may have its disadvantages?
6. What general principles can be drawn out of this article that have application for other forms of privatization?

Case Study—Private cash sought for new NHS hospital

Private developers are being invited to put up the money for a new £100m National Health Service Hospital in Newtown. The aim is to use private money to build a new 870-bed hospital in well under half the time it would normally take. In return for putting the cash up front in a project that could involve designing, building and equipping the hospital in as little as three years, the developer would, on completion, receive four NHS sites totalling more than 50 acres.

The Newtown, Basewell and Kidborough hospitals, with a total of 850 beds, are on three of the four sites. When the new hospital opens, they would close and the developer could then use the property for housing or commercial and retail development.

The scheme could be used as a test case for others so that new facilities could be provided by private capital investment with lower running costs.

John Bright, the manager of Newtown Health Authority, said that because health authorities at the moment are prevented from borrowing, it would take anything between 10–15 years for Newtown to get its new hospital built in stages, under present NHS investment arrangements.

'Under the new approach it would be possible to get the whole hospital built within three to five years,' Mr Bright said. A modern hospital on one site would release £2.5m of the health authority's £64m budget to be spent on better hospital and community services. 'At the moment we are having to run three intensive care units, three sets of operating theatres, three of everything. It is just not an efficient way of doing it,' Mr Bright added.

Questions

1. Who stands to benefit most from the proposed change? How will they benefit?
2. Who stands to lose from the proposed change? How will they lose out?
3. Do you think that the proposed change is justifiable? On what grounds?
4. Would the new arrangement for paying for the new hospital be a good thing for the people of Newtown?

Activity

Study an organization that you belong to, such as a club, team, or work organization. How effective is this organization? Start off by finding out what the objectives of the organization are:

- How are the objectives of the organization communicated to members?
- Are members aware of these objectives?
- How does the organization set out to meet its objectives?
- How does it measure the achievement of objectives?
- What does it do to remedy any failures to meet objectives?

Look at the organization in terms of the following categories:

- *Unity of purpose*: does everyone work to a common aim?
- *Effective leadership*: what are the strengths and weaknesses of the pattern of leadership.
- *Flexibility*: is the organization able to change when things are not going well?
- *Operational efficiency*: how well are operations monitored and evaluated; is there a global picture of operational efficiency?
- *Interrelationships*: does each member of the organization know their rights and responsibilities to each other?

Present your findings in the form of a report to the governing body of the organization with recommendations for improvements.

Activity

An organizational chart may set out a hierarchical structure and span of control for a large organization. This hierarchy can set out whom is responsible to whom. In addition, job descriptions will set out the responsibilities of each member of the organization:

- Look at an organization chart for a company.
- Try to find out how accurate a picture it gives of the way in which decisions are made in that organization.
- In what ways does it give an *accurate* picture and an *inaccurate* picture of the way that decisions are made in the organization.
- Is the organization chart helpful?
- Who is the organization chart primarily of use to?
- Is it possible to draw up a new organizational chart that more accurately reflects the way in which the organization is run?

Activity

Study an organization currently being privatized. Try to find out the following information:

- When will the privatization take place?
- Who were the old owners and who are the new owners of the organization?
- Who is handling the privatization?
- Is the privatization taking place all at once or is it being phased over a period of time?
- Who are the main supporters and opponents of the privatization?
- What are the main arguments for and against the change?
- Who stands to benefit and who to lose from the change?
- Is it possible to take up a neutral position to weigh up the advantages and disadvantages of the change?
- What are the main changes that will take place as a result of the privatization?

Essay title 1—'Public services today are accountable to the general public.' Discuss.

In recent years, the shape and style of management in the national public sector has changed enormously. Today, *all* three major political parties emphasize the role of accountability in the public sector. Labour attacks the Conservatives for the effect that privatizing monopoly utilities has on customers; the Conservatives accuse Labour of continuing to be more interested in the providers of, say, education and health than in the patients, parents and pupils who consume these services.

Both parties intend, across a broad range of services, to lend a new significance to output and performance measures. Providers who have only recently started measuring their performance in a detailed way may soon find that they will be penalized for failing to meet targets—public transport providers for example. From the Metropolitan Police Office to English Heritage, social security to Companies House, senior civil servants routinely speak about 'customers' and 'markets'. They run their own budgets and implement their own devolved decisions.

During the late 1980s and early 1990s, more than half of central government's work-force was hived off into 'Next Steps' executive agencies. Large areas of public sector enterprise have, additionally, been transferred to the private sector—a shift that none of the political parties would change.

More important than these structural changes, however, is the profound and continuing cultural change. From 1979 onwards, managers in government were repeatedly told that they were sluggish, inward-looking and even incompetent in comparison with their equivalents in the private sector. Public-sector managers were accused of being wasteful, unresponsive and resistant to new ideas.

This is rarely the case today. In schools, hospitals, transport organizations and many other areas of the public sector, business planning takes place today in a detailed way. Public-sector managers are explicitly defining tasks, pinning down who is responsible for doing them, measuring whether they have been done and how well and establishing clearly what they cost, as well as controlling the cost.

Consumer expectations are rising. As the customers of public services become aware of what is possible, they have started to demand higher quality. The Conservatives responded by introducing their Citizen's Charter, which places new demands on public-sector managers to meet given performance indicators in terms of the standard of service they provide to their customers. The Labour Party has proposed a quality commission for local government and education and incentive funding for the health service.

Ten years ago, managers would have argued that, because many public services are necessarily monopolistic, it would prove impossible to introduce effective performance measures equivalent to the competition in the private sector. Today, however, public-sector managers have increasingly devised sophisticated ways of measuring their progress against themselves, over time. Probably the biggest single change in government is the realization that the civil service tended to concentrate on covering its back against ministerial complaint. The devolution of executive responsibility means that decisions are being taken much closer to the customer. Powers have been passed from central powers to government servants working close to consumers.

Responding to consumers' wishes is never easy. The very large consumer base for public services is made up from many different segments. For example, in the Post Office, different kinds of customers have wishes that conflict. Professional people want speed, pensioners want time to chat with the person behind the counter, mothers with young children want accessibility. Similarly, the necessary absence of competition in some public service roles creates incentive problems. It makes little difference to turnover if you make a Post Office shop look more appealing; someone wanting to cash a giro cheque will have to use the Post Office whatever it looks like.

Equivalent difficulties regarding the value of 'customer' definitions have been posed throughout the public sector. Who are the 'customers' of the prison service, for example? The Courts? The police? The public? The prisoners? Ministers?

Nevertheless the very act of tackling these issues has gone a long way to helping civil servants clarify their own role. Management devolution has been welcomed by many in the public services. Surveys of staff at the sharp end of delivery unearthed considerable frustration and plenty of ideas for improving services. Today these issues are being explored internally by public-sector organizations. Undoubtedly great progress is being made towards public accountability.

Essay title 2 — What makes an effective organization?

Clearly there are many possible answers to this question. Emphasis needs to be placed on the words 'organization' and 'effective'.

A useful starting point is to show that an organization is a formally constituted body that sets out to achieve a particular objective. It is in the pursuit of objectives that organizations will prove to be effective or not.

At this stage of the essay, it would be helpful to set out some examples of possible objectives that organizations might have, as well as pointing out that organizations have both primary and secondary objectives. While a football team might set out to win promotion to a higher division, it might also seek to entertain spectators, so that gate receipts are maximized. A firm that seeks to maximize profits might also make it a priority to keep its work-force well paid and contented. Some organizations will be primarily concerned with health care and education while others will set out to sell hot dogs on a Saturday night. In the business sphere there are a range of possible objectives to be considered, such as profit maximization, sales maximization, market leadership, satisfying objectives and many other alternatives. In establishing objectives, different groups and individuals — both internal and external to the organization — will need to be considered (shareholders, managers, employees, customers, competitors, neighbours and so on).

Effective organizations will need to consider long-term as well as short-term results. Many organizations that appear to have got it right have failed to be effective in the longer period. The boom period of the 1980s threw up many such examples, including Polly Peck, Maxwell Corporation and Sock Shop.

An effective organization will need to coordinate its strategic and operational planning. The long-term vision of the company will need to be translated into high-level organization of operational detail.

An effective organization will need to plan effectively, implement policies and practices effectively and evaluate its decisions and operations effectively. Successful evaluation will then need to be fed back into the next phase of planning and implementation.

The success of an organization will rely on the correct combination of the following ingredients:

- *Unity of purpose*. All parts of the organization should be working towards a common aim because, if parts of the organization work in different directions, this can be very confusing and bad for morale.
- *Effective leadership*. Positions of authority and responsibility in an organization should be vested only in those who are capable of putting them into effect. Decisions can only be implemented if those in authority have the confidence and determination to see that they are carried out.
- *Flexibility*. An organization should not be too rigid. It should be able to alter course quickly if things are not going right and adapt to changing circumstances.
- *Operational efficiency*. This means that the operations that a company carries out must be studied and the results of this analysis used to ensure that things are done in the best way possible. At one level this will involve studying each operation and function separately to see that time is not wasted, that costs are kept down and that work is done accurately, and so on in order to ensure a smooth operation.

   At another level, the whole functioning of the organization needs to be studied at a global level. It is important that the various parts of the organization work smoothly together and in the same direction (this is called overall efficiency).
- *Interrelationships*. Each member of an organization needs to understand clearly his or her rights and obligations with regard to other members. Lines of authority and communications need to be clearly defined and acted upon.

In conclusion it needs to be stressed that there is no simple model for effective organization. When the work that an organization handles is routine and programmed, it may be possible to organize set procedures and methods for doing things (such as is done when running a prison or for various activities in the army).

However, in fluid situations, decisions may need to be made by managers 'on the ground', for example, in dealing with an unpredictable factory accident or a unique overseas selling opportunity. Today there is an increasing trend in large organizations to de-layer the command structure, to give more powers and responsibilities to grass roots managers. Of course, the development of information technology (IT) has been of great value in realizing this aim. Modern information systems provide individual decision makers with access to unprecedented quantities and qualities of information (as well as the means to rapidly process that information by means of expert systems, for example).

Finally, the essay should indicate that *no* organization can be effective if it fails to meet the needs of the people that belong to it and who it works for. Time and time again it comes to light that organizations that are effective in the long term are 'people organizations'. We are all familiar with organizations ranging from departments in schools to nation states that have been successful in the short term under charismatic leaders with little concern for those around them. In the longer term, however, such organizations are rarely (if ever) effective.

Essay title 3 — How can a business idea be turned into a business?

This is an interesting title. It focuses on (a) the business idea and (b) the business.

Nearly everyone at some time or another thinks about setting up an enterprise of their own. You will hear people say things like, 'Someone could make a fortune out of selling such and such' or 'If I had some money, I could run a business making this or that'.

However, the business *idea* will only be turned into an effective *enterprise* if it is carefully *organized*.

All too often, people fail to organize themselves properly so the good idea never gets off the ground or else falls at the first hurdle.

In the early part of the essay you should look at the genesis of business ideas. People start their own businesses for a variety of reasons:

- some have a bright idea that they think will make them rich;
- others find themselves unemployed and start their own business to survive;
- some are only happy when they are their own bosses;
- others want to make a particular contribution to their community and can see no other way of doing it except by setting up on their own.

Some ideas are new, others are copied:

- some ideas arise from spotting a gap in the market;

- some ideas are copied from other countries and areas;
- some ideas are brand new inventions;
- some ideas are adaptations of existing products;
- some ideas simply involve turning an existing interest or hobby into a saleable product.

There are others, too, so use familiar examples to illustrate each of these and other points.

The next part of the essay should focus on why a business needs to be organized. There are many factors that should be covered, briefly. A business needs to be organized:

- to provide a legal framework for disputes;
- to set out who does what and how profits are shared;
- to provide a framework for raising finance;
- to provide a framework for decision making;
- to provide a framework for marketing the enterprise;
- to provide a framework for the organization of production;
- to provide a framework for dealing with people both within and outside the company;
- for dealing with general administrative matters.

You could briefly cover the importance of planning and the sorts of areas covered in a business plan.

In the next section of the essay, you will need to consider different types of business—sole trader, partnership, company, franchise, cooperative, public enterprise and so on.

There will not be enough time available in the essay to detail each of these forms, so you should concentrate on looking at just a few of them in depth. The obvious choice is to look at the structure of a company. You would need to show how a company is set up and run, at the legal arrangements and how the company is organized to ensure that its main objectives are translated into day-to-day affairs. You would need to mention how the main aims of the company are codified in 'mission statements' and policies. Carefully selected examples from the real world will give your essay more impetus.

In the conclusion you will simply need to recap to show that effective organization and planning lies at the heart of long-term business success. You could use the example of a particularly effective organization such as Marks and Spencer whose organization is geared to meeting the requirements of its many levels, including consumers, employees and shareholders, as well as the whole community through its wider activities.

Essay titles

1. What is a business plan? What information should be included in this plan? Who are business plans written for?
2. 'Bureaucracies are no longer appropriate in a modern information society.' Discuss.
3. How can systems theory be used to understand how organizations function?
4. 'Small business organizations are flexible and responsible to the needs of consumers. Large organizations tend to be top heavy and cumbersome.' Discuss with reference to business organizations you have studied.
5. Explain why franchising is likely to become increasingly popular in the last decade of the twentieth century.
6. Who are the major decision makers in a public company? How influential are the owners of such companies?
7. In what situations is line organization likely to be the most effective way of organizing a business?
8. Functional organization is the easiest to understand and therefore the most desirable way of organizing a company. Discuss.
9. Why does business need to operate within a legal framework?
10. What constraints exist in the public sector that do not affect organizations in the private sector?
11. What advantages are available to public limited companies that are not available to private limited companies? Are public limited companies more likely to be effective organizations than private ones?
12. Has privatization increased the power and influence of the small shareholder in the economy?
13. 'In recent years we have seen a rising tide of privatization and public accountability—this trend is irreversible.' Discuss with reference to recent changes in the UK economy.
14. Are there some organizations and services that should always be part of the public sector?
15. Describe the functions of the main participants in the management of a public limited company.
16. In what ways are businesses accountable to consumers?
17. Show how each of the main decision makers in a company can influence company decisions.
18. 'The sole trader is the lifeblood of the economy.' Discuss.
19. Using examples, show how the process of privatization is a world-wide trend.
20. Is becoming a shareholder a responsibility of all citizens in a democratic society?

Short-answer questions

1. What details are usually covered in a deed of partnership?
2. What protection is given by limited liability?
3. What details are included in the Memorandum of Association?
4. What details are included in the Articles of Association?
5. What disadvantages are associated with becoming a limited company?
6. Why do public companies have non-executive directors?
7. What is the responsibility of the chairperson of a company?
8. What is meant by line organization of a company?
9. What is meant by grouping by function and grouping by process?
10. How are public corporations set up?
11. List three major public corporations and three major public companies.
12. What is meant by the public sector of the economy?
13. What is meant by privatization?
14. Who are the major decision makers in a public corporation?
15. Who are the major decision makers in a public company?
16. Who are the owners of public corporations and public companies?
17. Into which sector of the economy (private or public) could the following organizations be placed:

    - cooperatives;
    - municipal enterprises;
    - local councils;
    - partnerships;
    - franchises;
    - the civil service;
    - National Health Service?

18. What are the advantages of bureaucracies as organizational structures?
19. What steps need to be followed before a company can trade?
20. What is meant by franchising?

Projects

Perhaps the best projects on businesses will come from practical investigation inside real companies. This is quite easy when companies are small, for example sole traders, partnerships, franchise outlets and so on. It is not so easy for large public companies and public corporations where practical investigation will only reveal limited aspects of their total operation.

When studying large organizations, it is better to turn to published sources such as company prospectuses, newspaper and magazine reports, etc. Clearly, if you are going to build up a balanced picture of company activities, a range of sources will need to be surveyed. Company literature is bound to be one-sided and geared towards promotion. Companies should be studied by reading newspaper and other articles about them as well as through company sources. As you build up more business experience, you should be able to cut through the high-sounding text of promotional materials to see the actual underlying picture. However, even the most skilled financial analysts find it difficult (if not impossible) to uncover a completely true picture of company operations.

Suggested reading

Common, Richard, Norman Flynn and Elizabeth Mellor, *Managing Public Services — Competition and Decentralization*. Butterworth Heinemann, 1992.

Drucker, Peter F., *Managing the Non-profit Organization*. Butterworth Heinemann, 1990.

Hurl, B., *Privatization and the Public Sector*. Heinemann, 1988.

Old, John, and Tony Shafto, *Introduction to Business Economics*. Stanley Thornes, 1990.

Whitcomb, Dr Alan, *An Illustrated Business Studies Dictionary*. Stanley Thornes, 1992.

5

An introduction to decision making

Decision making is central to business studies. All individuals and organizations make decisions every day. Some of these decisions are routine, 'programmed' decisions that require little, if any, thought. When we clean our teeth or boil a kettle we go through a number of automatic steps. When a supermarket sells a certain number of items, new stock will be automatically ordered by means of a stock control system, which will probably be computerized.

Other decisions that individuals and organizations have to make, however, are not routine. Decisions such as whether or not to get married or to produce a revolutionary new product may happen just once in a lifetime. Such decisions need to be carefully thought through and planned. The more information that is available to the decision maker, the greater the likelihood that a 'good' decision will be made. Decision making in organizations needs to be carefully thought through. In some organizations, decisions will be made at the top and passed down. In other organizations decisions may be made 'on the ground' by teams of individuals with considerable powers.

When decisions involve quantitative information mathematical techniques and computer programs can be used to assist decision making.

Case Study—The role of the company chairperson

To what extent should the chairperson of a large public company become involved in day-to-day decision making?

It has been reported that at a meeting of executive directors of Marks and Spencer in February 1992, Richard Greenbury (the Chairman) ruled that there was too much satin, too many lingerie collections and not enough single garments in Marks and Spencer stores.

Minutes of the meeting showed that, while heads of lesser companies were striking huge deals, Mr Greenbury was concluding that a new method of displaying garments for ages two to four was wrong and was instructing stores to revert to the old display methods.

The meeting was attended by 11 of the executive directors. Four

Figure 5.1 A Marks and Spencer shop.

divisional directors were on hand to advise on particular product areas. Mr Greenbury heads a company with sales of £6bn a year and pre-tax profits of £600m, yet the minutes reflect a businessman who is particular about details, from the poor location of the Amsterdam store to the method of displaying casual jackets. Thanks partly to this attention to detail, returns of women's garments have come down from 25 per cent of sales to 22 per cent in the last six months. However, the minutes showed that this was still regarded to be unacceptably high and the target for 1992 was set at 20 per cent.

Questions

1. Define strategic, tactical and operational decisions.
2. In a large public company, who should be responsible for each of these layers of decision making?
3. What types of decisions were being discussed at the Marks and Spencer meeting described in the Case Study?
4. Do you think that this is the correct forum for this level of discussion?
5. Why were divisional directors present at the meeting? How could they have helped in the discussions that took place?
6. Explain the benefits and drawbacks of Richard Greenbury being involved at this level of decision making?
7. Are there wider lessons for other types of organizations that can be drawn from this example?

Case Study—From the world's biggest to the poor relation?

Figure 5.2 A branch of Midland Bank.

Until the 1950s, the Midland Bank was the biggest bank in the world. During the 1980s it has been the poor relation to the other British clearing banks.

The clearers were able to preserve an oligopoly market position until the Conservative government began to introduce competition into lending in the early 1970s.

Midland, founded in 1836 in Birmingham, was the least able to keep up with change as banks were forced to compete.

Midland's problems over three decades have stemmed from an inefficient and over-large branch network and poor management. Neither of these problems were tackled head on until the 1980s. Until 1980 there were two chief executives and their relationship was poor.

Midland's lack of leadership may have been partly responsible for a huge strategic error in the early 1980s when it joined a fashion among British banks to expand in the United States. Coming late into the game, it agreed a disastrous takeover of Crocker National Bank of California in which it invested money but failed to gain full management control.

Buoyed by new capital from Midland, Crocker went on a lending binge, producing heavy losses while its Latin American loans went bad after the Mexican debt crisis in 1982. Midland eventually took full control, but only in time to unscramble the deal and sell Crocker, though it was forced to keep the Latin American debts.

Sir Kit McMahon, former Deputy Governor of the Bank of England, was brought in as Chairman and was faced in 1987 with announcing the first full-year loss by a British clearing bank this century.

In the heady days of the stock market boom, Sir Kit was confronted with an informal takeover approach from the Saatchi brothers (owners of a large advertising business).

With morale devastated, there was a revolving door at senior level in the bank. Just as it began to recover from heavy Third World losses, it was hit by the effects of the recession in the UK.

Questions

1. What measures could be used to chart the decline of Midland Bank since the 1950s?
2. What evidence is given in the Case Study that Midland Bank had a poor decision-making structure?
3. How did this poor decision-making structure lead to poor decision making?
4. What evidence is given in the Case Study that Midland's strategy was weak?
5. What do you think would be the effects of Midland Bank's decision making for:

- managers;
- shareholders;
- employees;
- customers;
- competitors?

Case Study

Choosing a site is one of the most important decisions made by a retailer.

Granby is a rapidly expanding town in the East Midlands. The current population is 30 000, but this is expected to rise to 40 000 over the next 10 years. This is partly due to the development of a fast rail link to London, which has opened up the possibility of commuting. Employment is high in the town and incomes are increasing. There are also an increasing number of children and old people in the town. The nearest rival shopping centre is 30 miles away and, as a result, Granby attracts many shoppers from the surrounding villages.

The map in Fig. 5.3 shows part of the central section of Granby, including Market Place, Castlegate, a section of the High Street and Vine Street.

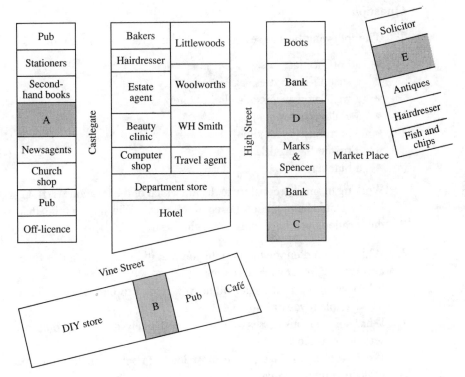

Figure 5.3 Granby shopping area.

The local council has carried out a frequency survey, counting people passing along these roads during an hour on an average shopping day. The results are as follows:

Castlegate (church shop side)	80
Castlegate (bakers side)	100
Vine Street	100
High Street (Marks and Spencer side)	1100
Market Place (Marks and Spencer side)	420
Market Place (antiques side)	310

The figures also show that for Castlegate and Market Place, two out of ten passers-by will be shopping on that street. For the High Street, four out of ten passers-by will be shopping on that street. For Vine Street, only one out of ten passers-by will be shopping there.

The costs of being on the High Street will be more because of higher rents and local taxes paid to the council. Market Place is the next most expensive location. There is not a lot of difference in cost between Vine Street and Castlegate.

Questions

1. The following businesses are thinking of setting up in Granby:

   - an off licence;
   - a second-hand dress agency;
   - a well-known women's clothes shop;
   - a children's toy shop;
   - Thorntons (sweet shop);
   - Trustee Savings Bank;
   - a butcher.

   Working in small groups, try to decide which of the locations A, B, C, D or E would be the best for each of the above. Why do you think that the locations you have chosen are the best?

2. Which location on the map would you regard to be the best one for a new café? Explain your reasoning.

3. Which location on the map would you regard to be the worst for a bank? Explain your reasoning.

4. What sorts of businesses would be most likely to make profits by setting up at location D?

5. What sorts of businesses are most likely to set up at location A? Explain your reasoning.

6. Select a line of business that you would like to set up in. Which location would you choose? Explain your reasoning.

Case Study—Decisions, decisions and changing prices

Imagine that you are the owner of a florist shop in the centre of town. Of your business, 90 per cent comes from the sale of flowers and potted plants. The flowers have a shelf-life of about four days, while the potted plants last much longer, up to a month or more. You buy most of your stock from one large nursery, but your supplier decides to increase prices by 5p in the pound. He tells you that every other grower has had to do the same, due to rising costs throughout the industry. You have enough flowers in stock to last three days and enough potted plants for a month. You bought all your existing stock at the old price.

You now have two main alternatives:

- to continue selling your stock to customers at the old price and try and make savings elsewhere (perhaps by cutting down on staff and services);
- to increase all prices straightaway (so that you can buy new stock at the increased price without difficulty).

Questions

1. What would you do? Explain your answer.
2. What if your supplier, instead of increasing prices, actually reduced them? Would you reduce your prices straightaway too?

Imagine that you are the managing director of a company owning a chain of five service stations. You have to buy all your petrol and lubricants from suppliers at the world price (set by the open market). Your stations hold a week's supply of petrol (which cost you £20 000 per site, £100 000 in total) and a month's supply of lubricants (which cost you £1000 per site, £5000 in total).

Suddenly, the world price of petrol and lubricants increases by 10 per cent. As a result, your stock of petrol has increased in value by £10 000 and your lubricants by £500. However, those increases exactly equal the increased price you have to pay for new stock.

You now have two main alternatives:

* to continue selling all your existing stock to customers at the old price and try to make savings elsewhere (perhaps by cutting down on staff);
* to increase all prices straightaway (so that you can buy new stock at the increased price without difficulty).

Questions

Explain your answers.

1. What would you do?
2. What if the world price for petrol and lubricants fell by 10 per cent. Would you reduce your prices straightaway too?

Case Study—Local council spending cuts

For this activity you will represent county councillors for Midshire. The County Council had previously approved the following increases in expenditure for the coming year:

* an extra 106 teachers in schools to reduce class sizes further as it had recently been noted that Midshire had a very poor pupil–teacher ratio when compared with the national average;
* an extra £350 000 (15 per cent) in home care for the elderly. (Midshire has a rapidly ageing population and the home care service has not been improved for the last five years);
* an extra 13 policemen in Middletown and more dog handlers as the crime rate in Middletown has risen by 100 per cent in the last year and the Chief Constable is 'seriously worried' by this development;

- new grants available to starters in industry—this policy has been found to be very successful in reducing unemployment figures;
- more money for books in schools as a recent survey has shown that many of the books used in schools are out of date;
- better services for the under-fives (at present there are only two pre-school nurseries in the whole of Midshire);
- an extra £100 000 on special education, for example to assist handicapped pupils who have special needs;
- more money to combat child abuse.

The County Council has now discovered that it had seriously overspent on its previous year's budget. Unfortunately it must scrap one of the above projects as it needs at least £80 000 to balance its books. However, the project will be restored as a priority in the following year. Two members of the class will be responsible for defending each of the above proposals in order to prevent it being cut. A chairperson should run the meeting and a vote should be taken to decide on the best way of making the cutbacks.

Activity

A network sets out all the activities involved in a project and all the links between events. It is usually set out in the form of an illustration. The purpose of drawing a network is to calculate how quickly a project can be carried out and to help you to sequence and organize work activities.

The critical path is the sequence of key activities that determine the time taken to complete the activity.

Think of an activity that you or an organization that you are familiar with has to carry out, then:

- list all the tasks that need to be carried out, how long each will take and in what order they must be done (are there some tasks that have to be finished before others can start and, if so, which are they?);
- draw a network to show the links between each task, representing each with a circle, identifying it with a letter or number and connect the circles using arrows showing the order in which the tasks must take place, pointing from left to right (write the time you estimate each task will take to complete above the arrow so that the time taken to complete the sequence can be calculated by adding up the length of time it takes to complete the tasks from start to finish; in the network in Fig. 5.4, tasks B, C, and D can all be started at the same time, but E cannot start until C is finished, although work on E and F can be going on at the same time and G can only be started when D,

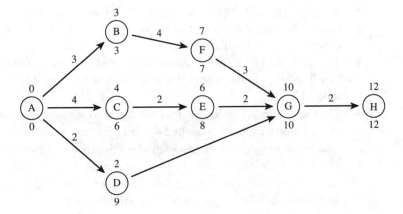

Figure 5.4 A critical path.

    E and F have been finished, so the earliest possible completion time is 12 days—A, B, F, G, then H being the longest path);

- work out the latest finishing times for each task and write them below the circles (the pathway that is most urgent—the one where if tasks are held up, then the whole project will be pushed behind schedule— is known as the critical path, which you can highlight using a colour to denote its route—in this case, route A, B, F, G, then H).

It is useful to find out this information as project managers may need to put more resources into critical path tasks.

    Try it out for yourself. There are all sorts of activities you can construct critical paths for, such as planning the use of study time, repairing an engine, building a house, constructing a new motorway, preparing a set of accounts and so on.

Activity

When the leader of a group or organizer of an activity needs to tell a particular group what needs to be done a *task briefing* will need to be carried out. Without an effective briefing, the performance of the task might turn into a shambles.

    Imagine that you are part of a group that is just about to carry out a task (any task will do). As part of the briefing, you will expect to be told about the aims and objectives of the activity and the part that you will play. List any other questions that you would expect to be answered during the briefing. (Compare your list with those given on page 248.)

Activity

Tannenbaum and Schmidt recognized four main leadership styles:

- *The Tell Style* The leader makes most of the decisions after thinking things through and then tells subordinates what they should do, expecting their compliance;
- *The Sell Style* The leader decides what should be done and then tries to sell the idea to the rest of the group in order to persuade them to follow his or her ideas;
- *The Consult Style* The leader does not make decisions until members of the group have been consulted about a particular problem or issue. The leader only makes the decision *after* this process of consultation;
- *The Joins Style* The leader allows the group to make decisions (the leader being one of the group). The leader initially sets the boundaries in which decision making will take place.

Study the way in which decisions are made over a period of time in a group with which you are familiar. Note how the leader makes decisions. For example, the leader could be your lecturer, teacher or work supervisor. What leadership style is employed? Does it vary depending on the types of decisions being made? How effective are the different leadership styles? You may want to compare different leaders.

Essay title 1—Business decision making should involve everyone in a company. Illustrate your answer by using examples from an industry with which you are familiar.

Decision making lies at the heart of business studies. It is important that you make this clear in your answer.

From the outset you will need to show the sorts of individuals and groups that make business decisions. Some of these decisions will be internal ones while others will be external. You will need to mention directors, shareholders, managers, employees, customers, pressure groups, competitors and so on and you will also briefly need to show that different organizations will be run and administered by different types of business participants (partners, cooperators, shareholders or others).

The central part of the essay could concentrate on the difference between strategic and operational decisions.

In an ideal situation, everyone in a company will be a decision maker. A company prospers best when everyone in it believes that success depends on the excellence of their contribution. Short-term decisions made many times a day by individuals determine the quality of that day's work. Long-term decisions, again by individuals, about their own career, training and ambitions, also affect the quality of their contribution but over a longer period of time.

The governing principle, whether recognized or not, is that everybody has a customer—either outside the company (the traditional customer) or inside it (the internal customer). *Both* kinds of customer expect to be supplied with the product or service they need, on time and as specified and neither should be considered to be more important than the other.

The principle holds good for everyone in the company, whatever their level of skill and experience, whether their 'product' is answering a telephone in a helpful way or masterminding a major new project. It works to everyone's benefit. It gives the individual genuine responsibility and scope for initiative and it virtually guarantees that the company's performance will improve as a result.

For *any* company, but particularly one with a wide geographical spread and a wide range of product types, decentralization of one kind or another is essential. Most decisions, especially tactical ones, cannot be taken effectively at the centre, which may be miles or continents away, because they have to be taken quickly, on the spot, by people who know all the circumstances. There is often no time for referral back to central office, even if it has a complete understanding of that particular problem.

The internal customer principle is one general way of encouraging decentralization, but there are others that involve changes in the structure of the company. One way is to 'flatten' the organizational hierarchy by removing one or more of its layers, so that each divisional head reports directly to the Managing Director rather than to other directors who themselves report to the top person.

Another way is to create separate profit centres—sections of the overall business that are given the responsibility and resources (and guidance where necessary) to run their own section as their own business. For instance, Shell's bitumen business is now run by Shell Bitumen UK, a separate profit centre within Shell Oil UK. Also, Emstar Limited is responsible for Shell's energy management business in the UK and Synthetic Chemicals Limited, a subsidiary of Shell Chemicals UK, specializes in fine chemicals.

Strategic decisions, with long-term implications for all parts of the company, however, have to be taken centrally. Even so, many different people will be required to contribute to them, simply because the amount of input needed when a major decision has to be made can be immense.

Of course, all decisions, at whatever level, are made in the context of the company's specific business objectives. These, finally, are determined and presented by central management, but have to be in line with the general directions, capacities and culture of the company.

Capital projects (projects that involve investing large sums of money that can only be recovered from profits earned over the years by the project themselves) nearly always compete with each other. A company must decide which projects best justify investment. For instance, is it better for an oil company to spend an available £50m on upgrading part of a refinery or building a new distribution centre, both of which may be justifiable commercially?

Every company is influenced by its achievements (or otherwise) in the past and by its hopes and plans for the future. It is also influenced by outside events, including government decisions and the activities of sister companies and competitors operating in the same country or elsewhere in the world.

The oil industry, perhaps more than any other, is affected by outside events as well as by its history. It all began in 1859 when Colonel Drake struck oil less than 21m (70 feet) beneath the ground in Pennsylvania and has been brought to its present level of sophistication by an unparalleled worldwide input of scientific and commercial energy that intensified over the decades and is still growing.

The benefits are considerable. Oil companies in the UK can learn from the experiences of their sister companies in other parts of the world and have learned from past experiences in the oil industry. The launch, say, of a new quality fuel in one year can provide commercial and operational guidelines for the launch of a new quality lubricant in the next or other years.

The most immediate and critical interrelationships, however, are between different parts of the business. The specialists in market research advise the marketing specialists on the latest customer attitudes; the marketing people translate these attitudes into a brief that the research laboratories can progress. The research laboratories in turn cooperate with the refineries regarding manufacturing feasibility and the refineries may specify a particular kind of crude for the traders to buy, but the traders may offer a slightly different crude although at a much enhanced price. The result is a high degree of flexibility in the identification and satisfaction of customer needs.

Essay title 2—How can you assess the quality of information available to a business?

In this essay you will first need to define what you mean in this instance by 'information' and then set out some criteria for establishing 'quality of information'.

A useful introduction might be to show examples of when companies have or have not had good quality information for decision making. For example, companies rarely have enough information about changes in the general economic environment in which they operate, hence the onset of a recession frequently catches many businesses by surprise. Many of the industrial giants, such as Shell and Marks and Spencer, buy in information from specialist agencies about market trends.

There is a common failure to distinguish between data and information. Information is communicated knowledge, while data only *becomes* information when it is communicated to someone and is used by them to make a more 'informed' decision. In a large organization, the accounts department will produce a great mass of financial information in the form of management accounts, ratios and so on. This is clearly *information* to the accountant. It *may* be used as information by company shareholders who are trying to weigh up the worth of the returns on their investments. However, it will only be viewed as information by the advertising manager when he or she feels a need to actually look at and use it.

In a large organization, managers often cry out for more information. They may be bombarded with *data*, but, unless this data is communicated in a manageable and understandable form, this will *not* be information. In designing information systems we therefore need to construct high-quality and relevant information—not masses of paper or meaningless computer records.

Managers at different levels in an organization will require different types of information. Management information systems need to be designed to provide appropriate information at each level.

When we have decided what we mean by information, it is necessary to set out some criteria for assessing the *quality* of particular information. This is neatly presented by Gilligan, Neale and Murray in the following way:

- *reliability*—it is important that the same observations yield the same information, regardless of *who* processes them or *when* they are processed;
- *timing*—clearly it is important that the information is available when the decision has to be made;
- *costs*—the information should not cost more to obtain than the benefit its knowledge produces;
- *necessity*—the information should contain no extraneous components;
- *sufficiency*—the information should make a maximum contribution to the elimination of uncertainty;
- *accuracy*—as far as possible, the information must be free from error;
- *usefulness*—the information should be presented in a form that enables it to be used directly;
- *relevance*—the information should be organized in such a way as to be relevant to the types of decisions to be made based on it.

Obviously some of these criteria pull in opposite directions. As with any other area of business, cost is always a limitation on effective information. However, it is pointless to just throw money at information systems if it is not providing substantial benefit. For example, many large businesses in the 1980s spent a great deal on IT. When these developments were not tied closely to the particular needs of an organization, the benefits were limited and the high expectations of it were crushed.

A management information system (MIS) is a formalized information system designed to provide managers at all levels with information from both internal and external sources that they need to make effective decisions when planning and controlling the activities for which they are responsible. Ultimately, the MIS will only be effective if it can be used effectively. This will depend on the function of the organization, its size and complexity, the degree of centralization in decision making, the importance of the environment to decisions, the management style and the balance between operational and strategic decisions.

In conclusion, we can say that information is vital to any organization and to its individual decision makers. Effective information can only be so if it meets the needs of its end users and can be used to good effect.

Essay title 3 — Teams work together most effectively when they consist of individuals with different contributions to make. Discuss.

This essay can be tackled in a number of ways. A useful starting point is to take obvious examples to show how different individual attributes can be contributed to a commonwealth. For example, in a sports team or the role of functional specialists in a company.

You could then go on to show that, in any team effort, there are three sets of needs that must be met.

First, there are the *task* needs. This is what the group sets out to achieve by working together — to win the league, to make a profit, to treat patients or whatever. It is concerned with products, deadlines, who does what, quality standards and so on.

Second, there are the *group* needs. To work together as a group, there needs to be some sort of maintenance or support activity going on. For example, somebody needs to give recognition and praise to the group for its efforts. Attention needs to be given to communication, discipline, fairness and openness.

Third, there are *individual* needs. Individuals' needs to be supported and recognized within the group. Attention must be given to individual targets, discipline, rewards and so on. It is necessary that individuals are given appropriate levels of support, authority, recognition, challenge, communication and so on.

How well a team works together depends on the mix of personalities and skills needed and brought to the task. When everyone wants to be the leader or everyone wants to be a follower, groups are not likely to be successful. Successful teams require a range of appropriate personalities and qualities. Over the years, a number of researchers have looked at the mix that makes an effective group.

For example, Robert Belbin, working in the early 1980s identified eight roles required in an effective group. Of course, it is possible that some individuals may be able to fill more than one role. Belbin's list included the following roles:

- *The chairperson*—someone who chairs the group and coordinates efforts;
- *The shaper*—a would-be chairperson who drives the team towards finishing the task successfully;
- *The plant*—someone with plenty of ideas who may be rather shy and quiet; the plant creates ideas and proposals;
- *The monitor evaluator*—someone who is able to analyse and evaluate progress and acts as a quality control check;
- *The resource investigator*—this sort of person is sociable and outgoing, bringing new contacts, ideas and developments to the team, but others will need to work on the resource investigator's ideas to make them work;
- *The company worker*—this person is an administrator rather than a leader, someone who is good at ensuring that tasks are carried out, but is unlikely to be a creator or leader;
- *The team worker*—this person works for the team and helps to keep it together, supporting others and encouraging and bringing the members of the team together;
- *The finisher*—the finisher plays an important part in getting the task finished well as he or she makes sure that the good intentions of the others are translated into a good end result.

Clearly these characteristics combine to produce a good team. Some people are good at fulfilling a particular role all the time, while others may take on more than one role. Individuals may take on different roles in different contexts, depending on how familiar they are with a particular task. For example, the team worker in the accounts department may not have the skill or experience to play the same role in the works' football team.

In conclusion, you might want to show that, while in some circumstances it is possible to get by using a fairly small range of individual skills and characteristics, this will not be the case in large organizations and in decision making that takes place in the longer term. In modern societies, many decisions require a lot of information and need to be made by groups of specialists working together. Group dynamics are thus an essential ingredient of decision making.

Essay titles

1. How does the size of group affect the way in which the decision-making process is carried out in organizations?
2. 'There would be no point in senior managers spending large amounts of time on routine tasks that can be done by somebody else.' Discuss.
3. Explain how an open systems decision cycle allows for changes and improvements to be made in business decision making.
4. Show how the human side of decision making is affected by factors influencing the individual decision maker and factors affecting group decision making.
5. What are the main factors that influence the way in which decisions are made?
6. What problems may be encountered in group decision making?
7. Effective decision making depends, to a great extent, on those in key central positions in an organization and on the quality of communications channels to them. Discuss.
8. What makes an effective leader? Illustrate your answer by reference to practical examples.
9. Are groups more effective at making decisions than individuals?
10. How can cost benefit analysis assist decision making in organizations?
11. 'We are now entering the age of information-based organizations.' Describe the role of the knowledge specialist in such an organization.
12. How can decision-making techniques facilitate the decision-making process?
13. Show how the decision-making network needs to be tailored to:

   - the size of the group;
   - the nature of the decisions that have to be made.

14. How can large groups work effectively together?
15. 'There is no single best style of leadership.' Discuss.
16. What makes an effective group?
17. 'Decision making is fundamentally the same in any type of large organization.' Discuss this statement.
18. 'Groups tend to concentrate on the task at the expense of the process.' Discuss.
19. 'Participative management gives an organization far more information at its fingertips.' Discuss.
20. Can all decisions in an organization be programmed?

Short-answer questions

1. Describe one decision that might be made by each of the following members of a small company:

    - shareholder;
    - manager;
    - employee.

2. Who should be responsible for the operational decisions of an organization?

3. Who should be responsible for the strategic decisions of an organization?

4. What is meant by 'the critical path'?

5. Identify the critical path shown in Fig. 5.5.

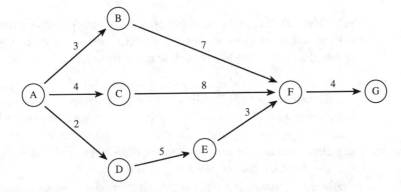

Figure 5.5 A critical path.

6. What is the difference between a hierarchical and a democratic form of organization?

7. Why might five be an ideal group size for decision making?

8. What is a decision tree?

9. Set out a diagram to illustrate the events and sequence that would be required to:

    - clean your teeth;
    - produce a set of accounts to trial balance.

10. Distinguish between a programmed and non-programmed decision that might be made by:

    - a school or college;
    - a supermarket chain.

11. Is evaluation the final stage in the decision-making cycle? Explain.

12. What is a game theory?

13. How are decisions made in a closed system?
14. What is a SWOT analysis?
15. In group working, what is the difference between:

    - task;
    - process.

16. Give three examples of situations in which computer simulations can be used as tools in decision making.
17. Why are clear objectives essential in decision making?
18. Define the term 'group'.
19. What is the role of the leader in a group?
20. What is participative management?

Projects

Decision making lies at the heart of business studies. All projects that you carry out will focus in some measure on decision-making processes.

Areas that you might like to look at could include:

- The study of a decision that you are involved in: who are the participants; what are the objectives; does everybody see the objectives in the same way; what are the responsibilities of the participants; what is the task or process and action schedule involved; what decision-making techniques are involved; is there a clear decision-making cycle; what are the intended or actual outcomes?
- Alternatively, you may like to examine the decision-making apparatus for a particular group, such as a school or college council: how has the framework been established; what are the rules; who is involved; how do different participants see their roles; how effective is the apparatus; is it possible to recommend changes to the machinery?
- Study the roles played by participants in a particular group: is it possible to identify different role types; do these roles change over time; is it possible to explore factors that influence the roles played, such as gender stereotypes, personality traits and so on?

Suggested reading

Clifford, Jim, *Decision Making in Organizations*. Longman, 1983.
Gore, Chris, Kate Murray and Bill Richardson, *Strategic Decision Making*. Cassell, 1991.
Gregory, Geoffrey, *Decision Analysis*. Pitman, 1988.
Needham, David and Rob Dransfield, *Exploring Industry and Enterprise*. Cassell, 1989.
Rawlinson, J. Geoffrey, *Creative Thinking and Brainstorming*. Wildwood House, 1986.
Richardson, Bill, and Roy Richardson, *Business Planning—An Approach to Strategic Management*. Pitman, 1992.

6

Using statistical and quantitative techniques

The importance of quantitative information

In order to make decisions at all levels, a business requires information from a range of sources. Much of this information will involve figures. Some of these may be relatively easy to interpret and understand, while others may be detailed and require extensive analysis. In the same way that everybody requires language skills to communicate, in business all employees will need some form of quantitative and statistical skills that they can use to interpret information. Such statistical analysis will help to reduce uncertainty and, ultimately, lead to better results.

The use of quantitative information will influence virtually all of an organization's activities. It might stem from a simple budget, the appraisal of an investment project, from detailed research of information from the market or possibly from extensive analysis of an organization's operations. The information gathered must be accurate, suitable for the intended purpose and have been obtained cost-effectively.

Case Study—The preserves market

The preserves market (jam, marmalade, lemon curd and others) was recently audited by Nielson as worth £130m. A.C. Nielson is a retail audit organization that collects data of items sold through supermarkets and large chains and then sells the figures to organizations wishing to buy them. Such figures provide a window into the market-place and enable manufacturers to work out market share, areas of growth, the performance of different products as well as the effects of any recent strategies.

Though the preserves market is a relatively traditional, mature market that has been suffering a 2 per cent yearly decline, it has recently been growing in value by about 9 per cent per year. Robertson's took over as brand leader in 1989 and their share of the total market now stands at 21.8 per cent with Chivers and Hartley close behind with a 20.1 per cent share. See Table 6.1 for the market shares of the various sectors of the preserves market.

Table 6.1. Market shares of the sectors of the preserves market

	% of Market	% Trend
Jam	55	−1
Lemon curd	5	−3
Marmalade	38	−4

Jam is today divided into three categories:

- *standard* with a minimum of 35 per cent fruit and over 60 per cent soluble solids;
- *extra* with a minimum of 45 per cent fruit and over 60 per cent soluble solids;
- *reduced or no added sugar* with a minimum of 35 per cent fruit and 30–35 per cent soluble solids.

The most important sector is standard jam, with 76 per cent of the total market. Of the other sectors, extra jam is by far the most dynamic area of the market, growing at 6 per cent per annum. This reflects increasing demands at home for premium and luxury products. As the only growth sector in a slightly declining market is extra jam, several new ranges have been launched over the last few months (see Table 6.2).

Table 6.2. Current trends in the jam market

Jam	% of Market	% Trend
Standard jam	76	−1
Extra jam	15.5	+6
Reduced or no added sugar	8.5	+1

Marmalade	% of Market	% Trend
Fine cut and sugarless jelly	50	−5
Fine and medium cut	28	−8
Non-jelly thick cut	19	−1

It is expected that the preserve markets will perform well up to and beyond the year 2000. With the greater likelihood of the adoption of the eating habits of the Continent, where they consume twice as many preserves as us, playing a wider role in our lives, the near future of preserves seems secure. With consumers becoming more health-conscious, the drive towards healthy, low-sugar products will probably also become more pronounced.

Assume that you work for a manufacturer of preserves as you answer the following questions.

Questions

1. Why might the type of quantitative information in the above case be useful for your organization?
2. Explain why your organization buys information from Nielson.
3. Using information extracted from the Case Study, construct:

   - a pie chart showing the percentage of the market taken by each type of preserve, marking the 2 per cent not accounted for 'others';
   - a bar chart showing the percentage of market attributed to each type of jam.

4. How might the information in the study influence any decisions that might have to be taken in the future?
5. Examine the relationship between a table or spreadsheet and any chart that might result from them.
6. To what extent does this case illustrate the importance of quantitative information in business?

Case Study—Production levels

A small company near Dulwich is concerned about what it considers to be massive variations in its production levels. Over a 60-day period it recorded the following:

```
10 11 15 10 18 19 20 12 13 14
12 11 20 13 18 11 11 15 12 16
12 14 12 17 15 13 18 18 12 17
12 15 17 15 16 13 12 17 18 18
14 13 17 16 18 12 13 13 16 17
12 14 15 14 12 13 13 14 13 15
```

The company wishes to analyse these production levels. The hope is that, by identifying where the problems lie, they might find what the problems are and then be able to take corrective action.

Questions

1. How might the company wish to present the above information?
2. Construct a frequency distribution from the figures.
3. From the frequency distribution, calculate the following measures of central tendency:

   - the arithmetic mean (to nearest whole number);
   - the mode;
   - the median.

4. Calculate the following measures of dispersion:

   - the range;
   - the lower quartile;
   - the upper quartile;
   - the interquartile range;
   - the mean deviation;
   - the variance;
   - the standard deviation.

5. Comment briefly upon the usefulness of the above data.

Case Study—British Steel PLC: analysis of shareholders

Table 6.3 analyses the composition of British Steel's shareholders by both category of shareholder and size of holding.

Questions

1. Produce both a component bar chart and a percentage component bar chart to illustrate the various categories of shareholder accounts. Classify shareholders under the headings:

   - male;
   - female;
   - joint;
   - others.

2. Produce a component bar chart and a percentage component bar chart to relate the number of ordinary shares to each type of shareholder (use the four categories given in the charts).
3. Comment briefly on the information highlighted by the presentation techniques used above.
4. Look carefully at the size of holding by shareholder accounts. Draw a histogram and frequency polygon from this table. Then construct a cumulative frequency table and use it to draw an ogive.

Table 6.3. British Steel PLC: analysis of shareholders as at 30 March 1991 (*Source:* British Steel PLC)

CATEGORY OF SHAREHOLDER	Accounts		Ordinary shares	
	Number	Percentage	Number	Percentage
Individual holders				
Male	202,372	60.37	169,949,913	8.50
Female	91,761	27.37	81,315,112	4.06
Joint	33,919	10.12	31,195,753	1.56
Banks (including clients' accounts)	503	0.15	1,387,166	0.07
Nominee Companies	4,682	1.40	1,296,678,874	64.83
Insurance Companies	138	0.04	157,347,632	7.87
Pension Funds	99	0.03	44,665,589	2.23
Limited Companies	1,385	0.41	172,149,316	8.61
Other Corporate Bodies (Colleges, Schools, Councils etc)	364	0.11	32,237,426	1.61
	335,233	100.00	1,986,926,781	99.34
British Steel Employee Share Ownership Trustees Limited	1	—	12,206,643	0.66
	335,224	100.00	2,000,133,424	100.00
BY SIZE OF HOLDING				
1 – 99	2,616	0.78	133,627	0.01
100 – 499	112,615	33.59	36,096,317	1.80
500 – 999	95,243	28.41	56,948,335	2.85
1,000 – 4,999	117,515	35.06	165,789,968	8.29
5,000 – 9,999	4,372	1.31	26,562,093	1.33
10,000 – 49,999	1,401	0.42	27,294,922	1.36
50,000 – 99,999	307	0.09	20,986,790	1.05
100,000 – 999,999	876	0.26	282,318,553	14.11
1,000,000 & Over	278	0.08	1,370,796,176	68.54
	335,233	100.00	1,986,926,781	99.34
British Steel Employee Share Ownership Trustees Limited	1	—	13,206,643	0.66
	335,224	100.00	2,000,133,424	100.00

5. You have been asked to relate the size of holding to the number of ordinary shares. Construct a Lorenz curve and comment upon the distribution shown by your graph.
6. Examine the usefulness of the above presentation techniques.

Case Study—British Coal summary

The summary in Fig. 6.1 appeared in the British Coal Corporation Report and Accounts 1990–91 submitted to the Secretary of State for Energy in accordance with sections 31 and 45 of the Coal Industry Nationalization Act 1946.

Look carefully at the table and charts and then answer the questions.

Questions

1. Comment briefly on the information shown in each chart in the summary.
2. Assess the presentation techniques used. To what extent are they useful in making:

    *   a year-by-year analysis;
    *   a comparison of different markets;
    *   user-friendly comparisons;
    *   an interesting comparison of data?

3. Explain why public corporations produce an annual report and accounts.
4. What other information could have been included in the summary?
5. Assume that British Coal wishes to improve its understanding of its market. It wishes to do this by undertaking both primary and secondary research. Comment on:

    *   the sampling methods available for undertaking primary research;
    *   the possible sources of secondary information both within the corporation and outside it.

Case Study—ICI Company news

Look at the information in Fig. 6.2 and then answer the following questions.

	1990–91 £m	1989–90 £m
Operating profit	238	133
Interest	(143)	(574)
Trading profit/(loss)	95	(441)
Exceptional items	(17)	(472)
Overall profit/(loss)	78	(913)

Sales by market
1990–91

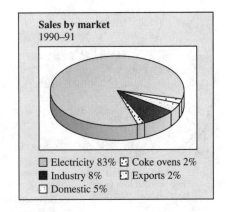

☐ Electricity 83% ⊡ Coke ovens 2%
■ Industry 8% ⊡ Exports 2%
☐ Domestic 5%

Deep-mined cost per tonne
(1990/91 prices)

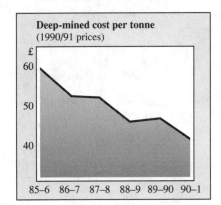

Productivity
(tonnes per man shift)

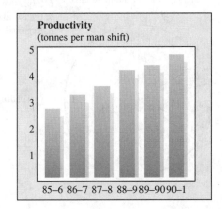

Opencast cost per tonne
(1990–91 prices)

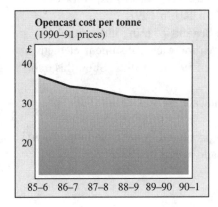

Accidents
(per 100 000 man shifts)

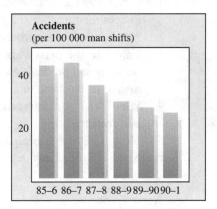

Figure 6.1 British Coal Corporation Report and Accounts 1990–91. (*Source*: British Coal Corporation.)

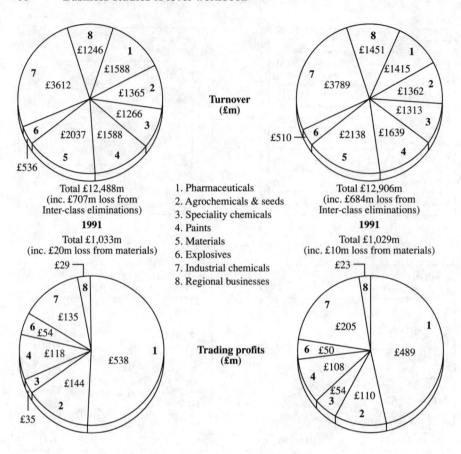

1. Pharmaceuticals
2. Agrochemicals & seeds
3. Speciality chemicals
4. Paints
5. Materials
6. Explosives
7. Industrial chemicals
8. Regional businesses

Figure 6.2 ICI Company News 1990–91. (*Source*: ICI.)

Questions

1. Using 1990 as a base year for turnover and profits, work out the indices for turnover and profits for ICI in 1991.
2. Assess briefly the purposes and benefits of using index numbers.
3. Calculate the percentage changes for each constituent element of turnover and profits/losses between 1990 and 1991. Show this information in the form of a table.
4. What does the information indicate to you about ICI's present performance?
5. How might the information you presented in the table in question 3 have influenced any decision made at ICI in 1992?

Activity

Construct a basic table of figures, for example, making comparisons between five years of turnover. Load a spreadsheet program into a computer. Enter the figures into a spreadsheet and then transfer the figures from the spreadsheet package to another for graph production. Display the figures in a variety of graphical forms and then print the results.

Activity

Obtain a recent annual report from a company. Read through it, looking for various 'understandable' statistics and tables. Interpret the information you find by using, wherever possible, various forms of presentation, measures of central tendency, measures of dispersion and index numbers. Using overhead projection transparencies, present your findings to the rest of your group.

Activity

This activity is concerned with finding out what sources of information and reference might be of use for a business. Visit your local library and scrutinize the reference section for books and other printed sources as well as any software that might be available. Make a list of useful business reference sources, indicating how and why they might be used.

Essay title 1—Examine the information requirements of a small retail business. How might such needs be supported by information technology?

Start by noting that all organizations will have different information requirements. Similarly, managers within every organization at strategic, tactical and organizational levels will also have different information requirements. Identifying these needs and satisfying them with information designed to improve the quality of decision making will undoubtedly improve the performance of the organization.

A small retail business will be concerned with buying and selling within a limited sphere. Yet, despite their small scale, their activities may be enhanced by research. Such information may be:

- *Internal*—that is, within the business, including:
  —data about purchasing;
  —information concerning sales;
  —financial data;
  —administrative data and so on;

  (wherever possible, each of the types of information mentioned should be supported with an example).

- *External*—that is, outside the business, including:
  —information about the actions of competitors;

—population/customer data;

—customer satisfaction;

—information relating to the external environment, such as the economy, political environment, legal matters and so on;

each point should be supported with an example and geared towards the needs of a small retail business.

Such information requirements may call for primary research, which involves collecting data for the business' own requirements, or secondary research, using materials that are either available within the organization or from external published sources.

How will IT help? IT should be briefly defined. IT may be used to:

- keep customer information such as names and addresses, methods of payment, purchasing patterns and so on;
- keep accounting records by means of accounting packages;
- store information such as letters, memos and so on;
- aggregate information and summarize data, such as sales figures;
- present information in a form that is easily understood;
- communicate information between managers, employees, share-holders and so on;
- verify data to check that it has been accurately recorded.

The quality of information obtained and the methods used to put this information to work will help to determine an organization's competitive advantage. In a modern business environment, no matter whether a business is large or small, it cannot afford to be complacent; it must be constantly analysing its information requirements and assessing how such information is gathered, stored, communicated and analysed.

Essay title 2—Distinguish between the collection of primary and secondary data. Describe four methods by which such information may be presented and analysed.

In your introduction you could say that the very nature of business activities means that much of the information a business has to deal with is likely to be statistical. Statistical and quantitative analysis involve three distinct stages:

- the gathering of information;
- the presentation of information;
- the analysis of information.

The above question requires an understanding of all three stages.

The data collected from research activities should be designed to satisfy an organization's information needs. Such needs will be directly related to the decision-making process. So, before collecting information, an organization has to decide:

- what information it requires;
- the level of accuracy needed;
- the cost-effectiveness of the exercise.

The information collected may be either primary or secondary.

Primary data is that collected from outside the organization. It is collected by the business for its own purpose. It might involve finding out about:

- the preferences of customers;
- consumer attitudes;
- the image the organization has;
- the nature of the market;
- external influences.

Primary data involves the business collecting information either on its own behalf or employing an agency to collect the information for it. As it would probably be impractical to interview all respondents, sampling techniques such as random, quota and cluster are used and the information is collected by means of some form of questionnaire administered either by post, personally or by telephone.

Though primary data is collected for a specific purpose and is usually more accurate, it can be expensive to collect.

Secondary data is that which is already available. Some of this might come from within the business. For example:

- customer records;
- sales information;
- purchasing patterns.

Other secondary data will be available from outside the organization, such as:

- trade magazines and journals;
- professionally collected marketing information;
- business reference sources;
- government statistics and so on.

Primary or secondary data may be presented in a variety of different ways. The four methods of presentation may include:

- types of grouped frequency distribution;
- types of charts:
  —pictogram;

—pie chart;

—bar chart;

—histogram;

—frequency polygon;

—Gantt chart;

—ogive; and others.

Define each of the four methods chosen by producing a rough sketch and description of each.

Such information must not only be presented, it must be analysed. Four techniques might include use of:

- arithmetic mean;
- median;
- mode;
- use of quartiles, deciles or percentiles;
- mean deviation;
- variance;
- standard deviation.

The four techniques chosen should be briefly defined.

In conclusion, information will have a variety of uses. The form of its presentation and the level of analysis will usually depend on its eventual audience.

Essay title 3—Benjamin Disraeli (1804–81), a British Prime Minister once said, 'There are lies, damned lies and statistics'. Comment on this statement by referring to the use of statistics in business.

This is a fairly straightforward question that, essentially, involves looking at the pros and cons of using statistical techniques in business.

At the beginning of your essay you could note that the very nature of the information a business has to deal with is financial and otherwise also frequently involves figures. Understanding such information will require a basic knowledge of statistics. 'Statistics' is a word that means a series of figures systematically collected. It is also used to refer to how such figures are used and presented, as well as how they are interpreted and analysed.

Statistics and quantitative analysis may bring greater certainty to decision making in business. They will be used in addition to common sense, problem-solving skills, business acumen and relevant knowledge necessary when taking decisions, and will improve the quality of that decision making.

The statement in the question infers that, though statistical analysis is extremely important in business, perhaps a business ought to take a wider view, not just look at a statistical report before taking a decision.

The benefits of using statistics are that:

- they can be used to summarize complex information;
- they enable quick and easy comparisons to be made with the past;
- different types of statistics can be constructed for different interested parties, for example, for strategic managers, tactical managers, operational managers, shareholders, creditors and so on;
- statistics organize data and make sense of numbers;
- they may form the basis for a decision and improve the quality of that decision;
- they provide a basis for complex analysis;
- they underpin many modern management techniques, such as investment appraisal.

There are, however, some dangers to using statistics for decision-making purposes, particularly for decisions that are entirely dependent on statistical information. For example:

- such decisions may only be as good as the quality of the information collected—a sample may not be sufficiently large or representative enough to enable a decision to be based on it;
- some figures may be biased or inaccurate because of the way the information has been collected or because of the types of questions asked;
- some statistics may gloss over detail by highlighting relatively minor aspects and ignoring other more important issues;
- some might use statistics subjectively to justify the decision they *wish* to make rather than the one they *ought* to make;
- there is always the danger that others will use statistics in a misleading way or misrepresent them;
- statistical information may not be fully understood by those who have to make decisions and they may not be willing to indicate that they do not understand them.

In conclusion, in an uncertain world, statistics make sense of data and provide a sound basis upon which decisions can be made. However, to ensure that such decisions are the right ones, a wider knowledge of the business environment is always likely to be necessary, as well as a knowledge of where the statistics are from and of how they have been constructed.

Essay titles

1. Examine the information and statistical requirements for:

   - different levels of managers;

- shareholders;
- providers of finance.

2. How might a large organization satisfy its information requirements? Comment upon the techniques it might use to obtain such
   information.

3. Using sample questions to support the points you wish to make,
   examine how a questionnaire should be constructed.

4. How might an organization wish to present data? Use at least three
   presentation techniques to support the points you wish to make.

5. What is frequency distribution? How might it be used to draw charts
   and graphs? Use examples to support your answer.

6. Examine the usefulness of a Lorenz curve in graphically displaying
   information.

7. What is meant by central tendency? Comment upon how and why
   analysis of central tendency might be useful when analysing business data.

8. How are measures of central tendency calculated and used? Use an
   example to support your answer.

9. What are the measures of dispersion? How will they help a business
   to make sense of data?

10. Maintaining production levels is very important for many organiza-
    tions. How might standard deviation techniques help an organiza-
    tion to analyse production information?

11. What is a normal distribution curve? Explain its relationship to
    probability theories.

12. Examine the importance of probability theories in business decision
    making.

13. What are index numbers? How might a business use them?

14. Using a numerical example, explain how an index number may be
    used. Why might some indices be weighted?

15. Examine the role of IT in gathering, storing, presenting and analys-
    ing business data.

16. Why might some statistically presented information be open for
    criticism? What must an organization do to improve the quality of
    information it receives?

17. Examine the various methods of analysing business data.

18. Assess the need for statistical analysis in business. How important is
    it for employees to understand any figures extracted or any analysis
    that has taken place?

19. Construct a frequency distribution to represent some business data.
    Using this frequency distribution, construct:

- a pie chart;

- a bar graph;
- an ogive.

Comment on the differences between each of the above forms of presentation.

20. 'Statistically presented information is only as good as the sources from which it has been extracted.' Discuss.

Short-answer questions

1. Define the word 'statistics'.
2. Distinguish between primary data and secondary data.
3. Name two techniques of sampling. Give one advantage and one disadvantage of using each technique.
4. Name three sources of government statistics.
5. What is a tally mark?
6. A company's sales figures are as follows:

	£m
toothpaste	20
dental floss	10
soap	80
others	60
	170

Using these figures, construct a pie chart and a bar chart.

7. What is a histogram?
8. Explain how a histogram might be used to construct a frequency polygon.
9. What is a Gantt chart and what might it show?
10. What is a Lorenz curve? What might it show?
11. Distinguish between an arithmetic mean, mode and median. Use an example to support your answer.
12. Explain what a quartile is and indicate one use it might have.
13. What is standard deviation? How is it used?
14. Examine the various uses of a normal distribution curve.
15. Name two benefits that may be gained from using index numbers.
16. Explain why some index numbers are weighted.
17. Describe briefly what is meant by significance testing.
18. Name two benefits of using IT for statistical analysis.
19. How might a grouped frequency distribution be used?
20. Name three types of internal data a business might generate.

Projects

There are very few areas where statistical and quantitative techniques are likely to form a basis for a project. There is, however, a much greater likelihood, if not a certainty, that statistical techniques will be necessary for whichever project you decide to undertake. It is important that you use such techniques wisely and bear in mind their purpose.

Two possible suggestions for project work are:

- an analysis of how information is presented to different groups of people both within and outside an organization;
- an analysis of how IT is used to store, generate, summarize and present information.

Suggested reading

Bancroft, G., and G. O'Sullivan, *Maths and Statistics for Accounting and Business Studies*. McGraw-Hill, 1988.

Galloway, Lee, *Statistics for Marketing in Business*. Stanley Thornes, 1989.

Morris, Clare, *Quantitative Approaches in Business Studies*. Pitman, 1989.

Whitehead, Geoffrey, *Statistics for Business* (2nd edn). Pitman, 1992.

Wright, Helen, *Statistics for GCSE*. Pitman, 1988.

7

A business in its environment

Businesses cannot afford to be inward-looking. Business takes place in a very far-reaching environment. All sorts of forces and pressures are exerted on business activity by this outside environment. Businesses need to keep a careful eye on:

- the economic environment and economic changes;
- the legal environment and legal changes;
- the social environment and social changes;
- the technological environment and technological changes;
- the political environment and political changes;
- what other organizations are doing in the same or similar lines of business;
- the international environment.

Clearly, this is a very challenging background to work against. This is why students of business studies need to have a broad understanding of general changes in society as well as specialist business knowledge and skills relating to specific areas.

Case Study—Subsidizing crofters

In Scotland there are 9000 active crofters and 17 600 registered crofts. The number of registered crofts has been declining steadily. The main crofting areas are Shetland, Orkney, the Western Isles and the north-west mainland of Scotland. Many of the crofts were set up in the nineteenth century when people were forced off the better land to make way for sheep. They settled on narrow strips of fertile land next to the coast. It is often very poor-quality land and crofters have a hard time just surviving.

Crofting has tended to become a monoculture, with sheep being the single product. This contrasts with the past when crofters carried out a wide range of activities, from growing potatoes, tending cows, and fishing to getting other jobs.

Sheep have increased as subsidies became more attractive and because they need little maintenance, which suits people busy doing other jobs, and this has discouraged more active crofting.

Despite declining prices, the value of Scottish sheep production rose by more than £30m to £218m—of which £130m, or 60 per cent, was subsidy in 1991. In the same year, the average hill farmer had an income of £11 000; without subsidy he would have made a loss of £7000.

Table 7.1. A typical crofter's budget (annual incomings and outgoings based on a 300-sheep flock)

	With subsidy	Without subsidy
Lambs sold (average £13 each)	1560	1560
Income from wool	420	420
Sale of ewes (£8 each)	360	360
Sheep subsidy (£26 each)	7800	0
Costs: feed/dip/vet	2500	2500
Rent on 5000 acres	42	42
Transport costs	1000	1000
Income	10140	2340
Less expenses	3542	3542
Overall profit/loss	6600 (profit)	1200 (loss)

One of the effects of the subsidy has been to make it more attractive for crofters to leave sheep packed on the hillside than it is to take them to market (particularly as the value of sheep's meat and wool has fallen).

Questions

1. Why do you think that hill farming is subsidized?
2. What is the effect of the subsidy on:

   - the number of sheep owned by crofters;
   - sheep provided to the market;
   - range of activities carried out by crofters?

3. Set out what you consider to be the main advantages and disadvantages of having the subsidy. Do you think that the subsidy could be modified in any way to make it more effective in supporting crofting?
4. Are the problems facing crofters more related to supply or to demand? Explain your answer in depth.
5. What do you think would be the effect of stopping the subsidy? Who would be affected and how?

Case Study—The spreading fats market

Nobody worried about eating butter until 1980. Then, suddenly, it was bad for you. Then good. Then bad again. Current nutritional thinking (1992) is that foods containing high levels of saturated fats—such as butter—can contribute to heart disease. However, in 1991, researchers had announced that butter-eaters were less likely to have a coronary than margarine-eaters!

Walk into any supermarket and you will find a wide range of spreading fats on sale (see Table 7.2).

Table 7.2. Types of spreading fats

Type of fats	Legal definition	Brand names
Butter	Minimum 80 per cent fat (all milk fat), maximum 16 per cent moisture.	Anchor Lurpak Country Life Kerrygold Wheelbarrow
Half-fat 'butter'	Fat 40 per cent (all milk fat), moisture 55 per cent.	Kerrygold Light
Margarine	Made from fish or animal fats and vegetable oils: minimum 80 per cent fat (up to 10 per cent of which may be milk fat)	Stork Echo (hard) Stork SB Blueband (soft)
Polyunsaturated margarine	Made from oils (e.g., sunflower oil) with high level of polyunsaturated fat: minimum 80 per cent fat, maximum 16 per cent moisture.	Flora Vitalite Blueband
Fat-reduced margarine	Based on vegetable oil: fat 60 per cent, moisture 35 per cent.	Krona Summer County
Mixed fat spread	Fat 70–80 per cent, moisture 15–25 per cent.	Clover Golden Crown Willow Meadow Cup
Reduced-fat spread	75 per cent fat or margarine, based on vegetable oil.	Mello Stork Light
Low-fat spread	Made from vegetable oils and 'dairy' ingredients, such as buttermilk: fat 40 per cent, moisture 55 per cent.	Outline Gold Delight Clover Light Flora Extra Light Half-fat Anchor
Very low-fat	Vegetable oils and dairy ingredients: fat 40 per cent, moisture 60 per cent.	Gold Lowest
Polyunsaturated low-fat	Made from oils high in polyunsaturated fat, sometimes with added milk products: fat 40 per cent, moisture 55 per cent.	Flora Light Shape Sunflower

The 'yellow fats market', including butter, margarine and low-fat spreads, is a £700m market (1992). There have been big changes in demand in this market: in 1973, butter had 75 per cent of the market; today it has only 22 per cent.

The biggest producer of non-butter yellow fats is Unilever, which has 35 per cent of the yellow fats market. The butter producers are very sensitive to challenges from non-butter producers.

A good illustration of this occurred in November 1991. Unilever introduced a new brand called I Can't Believe It's Not Butter!. The Butter Council complained to the Independent Television Commission that regulates television advertising and had advertisements for the product banned. The main cause for complaint was that the product's name contained a double negative, inferring that if you can't believe that the stuff is *not* butter, then you must believe it *is* butter. In fact, I Can't Believe It's Not Butter! is a polyunsaturated fat-reduced margarine.

Market research suggests that the 22 per cent of people who stick with butter do so because of the *taste*. If a product comes along that tastes like butter but is high in polyunsaturates—which reduce cholesterol levels—but low in saturates—which increase cholesterol levels in the blood—then that market could be blown wide open.

Clearly the yellow fats market is a dynamic one. Between 1983 and 1990, butter consumption halved, but margarine consumption also fell by 20 per cent, while sales of the new, reduced-fat products rose by 300 per cent. In the 1990s, with a renewed interest in the environment and purer foods, some people have realized that butter is pure and natural. They see the antioxidants, E numbers, emulsifiers, colourings and stabilizers in margarine and decide on butter instead, so maybe there will be a swing towards butter again.

Questions

1. How is the yellow fats market affected by direct and indirect competition?
2. What are the main factors that are likely to affect consumer buying decisions? How do these factors alter over time?
3. What factors have caused changes in the demand for butter and margarine?
4. How is a company like Unilever able to take a sizeable share of the yellow fats market?
5. What part does the government play in regulating the yellow fats market? Why is this regulation important?

Case Study—Changing patterns of consumer demand

Study the charts and diagrams shown in Fig. 7.1. Select three items that you know experienced increased demand over the period 1970–1990 and three items that experienced a fall in demand during this time. Describe

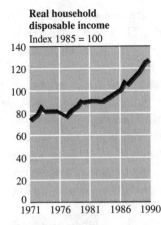

Real household disposable income
Index 1985 = 100

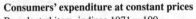

Work time needed to pay for selected items
Married couple with husband only working

Hours and minutes	1971	1981	1986	1990
White sliced loaf	9	8	6	5
1lb rump steak	56	60	46	40
500g butter	19	20	16	13
Pint of milk	5	4	4	3
Dozen eggs	22	17	15	12
100g coffee	22	20	21	14
Pint of beer	14	13	13	11
20 cigarettes	22	20	21	17
Motor car licence	40,31	27,11	25,39	17,55
Colour TV licence	19,27	13,12	14,37	12,32
Litre of petrol	8	8	6	5

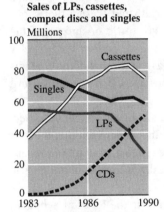

Sales of LPs, cassettes, compact discs and singles
Millions

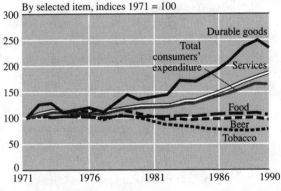

Consumers' expenditure at constant prices
By selected item, indices 1971 = 100

Figure 7.1 Changing patterns of consumer demand. (*Source*: Family Expenditure Survey.)

the change in demand and explain why it occurred. Draw on the data provided in the diagrams as well as on supplementary information that you have.

Case Study—Should we expand, or, how favourable is the economic environment?

The two young fashion designers Lesley Mensah and Carol Sewell who run Poise have a clear idea of their market. Lesley says, 'The woman we are selling to is between 25 and 35 years old. She has a job and the money to spend on clothes'. Lesley adds, 'Our target customer wants to be smartly turned out for work and wants more excitement than is offered by traditional classic lines'. Carol's research shows that this sort of woman is out there in the High Street and represents a growing section of the market as more and more women go back to work and concentrate on a career.

Lesley points out that, although the 25–35-year-old market is already catered for by well-known chains such as Next, there are still many women looking for something slightly different. They do not necessarily want to wear clothes that can be bought in any of the usual High Street shops. They prefer things that nobody else is wearing, so they buy in boutiques and it is to boutiques that Lesley and Carol sell most of their garments.

Before setting up Poise, Carol and Lesley spent two weeks interviewing women in London to ask what kind of style and finish they were looking for in clothes. They also interviewed boutique owners and fashion buyers to find out more about the market. Both Carol and Lesley see themselves to be typical young, well-dressed women and this gives them an insight into their market.

At school, Lesley used to sketch designs for clothes. One day she took her sketches along to an agency called Amalgamated Design that sponsors young designers. They advised her to go to the organizers of the London Fashion Show. They were very enthusiastic and, in 1985, Lesley exhibited a stand of her own designs. This was the turning point. She was commissioned to produce a range of clothes for C&A's three Oxford Street stores.

The workload soon built up and Lesley really began to feel stretched. At this stage she could not afford to employ anyone and felt that the only way to expand the business and cope with the existing demand was to take on a partner. In the fashion business, it really is almost impossible to design, produce, buy and sell all on your own.

It was at this point that Carol Sewell, fresh from the London School of Fashion, joined Lesley. Carol started making and designing clothes at school. She then went on to work for several leading fashion companies as a garment finisher, handsewer, pattern cutter and, finally, a designer. By building up a range of skills 'on the job', Carol developed a thorough understanding of fashion production before going on to the London School of Fashion.

Carol and Lesley can now share the design work. In addition, Lesley concentrates on the marketing and selling side of the business. Carol looks after the production and purchasing side of the business.

Poise is located almost immediately outside Kings Cross station. The workshop is very small, but the location is good because it is in the heart of the London fashion district and suppliers and buyers are not far away. Rent and rates for the premises are cheap.

Poise produces a wide range of items, including jackets, skirts, trousers and blouses. Materials are bought in twice a year and the business produces a Spring/Summer range and an Autumn/Winter range, each consisting of about 16 items.

Designers start creating their outfits well in advance of the shows.

Lesley and Carol consult the trend books that predict next year's fashions. They buy materials in bulk and keep designs simple.

Final production of the goods is contracted out to a factory. The final step is for Poise to deliver the goods to buyers.

Questions

1. What groups and individuals does Poise have to deal with? Make a list. Explain how each of these groups influence the fortunes of the business.
2. What were the main decisions involved in setting up the business? Explain how each of these decisions were affected by the external environment in which the business operates.
3. What factors are likely to influence the success of the business? Which of these factors are within the control of Lesley and Carol? Which do they have no control over?
4. What are the benefits of staying in their existing location? What are the drawbacks?
5. Lesley and Carol must take all their garments out to buyers, rather than invite the buyers back to the workshop. Because it is so small, the workshop might give a bad impression, even though the work is first rate. In any case, at busy times of the year, the workshop can be so full with materials or garments that there is hardly room to move. Would it be worth moving to a new larger location? Explore the pros and cons.

Case Study—New tobacco advertising agreement under attack

At the end of 1991, the Government signed an agreement with the tobacco industry to the effect that advertisements would thereafter carry tougher health warnings, namely 'Smoking kills', and that shop-front advertising near schools must be halved by 1995.

However, this deal was severely criticized by anti-smoking groups who felt it to be weak and spread over too long a time-scale.

Under the agreement, permanent shop-front advertising near schools has to be removed and advertising has been banned in young women's magazines.

The agreement had been awaited for a year, amid rumours that the Department of Health had threatened to ban *all* advertising unless a voluntary agreement was arrived at.

Questions

1. What do you think will be the effect of the agreement?
2. Do you think that the agreement goes far enough?
3. Can you find out what the position is of the European Community on cigarette advertising? How might this affect the position of the UK government?
4. The Secretary of the British Medical Association stated that, 'Children need the protection of the Government from the tobacco industry, not just when they are in the playground but when they are travelling about. Lung cancer is not a disease confined to school playgrounds'.

    Do you think that the government has a responsibility to protect school children? How should it do this? Why do you think that the government allows cigarette advertising? List six other industrial activities that are curtailed by government intervention.

Activity

You have been commissioned to produce a report seeking planning permission for a proposed service station. Your particular responsibility is to explain the benefits that the new station will bring to local people. In your report, you are expected to explain the various ways in which a service station adds value to the products it sells—fuels and lubricants, tyres and accessories, items for the shop—to the advantage of the customers.

What is a report? Many people when they hear the word 'report' immediately think of a school report; others think of a newspaper report, but a report is simply a written (or spoken) statement from someone who has made a study of something. That 'something' can be anything from a local newsworthy event (such as a local football derby) or how a school or hospital or business actually works.

There are many ways in which to set out your report. The basic essential is clarity and ease of reading. The sequence of thoughts must be simple to follow (subheadings can help here).

Here is one possible sequence:

*   *title*—this tells the reader what the report is about;
*   *contents list*—this tells the reader in more detail what the report is about;
*   *terms of reference*—this tells the reader what you were asked to do in the first place, so, in your case, you could say, 'I have been asked to study the proposed service station and report on the benefits it would

provide for the community. The report will be presented to the Planning Committee';

- *procedure*—this explains how you set about collecting the information (did you write to people, asking their opinions, or did you carry out some face-to-face interviews and what else did you do—did you visit other service stations in nearby towns?);
- *findings*—this could be the longest part of the report;
- *summing up*—this is a brief reminder of your findings—for instance; this service station will provide employment for eight people; will be used by over 2000 motorists every day, most of them local people; the shop will stock a range of 900 different consumer goods and local people will find it convenient to pop in because it stays open until late and so on;
- *recommendations*—these are the actions you think should be taken by the Planning Committee as a result of your findings;
- *signature*—this tells everyone that it is your work.

Activity

Figure 7.2 shows the top 20 brands in the UK in 1991.

	TOP TWENTY	
	Product	£m
1	Persil	£205.6
2	Coca-Cola	£203.0
3	Ariel detergent	£201.1
4	Nescafé coffee	£188.5
5	Andrex toilet paper	£181.0
6	Whiskas cat food	£178.1
7	Silver Spoon white sugar	£144.5
8	PG Tips tea	£140.7
9	Flora margarine	£125.3
10	Tetley tea bags	£116.6
11	Heinz baked beans	£111.4
12	Robinsons squash	£106.4
13	Walkers crisps	£105.6
14	Pedigree Chum dog food	£105.3
15	Heinz soup	£95.9
16	Mr Kipling cakes	£92.6
17	Kellogg's Corn Flakes	£85.2
18	Tate and Lyle white sugar	£84.9
19	Kit Kat chocolate snacks	£84.9
20	Anchor butter	£80.2

Figure 7.2 Top 20 products in the UK in 1991.

What do these brands have in common? Make a list of factors. Carry out some research to find out how aware consumers are of these brands. How do consumers know about these brands? What makes consumers buy them? All 20 were in the top 20 brand list for 1990 as well. How do the firms concerned maintain this brand loyalty? German-made Müller yogurt shot up to 41st place, making the fastest increase in sales, even though it was only launched in the UK four years ago. How can you account for this rapid rise in popularity?

Activity

Make a study of a local business to find out how it is affected by individuals and groups that make up its environment. How is it affected by the following:

- consumers;
- competitors;
- national and local government;
- neighbours;
- suppliers?

Essay title 1—Reconcile the following statements: 'A decrease in demand leads to a decrease in price' and 'A decrease in price leads to a rise in the quantity demanded'.

This is a straightforward essay, asking you to show your understanding of simple changes that take place in the market-place.

Start off by defining 'decrease in demand' and 'decrease in price'.

A decrease in demand (see Fig. 7.3) occurs when a smaller quantity is demanded for a good or service at any given price than previously.

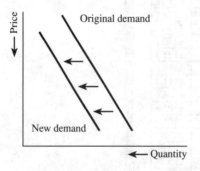

Figure 7.3 A decrease in demand and its effect on prices.

A decrease in price is simply a fall in the market price of a particular good or service.

The quantity of a good that is demanded is inextricably tied up with its price. The price is usually the first thing that a buyer looks at when considering a purchase (although this is not always the case).

The main body of your essay should be concerned with explaining the two statements and showing that they are an integral part of dynamic price theory. Use plenty of applied examples.

A decrease in demand leads to a decrease in price. There are a number of major factors that may cause demand to decrease. These would include:

- *A change in tastes*. With greater environmental awareness and increased traffic delays on the road, a number of people have switched to buying smaller cars, leading to a decrease in demand for 'gas guzzlers'. In the pop and fashion industries, tastes and fashions can change very rapidly—this month's sensation can become next month's has been. When Scotland went to the World Cup finals in Mexico, many copies of the football record 'We're All Part of Ally's Army' sold at standard prices in the shop, but after Scotland had lost to Peru, shopkeepers couldn't give them away.

- *A fall in incomes*. In most countries, average living standards increase year by year. In a recession, incomes may drop for a large number of people. At these times, demand for a number of items is likely to fall—say, for foreign holidays, cars and consumer durables in particular.

- *A fall in the population*. A falling population in a country can lead to a general fall in demand, which will pull down general price levels. What is more likely to happen is that there will be a fall in a particular *age group* as a result of demographic trends. For example, between 1990 and the year 2000, the population of 15–29-year-olds in the United Kingdom is expected to fall by 16 per cent. Clearly this may lead to a fall in demand by this group for all sorts of items—clothes, starter and second homes, cars, leisure services. This will therefore bring down prices of some goods typically bought by this group. Producers may switch their production to expanding age groups—for example, in the same period, the number of 30–59-year-olds is expected to rise by 12 per cent.

- *A fall in the price of substitute products*. When the price of substitutes that compete directly or indirectly with your product fall, then demand is likely to fall for your own product. A reaction to this may be to lower prices in order to compete. Recently a number of estate agents have reduced the commission they charge in order to win over customers. Rivals have tried to match these actions to win back demand. Equally, a rise in the price of a complementary product is likely to reduce the demand for its complement. If petrol becomes more expensive, companies may reduce the size of their vehicle fleets. The knock-on effect is to leave unsold cars on garage forecourts, putting downward pressure on prices of cars generally.

- *A reduction in wealth.* When people's wealth falls, they have less of a capital base on which to borrow and to spend. In the recession of 1991 and 1992, people found that their houses were falling in value. They therefore became more reluctant to borrow and this helped to dampen down demand in the economy and, thus, pull prices down for specific goods, such as household furnishings.

A decrease in price leads to a rise in demand. When prices in an economy fall (as measured by the Retail Price Index—RPI), if people's incomes remain constant or rise or fall by less than prices, then the standard of living will rise. People will have more money and are therefore likely to spend more, therefore creating a rise in demand.

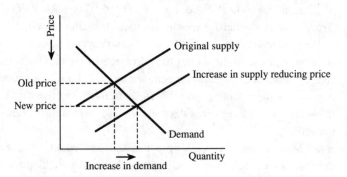

Figure 7.4 A decrease in price leads to a rise in demand.

When the prices of individual goods fall, they are likely to become relatively more attractive and people may buy more of them. If a particular cheese is on special offer, for example, its sales may boom. When items such as the ballpoint pen, the home computer and the pocket calculator were first invented, they were costly to produce and hence expensive to buy. As mass production methods were introduced and the prices of these items fell, then demand increased enormously.

In conclusion, you should point out that prices are very important signals to consumers and producers. When prices are falling, consumers may be attracted to buy more of a particular good. However, if price is falling as a result of an original fall in demand, then the price fall may serve only to staunch the loss of demand rather than to reinstate it to former levels. Business owners will need to react to the fall in demand by examining their marketing mix. They will have to look to price, product, promotion and place to try and re-inject some vitality into their product. While some products can be re-launched and revamped, others will have reached a stage of maturity from which there is no turning back.

Essay title 2—How can a particular group of consumers influence business behaviour?

All businesses need to be aware of the market-place in which they operate and, hence, consumer wishes. Marketing (and market research in particular) is the means by which businesses anticipate and identify consumer needs and wants. Businesses will then be able to take strategic decisions to make sure that they fulfil consumer requirements. Businesses need to be aware of the consumer characteristics of particular segments of the market-place. The typical consumer of a product (if such a thing exists) is constantly changing. Today's consumer, for example, is more environmentally and technologically aware than ever before. Moreover, consumers are increasingly well-informed about product characteristics and requirements.

The central part of the essay could focus on a particular group of consumers. For example Mintel carried out a survey on children as consumers. It reported that children are becoming increasingly sophisticated consumers, with a growing influence over their parents' shopping habits. Parents are increasingly nagged by their offspring about what they should buy for the entire family.

The Mintel report, *Children—The Influencing Factor* (1991) says that, in all social classes, children have the greatest effect on their parents' shopping from the age of 5 until about 11 or 12. At this stage, children are old enough to be aware of products and of the power they can exert in determining which ones are bought, but young enough for the family still to be the hub of their existence.

The report added that this is the age group that will show the biggest increase in the last decade of the twentieth century.

Parents are affected by their children's health needs, eating habits, such as the growing number of child vegetarians, and increasing fashion-consciousness.

The main influences on what children want are their friends, followed by their schools and advertising.

Mintel also asked nearly 7500 households about their weekly expenditure. Those with children spent almost £60 on food a week compared to just over £40 by those without.

Looking at the graph in Fig. 7.5, it becomes immediately obvious that households with children spend considerably more than those without. Clearly businesses need to respond to the needs and wishes of this group of consumers. It is all too clear that a lot of television advertising of branded foods is already aimed at this group.

The Mintel report also indicated that children are educating their parents about green issues and persuading them to buy environmentally

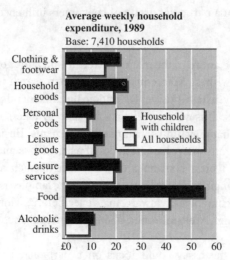

Figure 7.5 Average weekly household expenditure, 1989. (*Source*: FES/Mintel.)

friendly products. Mothers who took part in discussions with researchers admitted to being so influenced that they bought green products even when the children were not there.

Surveys like the Mintel one, Social Trends and the Family Expenditure Survey are widely used by businesses. In a competitive market-place, the more information that businesses have about consumer requirements, the better they can respond. Business organizations try to chart the benefits that consumers are looking for and to translate them into products. A key question is, 'Who makes the buying decisions?' closely followed by, 'What do they require?'

At the end of the day, consumers may choose *not* to buy products. Green consumers may buy publications outlining which products are or are not environmentally friendly. They will look carefully at such issues as packaging, nature of ingredients, use of resources and so on. Sometimes groups of consumers may actively boycott products. For example, in the 1960s and 1970s, many consumers refused to bank with Barclays because of its links with South Africa. Other consumers have boycotted firms involved with testing products on animals.

Consumers can also orchestrate pressure by means of organized consumer groups. Complaints can be taken to groups such as the Consumer's Association, which publishes *Which?* magazine, and to the local Trading Standards Office. Many industries have their own regulatory groups, too, such as ABTA for travel agents, Oftel for Telecommunications and so on. Each of the public corporations has its own Nationalized Industries Consumer Council. Industries that have been privatized have each got a consumer council. Consumer complaints can be taken further, through the courts or raised with a local Member of Parliament. There are many regulations covering consumer rights and business responsibilities, but pressure from consumers is sure to bring about more legislation in this area.

In conclusion, you might want to argue that consumers have many rights in the market-place. Clearly, in many areas these rights are not being effectively enforced. In the final analysis the consumer's greatest right is not to buy. In the long run, any firm that fails to work for its consumers is likely to fail.

Essay title 3 — 'Markets that are dominated by a small number of firms will rarely be competitive'. Discuss this statement.

Sometimes a simplistic generalization is made — 'Lots of competitors, good; few competitors, bad'. When there are a few firms operating in the market, they have the potential to restrict output and raise prices.

You may find it helpful to set out some simple explanations of monopoly, oligopoly, monopolistic competition and perfect competition at this stage.

The great advantage that large firms have over smaller ones is their ability to rationalize the way resources are used. These advantages are referred to as *economies of scale*. You might briefly explain technical, financial, managerial, marketing, commercial and risk-spreading economies. What these economies add up to is the ability of large firms to produce large outputs at low unit costs.

Because of their ability to produce at low average cost, firms are able to gain a large market share and, also, to create an artificial monopoly position. As a result, barriers to entry are created in the market-place. New firms cannot enter freely because of the prohibitive cost of tooling up to produce in bulk.

Will the large firms then use their market dominance to exploit consumers? Clearly, if we assume that a firm sets out to maximize profits, it may then choose to restrict output and raise prices. Indeed, the Monopolies Commission has been kept busy over the last 45 years investigating a host of suspected monopoly positions. For example, it regularly investigates the sale of washing powders (dominated by two large firms), petrol retailing (dominated by Shell, Esso and BP), High Street banking (dominated by NatWest, Barclays, Lloyds and Midland), condoms (dominated by the London Rubber Company) and many other industries.

However, it frequently reports that there is no case to answer in these industries. In fact, oligopoly markets can be highly competitive. Because there are only a few large firms jostling for position, they may be forced continually to out-guess each others' strategies — that is, to be highly competitive. The theory of games explores ways in which a few players may try to devise strategies that will outflank each others' next move. This is a fair description of what frequently happens in oligopoly markets. One key implication of oligopoly competition is that competitors will plough substantial sums into market research and product development. Often this research and development is a prerequisite of quality. For example, although the Monopolies Commission has found prices charged for drugs and medicines to be high, it has been felt that this is an acceptable price to pay for medical developments and quality.

Large companies can use the advantages of economies of scale to add value to products. 'Value' is a blend of price and benefits and both are critical. Unless the price is right, the best combination of desirable benefits will not be considered good value by the customer. Nor, in the long term, will the customer think it good value if the benefits are added irresponsibly, by damaging the environment for instance. The customer's decision is final.

Benefits, whether tangible—in the form of scientifically measurable product differences—or intangible—in the form of 'image' or service—are comparatively easy to add.

The difficult part is determining which benefits people want and then producing them at an acceptable price and in an environmentally acceptable way. Both these requirements can only be met by more efficient operations at all stages of production and marketing. 'Efficient operations' are those operations that produce the desired end result at the lowest financial and environmental cost. The two aims are fully complementary. In fact, cost reduction, which helps achieve the financial target, is essentially the same as waste reduction, which helps achieve the environmental target. Of course, both cost and waste reduction involve initial investment.

Large companies, therefore, have the *means* to achieve efficient operations as well as the *incentive*—other large competitors striving for their own efficient operations.

It is not surprising that in the real world many of the UK's 'best' companies operate in oligopoly market situations—Marks and Spencer and Tesco, Shell and BP, Cadburys and Rowntree Macintosh.

In its recommendations, the Monopolies and Mergers Commission in recent years has tended to consider whether the benefits of a monopoly situation outweigh the costs or not. Concentration has not been seen as being a bad thing *in itself*. More important has been the ability of new firms to enter an industry and the way in which firms in concentrated markets have behaved. The Competition Act 1980 stressed that the Monopolies and Mergers Commission should be more concerned with the *general competitive environment* in an industry than with the level of concentration.

In conclusion, it is important to note that we need to look at how firms operate in practice before we can draw out general conclusions about competition and its effects. Undoubtedly, large firms have the ability to carry out restrictive practices, to charge high prices and to restrict output. It is sound business practice, however, to aim for a competitive edge, to invest and research for the future and to constantly seek ways of leading the market through quality.

Essay titles

1. 'Business behaviour is determined as much by the environment in which it operates as by the people that run it.' Discuss.
2. Explain why market forces are constantly changing market conditions.
3. 'Monopolies situations should be assessed according to whether the benefits outweigh the costs or not.' Discuss.
4. 'Markets that are dominated by a small number of firms will rarely be competitive.' Discuss this statement.
5. How does the UK government seek to make markets more competitive?
6. What are the most important factors influencing the supply of products to markets?
7. 'Markets should never be interfered with.' Discuss.
8. Explain how UK businesses stand to benefit from the development of the Single Market.
9. 'Competition will always lead to the best use of resources in society.' Discuss.
10. In what ways does business activity involve competition for and cooperation in the use of scarce resources?
11. Discuss the view that steadily rising demand is always good for business.
12. Show how the forces of demand and supply interact to create a market price.
13. How stable are market forces in the real world?
14. Why are some prices more volatile than others?
15. What should be the role of the government in creating a climate favourable to business enterprise?
16. What influence can a business exert over its environment?
17. How has new technology changed patterns of business development in recent years.
18. 'Supply creates its own demand.' Discuss.
19. How can government increase the level of competition in the UK economy?

20. Is the opening up of the Single Market the most significant development for firms in Britain in the 1990s?

Short-answer questions

1. List five reasons that might lead to an increase in demand for pork.
2. List five factors that might lead to a rise in the supply of camcorders
in shops.
3. What is a monopoly?
4. What is a restrictive practice? Give an example.
5. Give three examples of competitive oligopoly markets.
6. Does the demand for consumer goods always increase with rising
incomes? Explain.
7. Why does a typical supply curve slope upwards from left to right?
8. Why does a typical demand curve slope downwards from left to
right?
9. What are the conditions of perfect competition?
10. What is meant by the 'external environment' in which businesses
operate?
11. What is a merger?
12. Who are the members of the European Community?
13. How can changes in technology affect the supply of a particular
product?
14. Give three examples of pairs of complementary goods.
15. Give three examples of pairs of substitute goods.
16. What is:

   - a natural monopoly;
   - an artificial monopoly?

17. What is the Monopolies Commission?
18. What is monopolistic competition?
19. What happened to 'national standards' for EC member states after
1992?
20. How can government taxes affect business activity?

Projects

There are many project titles that could be used to look at a firm in its
environment. For example:

- You may want to examine Social Trends or the Family Expenditure
Survey as well as work produced by private market research agencies
to find out about changes in demand in particular product sectors.

This sort of research could support work you have carried out to identify gaps in the market for new products. You could then produce a report to show that you have identified a clear pattern of potential demand for a new good or service.

- You may want to look at changing demand patterns for a particular good or service in your locality. What factors influence demand, say, for hairdressing? How have these demand patterns changed over time—what have been the implications for supply?
- You may want to investigate the effect of 1992 on local businesses in your area. Carry out a survey and present your findings in the form of a detailed report.

Suggested reading

Cannon, Tom, *Enterprise—Creation, Development and Growth*. Butterworth Heinemann, 1991.

Danks, S., *A First Course in Business Studies*. D. P. Publications, 1991.

Hobday, Ian, *Economics—A First Course* (2nd edn). Hodder & Stoughton, 1991

Huggett, Renée, *Markets*. Macmillan, 1990.

Kent, Penelope, *M + E European Community Law*. Pitman, 1991.

8
Marketing

We live in a world where new products and services designed to improve our quality of life are constantly being made available. Such improvements are due to the process of marketing. Marketing is the link in a chain that communicates the wishes of consumers to producers, who respond by making goods and/or services available in the market-place. It is, therefore, the essential point of contact between an organization and the users of its products.

The Chartered Institute of Marketing defines marketing as, 'The anticipation, identification and fulfilment of a consumer need—at a profit'. It is thus a *strategic* discipline that enables an organization to provide products which make it more competitive so that it can achieve its objectives. Marketing services are the *tools and tactics* used to support the marketing process.

Case Study—Waning thirst for electronic wizardry

Japan seems to have an endless appetite for electronic gadgets. The ultimate in such consumption has to be the remote controlled lavatory. At the mere touch of a button, you can raise or lower the lid and seat, set the heating level inside the toilet seat, flush and then produce a jet of water for the bidet effect!

In post-war Japan, families had to worry where the next meal would come from. Yet today's generation is one of the richest groups of consumers in the world. The problem is no longer how to find the money to survive, it is one of finding new things to buy. Electronic companies in modern Japan provide continuously upgraded 'fuzzy logic' implements for householders to cater for the multitude of different needs and demands in the home. These include washing machines whose fuzzy logic programs adapt to different types of washing and dirtiness and vacuum cleaners that adapt to different floor surfaces. Consumers, however, cannot be fooled all of the time. When it appeared that a shirt washed by fuzzy logic showed little difference to the one washed by a standard machine, consumers began questioning whether the higher price tags were really justified. At the same time, there is a general feeling that many consumer markets in Japan are beginning to reach maturity. Car sales fell from 5.1 million in 1990 to 4.8 million in 1991, with nearly 80 per cent of households owning a car already.

One economist thinks he has the answer for the downturn in the Japanese market. Paul Summerville, Chief Economist for Jardine Fleming in Tokyo, argues that the next big growth area will not be in gadgets for houses, but in the houses themselves. He feels that the boom will be a selective one and will affect those properties that have an owner and are in need of renovation and rebuilding. Today, despite all of the hi-tech gadgets in bathrooms and elsewhere, many Japanese properties look decidedly shabby. In fact, 37 per cent of Japan's existing housing stock was built before 1965. Given the difference in average incomes between 1965 and today, housing standards are totally out of sync with income levels.

This reflection is borne out by looking at the quality of Japanese homes. A typical home would have non-existent insulation, cardboard walls and low ceilings. If a massive building and house improvement boom is to take place in Japan, the path to the consumer's yen is clear: forget about providing gadgets and elaborate electronic goods and move into the home improvement market.

Questions

1. How does the Case Study highlight the changing needs of consumers in Japan?
2. Explain why continuously updating products shortens product life cycles?
3. How will shorter product life cycles affect the environment?
4. What is meant by 'many consumer markets in Japan are beginning to reach maturity?'
5. If consumer markets seem to be reaching maturity, what should Japanese manufacturers be doing?

Case Study—The video game war

THE WEEK

VIDEO GAMES

Nintendo fights off Sega with an early launch for Super NES console

By Mat Toor

Nintendo has brought forward the launch of its next generation video game in an attempt to cut short the success of arch-rival Sega in the top end of the £200m console market.

The Super NES was originally due to launch in the UK at the end of 1992 or early 1993. But now Nintendo plans to bring the machine to market in either May or June of this year.

The £150 Super NES, packaged with the latest adventure of the brand's spokesman Mario, offers improved sound and visual detail and competes directly with the £130 Sega Megadrive.

Both are called "16 bit" machines because their computer brains are twice as powerful as the "8 bit" silicon chips in the ordinary NES.

The launch of the Super NES will take the bitter marketing struggle between Sega and Nintendo to

Mario: part of the Super NES package brought forward by Nintendo

a new battleground – for both teenagers and adults.

Observers believe that it was the success of the Megadrive in the run up to Christmas – many retailers sold out and supplies had to be air-freighted from Japan – that forced Nintendo's hand.

"They've had to bring forward the launch otherwise they would concede the 16 bit market totally to Sega," says John Salisbury, editor of *World Toy News*.

But Mike Hayes, marketing manager for Nintendo's UK distributor Bandai, denies the compa-

ny was "panicked" into its decision.

He says the explosion of the video games market in the past two years means the UK is "catching up" with the US and Japanese markets where the Super NES has already been launched.

Hayes anticipates that the new machine will actually outsell the standard NES console in 1992 by 600,000 to 450,000.

Sega is likely to respond to the Super NES with a further price cut to £100, although marketing manager Simon Morris is reticent about the company's plans.

In the US the Sega 16 bit machine, branded Genesis, ran the Super NES very close over the Christmas. Some analysts even maintain that the Genesis emerged the winner. That prompted an unprecented corporate statement from Nintendo that the Super NES would reach its sales target.

Figure 8.1 The video game war. (*Source: Marketing*, 9 January, 1992.)

Questions

1. Explain why the Sega Megadrive was so successful in late 1991.
2. Why has Nintendo brought forward the launch of the Super NES?
3. Define the term 'direct competition'.
4. The Super NES uses the brands spokesman, Mario. Using other examples of characters identified with brands, explain how such characters help to promote a product or service.
5. Identify the various segments of the market for computer games. Describe briefly how Nintendo's promotional mix should differ for each market segment.
6. Explain why Nintendo uses Bandai to distribute its products.
7. How is Sega likely to respond to this direct competition for its Megadrive?

Case Study—Benetton moves into moral issues

Luciano Benetton, President of the Italian clothing giant, masterminded the company's move away from promotions depicting pictures of jumpers into moral issues and a sea of controversy. For the past four years, Benetton has tested the patience of regulatory authorities with pictures of black surrogacy, graveyards and condoms. Recently its advertising agency J. Walter Thompson and UK poster contractors were caught up in the furore over Benetton's refusal to tear down its newborn baby posters.

Figure 8.2 Benetton shop.

In a strong attack, the Advertising Standards Authority heavily criticized not just the advertiser but also its agency and site contractors for not rejecting the campaign. A spokeswoman for the ASA said that, 'Benetton has displayed a conspicuous disregard for the sensitivities of the public. We are concerned it has ignored our advice to scrap the advertisement'. Now, media owners and agencies are being warned to check with the ASA before accepting any future work from Benetton. So far, the new-born baby campaign has provoked more than 800 complaints. Council planning departments have been inundated with requests from residents asking for posters to be removed. At least one airport authority has banned it and one pub landlady was furious and pointed to loss of business when the picture was posted opposite her beer garden. In other locations, many posters have been defaced or ripped down.

Benetton feel that UK advertising legislators should pay to take down the ads if they are unhappy with them. They are now planning a repeat run of the ad showing a black child sitting next to a white child with its hair made into horns.

Questions

1. Does the controversy over the Benetton campaign point to their success or failure to communicate a message? Explain why.
2. Briefly describe the role of an advertising agency in such a campaign.
3. Explain how the Advertising Standards Authority functions.
4. To what extent does the case indicate that the UK requires a stronger regulatory framework controlling advertising?

Case Study—The instant coffee market

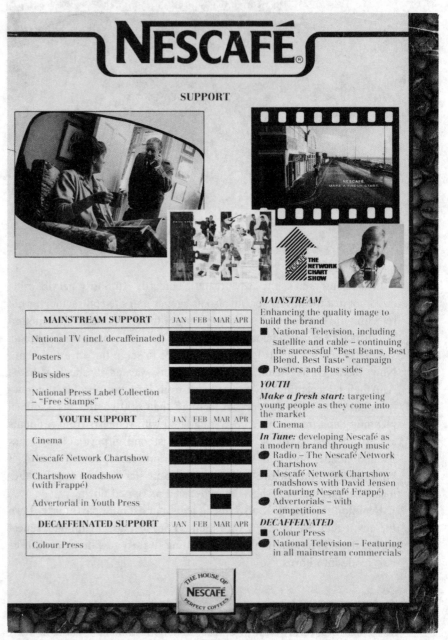

Figure 8.3 Nescafé support. (*Source*: Nestlé.)

Questions

1. Comment generally upon the changing trends in the sale and consumption of instant coffee since 1976.
2. Explain how such information would be used by manufacturers.

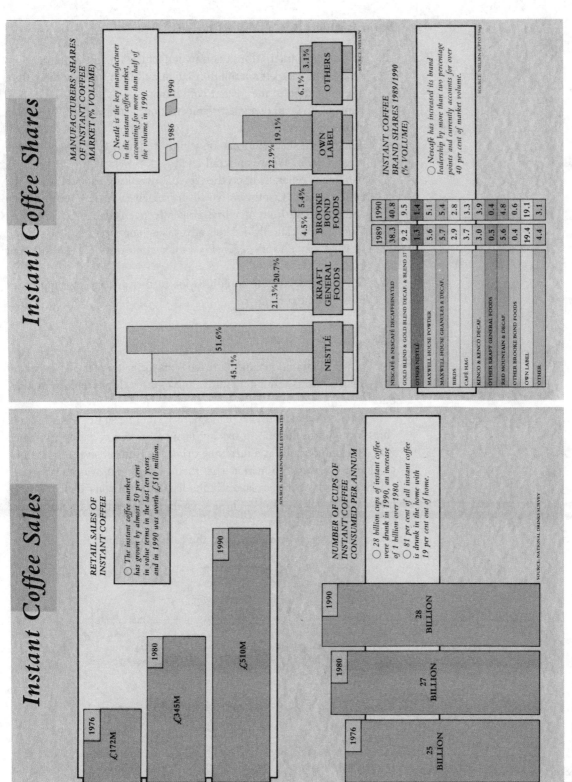

Figure 8.4 The instant coffee market. (*Source: Hot Beverages Report 1991*, Nestlé.)

3. List other market information manufacturers might require.
4. Analyse the market share information and then indicate the nature of competition in the instant coffee market.
5. Explain how market share information will be used by coffee manufacturers.
6. The market share information is provided by A.C. Nielson through a retail audit. What is a retail audit?
7. Comment generally upon the type of advertising expenditure in the coffee market. List the coffee advertisements you have recently seen and can recall from memory. How effective is each?
8. How do Nescafé divide their advertising support?
9. In what way do they *differentiate* their strategies between different groups of consumers?
10. Suggest how Nescafé could provide further advertising support for each type of consumer.

Case Study—Lyons Tetley

Tea is Britain's traditional drink. It accounts for just under 50 per cent of everything we drink, excluding water, and tops the drinks table as number one.

In the hot beverage market, tea is perceived to be as British as fish and chips or a pint in the pub. It has heritage and tradition and is associated with a morning cuppa, as a mealtime drink or as afternoon tea. It is drunk by almost everyone, no matter what their background or occupation.

There are three major players in the tea market: Lyons Tetley; Brooke Bond and Premier Brands. These account for more than 50 per cent of total tea sales in Britain.

The market can be divided into the categories shown in Fig. 8.5.

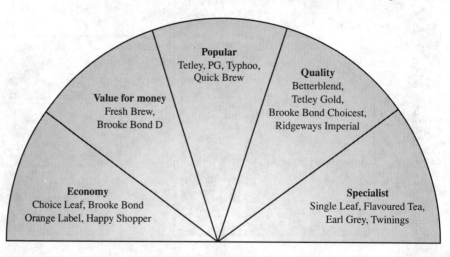

Figure 8.5 Segments of the tea market.

As well as divisions in the market according to the segments shown in Fig. 8.5, there are also variations according to buying behaviour. For example, Tetley traditionally performs well in the North, whereas PG performs well in the South.

Tetley teas are manufactured by Lyons Tetley, which belongs to the food division of Allied Lyons. The group's key strengths lie in the following:

- building brands;
- meeting changing consumer needs through new product development;
- international thinking and operation;
- having the financial resources and quality of staff to meet these objectives.

Tetley's Greenford factory produces over 100 different tea packet styles and around 30 different blends of tea. Styles of pack range from loose tea in cartons to tea bags in plastic boxes.

Tetley's advertising agency is DMB & B, whose main function is to develop and produce advertising for Lyons Tetley. At the same time, it also provides other specialist agency services, such as public relations and sales promotions. The advertising agency has to become an authority on the market it is handling. By placing itself in this position, it is able to produce advertising that is attention-grabbing and entertaining by communicating a message that is relevant not just to the brand, but which also addresses competitive activity in the market at that point in time. As a result the client–agency relationship is a close one, though there are some areas of overlap between the functions and expertise of each.

Tetley tea advertising involves communicating different messages as the market situation develops. Its key feature is its ability to be memorable and amusing. For example, the 'tea folk' have supported the brand since 1973 and have given Tetley an identifiable trademark with a craftsmanlike connotation and a depth of support. As well as projecting the qualities of the brand, they have reflected major product innovations, such as the round tea bag designed to maintain and develop Lyons Tetley's market share.

Questions

1. As there are three major players in the tea market, what sort of competitive activity would you expect?
2. Comment generally on the consumer profile of a tea drinker. Mention:

   - factors affecting demand;

- consumer needs;
- image of tea;
- socio-economic grouping;
- lifestyle.

3. How would a knowledge of this consumer profile affect the way in which tea is marketed?
4. Look at the different market segments for tea. Explain how a promotion for the popular sector would differ from a promotion for the specialist sector.
5. Explain why Allied Lyons identify one of their group strengths as 'meeting changing consumer needs through new product development'.
6. Research and then identify the roles of an advertising agency.
7. Explain why the marketing process must be a dynamic and progressive activity.

Activity

Work in small groups to complete the following activity:

- choose a product or service;
- using both desk and field research, obtain details about the market in which this product or service operates:
  —the market segment it is designed to appeal to;
  —the image it portrays (if necessary conduct an image study);
  —its stage in its life cycle;
  —further product possibilities, line extensions and so on;
  —environmental, social implications of product development;
  —current strategies;
  —the elements of its marketing mix and so on;
- conduct a SWOT analysis;
- use appropriate presentation techniques to display feedback from your research.

Put yourself in the position of the marketing or brand manager responsible for this product or service. With the help of all the information you have obtained and, using a report format, indicate the strategies you would adopt to increase its market share. Present this report to the rest of the group and be prepared to discuss your findings.

Activity

Write to a marketing manager or brand manager of a local company.

Arrange a convenient time and date to interview him or her. Before attending the interview:

● make a list of questions, topics and areas you would like to discuss with them;
● familiarize yourself with brands and products from their organization.

Write up the results of your interview. Indicate what you have found out and how this has improved your understanding of marketing.

Activity

You are responsible for the launch of a new model of Vauxhall motor car:

● What will you call the car?
● What market segment is it going to operate in?
● What differential advantages is it going to have over its competitors?

Prepare a campaign plan for the launch of this car:

● What media slots would you use to attract the attention of buyers?
● How will you build upon the loyalty of users of other Vauxhalls?
● What other areas of the promotional mix will be used to support the launch?

How will other areas of the marketing mix be used?
Compare your strategies with those of others.

Essay title 1 — Why might an organization wish to change the position of a product in a particular market or relaunch an existing product?

In your introduction to the essay, the answer should indicate that the environment in which organizations exist is constantly changing. At the same time, consumer preferences change. Both points would, ideally, be supported with examples. Marketing is the dynamic function that allows organizations to respond to such changes. It should be defined.

As a product goes through its life cycle, more competitors will appear in the market-place as the market matures. Define the product lifecycle. As the market reaches maturity, we would expect more marketing activity, which might necessitate the changing of a product's position or the relaunch of an existing product.

Changing the position of a product in a particular market involves the company in establishing where its product is in relation to its competitors — downmarket, midmarket or upmarket and so on. Market research with, perhaps, an image study would reveal this. Then, to reposition a product (change the position of a product in a market), for example, move it upmarket, the company would have to look at the ingredients of the marketing mix (defining marketing mix here). For example, how would you make a car seem more upmarket? This can be achieved in several ways:

- *the product*: add extras—electric windows, tinted glass and so on;
- *the price*: increase the price and use the increase to pay for the extras and the change of perception;
- *the promotion*: show the product in more upmarket surroundings, being used by more exclusive people and so on, use less mass-market media and more selective media; consider a re-imaging process, such as the Rover group have used;
- *the place*: look carefully at dealerships and the process of delivering cars to consumers.

Relaunching an existing product involves a massive injection into the product life cycle as the product begins to mature. An organization might need to make people aware of the product again, re-establish loyalties, emphasize brand heritage, identify with the product again and so on. To do this, they would have to look again at the ingredients of the marketing mix. For example:

- *the product*: whether cosmetic or radical modifications are required, line extensions and so on—use examples;
- *the price*: consider tactics—short-term and long-term, competitive pricing, penetration pricing and so on, each type of pricing being supported by an example;
- *the promotion*: consider the campaign plan;
- *the place*: make the product more accessible, perhaps with a wider range of product sizes.

A good answer would be supported by examples throughout.

In conclusion, say what the net results of each strategy are—greater market share, profits and so on. The aims of such an exercise must be to provide a firm foundation for an organization to meet its range of objectives.

Essay title 2—Explain why the marketing mix for each product will be unique.

This is a fairly straightforward question, which is best answered with constant reference to examples.

In the introduction, mention that every organization will have different objectives, such as maximizing profits, brand leadership, market domination and so on, that will lead it to adopt different strategies to another. At the heart of corporate strategy is the need to match marketing practices with corporate objectives. Marketing should be defined here. For example, British Airways seeks to lead the world's airline industry, but such an objective involves setting standards for others to follow.

What is the marketing mix? The mix should be defined. It should be viewed as a device to suit the precise requirements of each market. An example of a well-known product should be used to illustrate each of the ingredients.

The crucial element in answering this question is to respond to the 'why'. For example:

- all organizations have different objectives and will need to develop mixes to meet such objectives;
- every mix must be designed to suit the precise requirements of the market and markets vary enormously;
- mixes have to be constantly modified to respond to the changing conditions in the business environment;
- marketing is a dynamic function, so no mix remains static for very long;
- the mix has to be constantly modified to respond to changing phases in the product's life cycle.

The answer should then briefly analyse each of the ingredients of the mix to highlight why even products or services that seem to be similar would have completely different marketing mixes. Marketing mixes cover:

- *the product*—tangible features, such as colour, size, design, packaging, and intangible ones, such as guarantees, after-sales service and so on, and product benefits, such as generic dimensions, sensual dimensions and extended dimensions.

- *the price*—pricing objectives, and pricing strategies, both long and short term;

- *the place*—different forms of transport and different forms of distribution systems;

- *the promotion*—promotional mix, controllable methods and non-controllable methods, advertisements, sales promotions, personal selling techniques and public relations as well as various uses of creative elements to communicate with consumers.

It is essential that the answer is constantly put in context and the best way to do this with this question is to use examples of how rival products use different mixes to differentiate between each other.

In conclusion, then, every product is as individual as each and every human being. Though some products seem to be similar superficially, when you analyse their mixes, you begin to realize how completely different they are.

Essay title 3 — 'The fault of much of British industry has been a failure to recognize the importance of marketing.' Discuss this statement.

This is a difficult question to answer because of its very general nature. Many would automatically respond to it because it mentions marketing and then, perhaps, become 'bogged down' in it at a later stage. A good answer must show wide-ranging knowledge, understanding of the question, analysis and substance.

In the introduction you could say that there have been many criticisms of British industry over recent years. Throughout the two major recessions during the 1980s and early 1990s we have seen:

- a changing structure of British manufacturing and service-based industries;
- some industries go into decline while others continue to develop;
- some industries remain product-orientated;
- uncertainty in British markets.

The question is, have the successful organizations *always* been market-orientated and the unsuccessful ones product-orientated? The answer would then attempt to show that marketing cannot and, indeed, can never hope to *eliminate* risk, but it can certainly *reduce* it. To understand how, we have to analyse what marketing is.

The body of the answer could then look at marketing, its definition, key features and benefits. Such an answer must be supported with numerous examples to show how marketing works and what happens where marketing does not take place, such as in the motor-cycle industry.

The answer should also attempt to clear up any misapprehension about the role of marketing. For example, in the 1970s, many organizations had a token marketing department with a tactical function. Today, marketing assumes a significantly greater importance for many organizations in leading them towards the achievement of their overall corporate objectives. In fact, today, many organizations have a 'total product' approach towards marketing, whereby all of the activities of the organization are designed to fulfil the needs of the consumer. Such an approach relates quality to marketing and ultimately to success in the market-place.

So what of the organizations that ignore marketing? They will:

- be less responsive to consumer needs;
- be less competitive;
- lack overall direction;
- rely on past achievements.

For the conclusion, mention that it must be remembered that marketing is not only a way of responding to consumer needs, it is also a system of planning—taking decisions today about what is to be done tomorrow.

Essay titles

1. Explain what is meant by each of the following:

    - market segment;
    - positioning;
    - differentiation.

    How do each of these terms interrelate?

2. Using an example known to you, show how an organization segments one of its markets. Explain why it does so.

3. Describe the difference between marketing *strategy* and marketing *tactics*. Explain why marketing is essentially a planning process.

4. Show why different groups of consumers have differing needs. Explain how market research helps organizations to identify such different needs.

5. An organization wishes to initiate market research of its main market for a consumer durable good. How would it go about doing so?

6. What is meant by the marketing mix? How does the marketing mix relate to the product's life cycle?

7. Analyse the marketing mix of a product that is reaching maturity. Show how the mix has been changed over the product's life cycle.

8. Describe the processes leading up to the launch of a new product.

9. 'Pricing is an important ingredient of the marketing mix.' Discuss.

10. Using examples wherever possible, comment upon the factors, both long and short term, that might influence the pricing strategies of a large organization.

11. 'Distribution is the underrated ingredient in the marketing mix.' Discuss.

12. Analyse each of the ingredients of the promotional mix. Using examples, explain how each may be applied in practice.

13. Describe the role an advertising agency would have in the launch of a new product.

14. Describe the functions of a marketing department in a large organization.

15. Explain why a positive response to consumerism, business ethics and environmentalism are of increasing importance for marketeers.

16. To what extent might the marketing mix of an organization be influenced by its competitors? Use examples to support your analysis.

17. Why might marketing considerations cause a motor car manufacturer to delay the launch of a new vehicle?

18. Using the report format, explain why marketing should be generally regarded as the overriding business activity.

19. Explain the difference between primary research and secondary research. Why are both important for the marketeer?
20. 'Marketing is the essential point of contact between every organization and its customers or clients.' Discuss.

Short-answer questions

1. Define marketing.
2. What is meant by market segmentation?
3. Distinguish between primary research and secondary research.
4. Name two pricing strategies.
5. Describe two differences between marketing goods in the home market and marketing overseas.
6. Name two controls over advertising.
7. What is the difference between consumer marketing and organizational marketing.
8. Name two economic determinants of consumer demand.
9. Explain how the needs of consumers from socio-economic groups A and B would differ from those of groups D and E.
10. What is undifferentiated marketing?
11. Name two phases in a product's life cycle.
12. Name two functions of a wholesaler.
13. Describe what is meant by personal selling.
14. Define what is meant by advertising.
15. Name two advertising agencies.
16. Provide an example of a strapline.
17. Explain what is meant by a dealer loader.
18. What is meant by telemarketing?
19. Briefly describe the role of the Advertising Standards Authority.
20. What does BSI stand for?

Projects

Projects in the field of marketing are always exciting because it is a dynamic area that is constantly changing. It is also an area in which you can engage in marketing activities yourself and use your creative talents. For example, you might like to:

- consider your own ideas, research them to see if they could be successful and then produce a report on the outcome;
- follow an organization's marketing strategy and observe their behaviour as well as the behaviour of their competitors;
- consider how you might attempt to revive the fortunes of a flagging product.

Some of the problems that you might encounter are that:

- by the very nature of their activities, those involved in marketing activities are often very busy, so it may be difficult to establish a firm and reliable contact;
- marketeers have to be extremely careful about the information they give you as it is often confidential, for example, profit figures for different brands;
- marketing strategies are very complex.

Suggested reading

Hill, Nigel, *Marketing for BTEC*. Business Education Publishers, 1989.

Leader, W. G., and N. Kyritsis, *Fundamentals of Marketing*. Stanley Thornes, 1989.

Needham, David, and Robert Dransfield, *Marketing—Everybody's Business*. Heinemann, 1991.

Sutherland, J., and N. Gross, *Marketing in Action*. Pitman, 1991.

The European Marketing Pocket Book. NTC Publications, 1992.

9

Production

The process of producing goods and/or services by means of wealth-creating or value-adding activities is generally known as either *production* or *operations management*. It is the central activity for any organization as it actively involves the processes necessary to provide the goods and/or services to satisfy customer needs. This area usually accounts for the largest single section of an organization's resources and it is essential that managers have proven strategies for carrying out this function.

All activities, whatever the industrial sector, create wealth. Production or wealth-creating activities would, therefore, include primary, secondary and tertiary production. Managing the resources necessary to produce goods and/or services will involve the five P's of production: product, plant, process, programme and people.

Case Study—The development of the factory worker

Not so many years ago, when we thought of Japanese goods, we automatically associated them with cheap or shoddy copies of British goods. How things have changed! Today, the Japanese approach towards quality has overwhelmed us. Japanese manufacturing has moved from a position of low competence to one of clear supremacy over European and US manufacturers.

The first success in this battle for markets has been on the basis of Japanese *quality*. Having achieved quality, Japanese manufacturers are today working on a new area and redefining their rules for engagement on the basis of *flexibility* and *customer response*. In this new war, quality will be a basic, assumed manufacturing skill.

In order to understand how the Japanese have achieved quality we need to look at the 'seven ages of factory man'.* The best and most capable of British producers tend to exist towards the top of this evolutionary scale.

*Adapted from the October 1991 issue of *Director*, by kind permission of Director Publications Limited. Article by David Pearson, Chief Executive, The Strathclyde Institute.

However, many still lie around the middle and some are in the early stages of development. The stages are:

- *stage one—Fordian man*—this organization is characterized by long flow lines, lengthy change time and large batch sizes; the Fordian man provides low variety, lacks flexibility and has high direct labour and inventory costs;
- *stage two—Automation man*—in this age, organizations become obsessed with automation, mainly directed at reducing direct labour costs, and the weaknesses at this stage concern a change of focus away from manufacturing issues and on systems issues instead, poor labour relations, high capital and white-collar investment levels and, often, poor product quality;
- *stage three—Low inventory man*—in this stage, managers begin to understand that equipment and people should be driven by market demand, but, at the same time, there is a growing recognition of the importance of developing employees; the negative tendency at this stage is to reduce market flexibility and limit the number of suppliers;
- *stage four—Balanced man*—this stage focuses upon chasing and eliminating bottlenecks and results in higher throughput operations, but, the negative consequences of this include high levels of capital investment;
- *stage five—Integrated man*—this age is heralded by the understanding that marketing, R&D and production functions are all part of the same company rather than deadly warring enemies and so they share information and systems; the growing strengths in this stage include better customer delivery and service, higher quality products and more choice, while the weaknesses include a growing dependency on expert systems.
- *stage six—Low overhead man*—in this factory, IT is used as a primary vehicle in the displacement of administrative and middle management jobs; the strengths of this age include improving product cost structures and margins, a clearer vision of the strategic role of IT and shorter decision and information structures and its weakness is that it becomes a much flatter, stress-laden organization with a heavy dependency on expensive 'knowledge' workers;
- *stage seven—Quality man*—this age is characterized by organizations producing quality goods and services in the market-place, where faults are measured in one or two parts per million, so quality, service to the customer and internal communication is excellent, but its weakness is the belief that quality is the ultimate business goal, a cost structure that becomes inflexible and an inability to make production compromises.

In the UK, though electronics companies tend to be towards the top of this scale, many traditional industries, such as chemicals, plastics, pharmaceuticals, textiles and food processing, tend to be stuck at around levels two to four. Japanese companies, however, not complacent about their present success, are moving further ahead with three more strategies designed to improve their competitive advantage. These appear to be:

- *Flexible man* — this represents the major challenge from Japan over the next decade as 'flexible' factories will be designed to give short delivery times, have high levels of demand change and will be optimized to provide maximum product variety and choice;
- *Service man* — in this development, customer response will be taken a step further — the factory will be opened up directly to the consumer, operating a direct dialogue between production line and customer, so production capability will become the key element in market penetration and the customer will have more control over the making, timing and features of the product order;
- *Enterprise man* — this development carries the mantra: 'To make is to be' and at this stage, manufacturing capability becomes so significant as a competitive force, that it influences all other elements of corporate strategy.

Questions

1. What are the 'seven ages of factory man'?
2. Compare and contrast the operations of Fordian man with those of Quality man.
3. Why do you think that many British companies are floundering between stages two to four?
4. What does the case indicate about the advantages and disadvantages of:
    - automation; and
    - IT?
5. Discuss the seven ages of factory man with somebody working for a large organization (the organization could be in either the manufacturing or services sector). Find out which age they feel their organization belongs to and why.
6. Explain what is meant by the following terms:

flexibility	customer response
large batch sizes	direct labour
inventory costs	labour relations
white collar	market flexibility
bottlenecks	expert systems
margins	flatter organization

- stress-laden
- inflexible cost structure
- maximum product variety
- internal communication
- short delivery times
- market penetration.

7. Explain why the consumer benefits as organizations work through each of the stages.
8. How has quality become an assumed manufacturing skill for the Japanese?

Case Study—The software revolution

In the next decade, sales of industrial software are anticipated to exceed hardware sales. In industry today, whereas the hardware for controlling machinery is becoming more and more standardized and less and less expensive, the potential for new industrial software is practically limitless. In fact, new software is becoming available that actually reduces the labour of writing the software itself!

Managers today are concentrating upon three concepts that require 'soft' as opposed to 'hard' automation. These concepts are:

- Computer Integrated Manufacturing (CIM)
- Just-in-Time (JIT) manufacturing;
- Total Quality Control (TQC).

CIM is the effective use of computers to receive, process, communicate and output information in order to enhance productivity and serve the needs of the customer more precisely. It is concerned with coordinating the activities of the whole organization, including purchases, accounts and sales in order to assure a smooth and integrated operation.

JIT manufacturing ensures an even flow of materials designed to minimize:

- parts;
- work-in-progress;
- finished products in stock.

It has been recognized that JIT improves production flows and can lead to massive savings by contributing to the provision of efficient flows of materials through flexible product mixes.

TQC requires all of those providing the good or service to be responsible for the quality of the product. This eliminates the need for testing and reduces the number of faults. TQM requires that faults with purchased and manufactured parts be tracked through the system and software helps to unearth weaknesses so that they can be dealt with quickly.

In the short term, software solutions are still being found today to implement CIM, JIT and TQC. However, as such systems develop, software in the future will eventually become more *expert* until one day *artificial intelligence* (AI) will become a reality. Whereas expert systems of the future will respond to collated knowledge, AI will take this a step further by testing knowledge, applying reasoning and then using it in a creative way.

The key to such developments is the successful creation of software solutions. The beginnings of this software revolution are already underway.

Questions

1. Explain why software sales are expected to exceed hardware sales.
2. What is meant by CIM, JIT and TQC? How would each improve the operations of an organization?
3. Describe the difference between an expert system and one that has artificial intelligence.
4. Comment briefly on how the above implications for software might have affected the operational activities of a small manufacturing or service organization in 10 years' time.

Case Study—Unilever's research and development

Unilever's research and development effort knows no scientific boundaries. Its scientists and engineers operate in teams across the corporate laboratories turning their ideas into realities. Molecules are designed and synthesised, new products formulated and manufacturing technology developed for ongoing projects. The interaction of teams allows ideas to flow freely between scientists from different science backgrounds – creating opportunities which would be denied in a less diverse company.

Global research allows Unilever to leverage the science across a range of product types. For example, an understanding of fats and oils technology can be utilised within the manufacture of soaps, skin creams, ice creams and spreads. Centralising of information in this way reduces the innovation cycle time; the time-lag between the first germ of a product idea to its eventual manufacture. This factor is commercially vital in fast moving consumer product markets.

'We believe that our tradition of keeping close to our markets will be the key to transforming innovation into competitive advantage.'
A presentation to Japanese investment analysts, 1990 by Dr Ashok Ganguly.

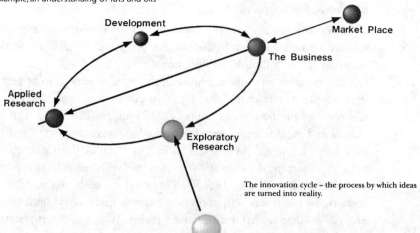

The innovation cycle – the process by which ideas are turned into reality.

Figure 9.1 Unilever's research and development. (*Source*: Unilever).

Questions

1. What range of expertise might a product development team at Unilever include?
2. What stages do products go through from development until they are launched?
3. Describe what is meant by 'global research'.
4. How important is the 'centralizing of information' for Unilever and where might this information have come from?

Case Study—BS 5750

Figure 9.2 BS 5750. (*Source*: Logo reproduced by kind permission of BSI quality assurance.)

The increasing demands for quality from customers and suppliers alike in the 1990s have meant that more and more organizations today are formalizing their quality standards with BS 5750 accreditation. BS 5750 stipulates that 'The supplier's management shall define and document its policy and objectives for, and commitment to, quality'. Once the system is set up, 'the supplier shall carry out internal audits to verify whether quality activities comply with planned arrangements and to determine the effectiveness of the quality system'.

BS 5750 was first introduced in 1979 and updated in 1987 to bring it into line with European and international standards. It comprises a series of national standards that can be used by any organization, whether it employs 10 or 10 000 people. Such standards identify basic procedures and criteria that help to ensure that organizations provide goods or services that meet customer requirements.

Achieving BS 5750 accreditation may take an organization between one and two years, depending on the size and complexity of the business and the amount of work already achieved. The costs will also vary. Many organizations employ a consultant to take them through the process.

The great benefit of BS 5750 is the economies created in its wake. For example, systems are improved, customer needs are identified and then satisfied and overall product requirements provide genuine market and competitive benefits.

Mike Beaman, joint managing director of Beamans Bodyworks in Barnstaple, Devon, is proud of his company's membership of the exclusive BS 5750 club. Beamans had always had a well-established name for quality in the automotive refinish industry and, after meeting a BSI assessor in 1985, their interest turned into active involvement.

In order to achieve BS 5750 accreditation at Beamans, they used a democratic route that initially involved the management team presenting the Total Quality programme to the work-force. Quality work groups evolved to identify and resolve any potential problem areas and to add their expertise to developing the system. BS 5750 has created a system at Beamans that today allows someone to take over another person's role because of centralized control of systems. Their management feel that the process has been very much a two-way learning process that has contributed to a successful outcome.

Questions

1. Discuss why organizations should develop quality standards.
2. What is BS 5750?
3. Would implementing BS 5750 be useful to the organization you work for or the college you attend? Explain why.
4. In what ways does BS 5750 link with the marketing function?
5. What are the benefits of BS 5750 accreditation?
6. Explain how Beamans introduced BS 5750.

Case Study—The relocation strategy

For many companies, relocation had become a major business strategy, designed to cut costs, expand, improve the quality of space or to rationalize. For example, in recent years, Barclays chose to move to Coventry, Argos moved to Milton Keynes and Bosch went to Wales.

The question is, has the migration from London begun? How many organizations are leaving in search of lower-cost locations? Why are they going and where are they going? Evidence from property agents Jones Lang Wootton showed that, of 189 large moves between 1983 and 1992, nearly half stayed within Greater London and only 50 abandoned the South East. They also showed that it was very difficult for a provincial town to encourage or persuade large companies to relocate outside London. Despite this, many towns use slick marketing techniques to extol the virtues of their locations to try to encourage large organizations to move there.

Councils and development corporations have frequently used a variety of strategies to attract organizations to their areas. Incentives have included a range of grants, such as regional selective assistance, relocation grants and rates equivalent grants. Enterprise zones have attracted many companies and some, only designated over the last two years, will keep their benefits until the end of the century.

Some of the benefits offered by enterprise zones include rates exemption on industrial and commercial property, 100 per cent corporation and income tax allowances and exemptions on supplying certain information.

TV, newspapers and magazines have been successfully used to promote the virtues of certain areas. For example, Telford's transformation has been profound. The town has grown from being a downtrodden coalfield in East Shropshire to winning the Europe in Bloom award. Telford Development Corporation has spent about £1m per year on promoting its activities and the return has been tremendous. They have successfully 'sold' the town to the Americans, the Japanese and Europeans.

In the end, however, major factors affecting any move are industrial inertia and whether key employees think that their life-style or children's education might suffer from a move. A move may be such a massive step that organizations may only commit themselves if they can guarantee success.

Questions

1. Explain why an organization might wish to relocate.
2. What factors should an organization take into account before relocating?
3. In your judgement, what benefits has the South East got over other locations?
4. Outline the dangers of subsidizing an organization's move.

Activity

Analyse the location and activities of a local organization. Consider:

- why the organization exists in that particular location;
- the factors that influenced its choice;
- some of the alternative locations available to it;
- the sort of inducements that might have influenced the location;
- how long the organization has been there;
- whether another location might provide it with greater benefits today;
- the reputation of the organization locally;
- the nature of its value-added activities.

Present your findings in a report.

Activity

Working in groups, choose a simple product that you could make and sell within your organization. Discuss:

- the nature of the product;
- who it would appeal to;
- how you would design it;
- where you would need to make it;
- forecast direct costs, indirect costs, selling price and turnover;
- the production process—job, batch and so on;
- technology, quality, people;
- other factors relating to manufacture.

If it is feasible to do so, make samples. Present your findings to the rest of your class.

Activity

Arrange a visit to a local manufacturer.

Before going, prepare a list of questions to ask about their operational and value-added activities. Make notes while visiting and later analyse the organization's activities.

Using the title 'The way forward for _____', discuss how you think the organization's operations will change over the next five years.

Essay title 1—A company in London is contemplating whether to move its head office closer to its operational activities in west Wales. Before making any decisions it has extensively researched the benefits this particular part of west Wales will offer staff who choose to relocate there.

Explain why factors such as schools, desirable and affordable properties and social amenities might be considered more important locational influences for a head office than other conventional factors.

The introduction would need to consider why location is an important decision for all organizations. For example, influences upon performance, reduction of costs, the finding of an appropriate site, competitive influences, maximizing benefits and minimizing costs.

A wide range of factors have traditionally influenced location. These have included:

- transport;
- integration with group companies;
- labour/housing;
- amenities;
- land;

- regional advantages;
- safety requirements;
- communications;
- government influences.

Brief examples and descriptions should be used to support each factor.

In the past, a combination of the above factors have influenced location. However, whereas firms locate and remain relatively static, factors and influences constantly change. This means that, though it might have been good to locate to a particular area 20 years ago, today other locations may offer more attractive benefits at lower cost. For example, many companies located in London because of communications, infrastructure and regional advantages, but today factors such as high land prices and congestion mean that it is not such a desirable location. At the same time, communications and infrastructure outside the capital have improved. The real question, however, influencing companies who would wish to move from London is whether their staff will follow the move. If staff do not follow the move, they could be placed at a severe competitive disadvantage. In order to encourage them to move, they therefore have to look at schools, properties and amenities.

In conclusion, although the influence of traditional factors is clearly important, staff and their experience cannot be replaced overnight. Any move would be an important step, both for staff and the organization and would have to be carefully promoted to them.

Essay title 2—How important is it for marketing and production objectives to match each other?

In the early stages of your answer, it is important that you show what is meant by both 'marketing' and 'production' and that you understand why and how they differ.

For example, to define marketing, indicate:

- its strategic elements;
- its tactical requirements;
- the importance of flexibility;
- the need to enter the market first;
- the need for short production times and the ability to be able to respond to demand;
- why it involves responding to research;
- the need for product variety, generic, sensual and extended product dimensions.

Then define production. What does it do and what is it limited by? For example, production is the most difficult area to understand, coordinate and carry out. It usually involves a complex series of operations covering a massive range of resources. Mention relevant constituent parts of each of the five broad areas of production. Production is an area:

- that is often inflexible;
- where managers would prefer large production runs of identical products;
- that carries stocks;
- that can respond more efficiently where there is continuity of demand for one type of product;
- that benefits from economies of scale;
- that requires careful planning, programming and control.

What is easy and more efficient in production may, therefore, not be suitable for the market. On the other hand, if tastes in the market continually change and are factionalized into too many market segments, it may be almost impossible for a production department to provide the required goods or services in a profitable and coordinated way. The solution is simple—they must work together.

Both marketing *and* production objectives should be based on the overall objectives of the organization. The overall marketing plan must be carefully matched to production capabilities. Research and development, product modifications, line extensions and other injections of life into any product should, therefore, materialize when marketing people and operations managers work together and coordinate their activities.

In conclusion, the changing emphasis in recent years has been away from traditional product orientation towards market orientation. This has placed a huge burden on operations to be more efficient, responsive and capable of handling greater variety. Improved technology has enabled production teams to respond to and work effectively with marketing teams.

Essay title 3—Explain why many organizations pursue the objective of growth. What are the benefits gained from such a policy and the dangers it may face?

In your introduction explain that modern organizations have a range of objectives, one of which is often growth and say what growth is. For example, market share, assets, size of the organization, more control of a market and so on. Organizations can grow by acquiring assets, developing markets and expanding sales. This is organic growth and is often a slow business. Alternatively, a quicker and more dynamic form of growth occurs by means of mergers or takeovers, which involve integration with other business units.

Organizations pursue growth for several reasons:

- *economies of scale*—internal, such as technical, labour and managerial, commercial, financial and risk-bearing; external, such as concentration, information, disintegration; such economies reduce unit costs;
- *experience effect*—over a larger output organizations build up experience that affects unit costs and increases productivity and resource specialization.

Both of the above improve the organization's margins. Operators with the largest market share will, therefore, enjoy a price advantage and have greater flexibility to sustain market dominance.

The dangers of such a policy may include:

- diseconomies of scale, for example, human relations, decisions and coordination and external diseconomies;
- overtrading;
- becoming too highly geared;
- loss of markets;
- loss of identity.

Wherever possible examples should be used to support each of the above.

In conclusion, growth clearly brings many benefits but, if it takes place too quickly, it may also pose many risks. Examples should support your conclusion.

Essay titles

1. Explain what is meant by operations management. To what extent has operations management changed in recent years?
2. Describe what is meant by value-added activity. Using two contrasting industries, explain how each adds value to the goods and/or services they provide.
3. A large company is intending to build a factory in a new town in South-West England. Discuss the issues that would need to be considered before implementing such a proposal.
4. Examine the phases a new product would have to go through before it is launched.
5. How has manufacturing technology improved the process of supplying goods and services in recent years? In what ways has it enabled modern organizations to become more responsive to consumer needs?
6. 'Changes in the product life cycle clearly influence research and development.' Discuss.
7. Explain why many organizations seek to merge with others. Examine the dangers of doing so.

8. Examine the factors that would influence the location, design, layout, safety and performance of a manufacturing plant.
9. Explain how batch production differs from other types of production. What problems might be encountered with each system of production?
10. 'Effective purchasing makes a distinctive contribution to a business.' Explain why.
11. What types of stocks would a small manufacturer hold? Why would it attempt to control its levels of stock and how would it go about doing this?
12. A central management objective is to identify any product that deviates from expectations. Examine the role of quality assurance.
13. Explain how just-in-time (JIT) may benefit a manufacturer.
14. To what extent does the success of the production process depend upon people? Examine the importance of people in the work-place.
15. In what ways will the operations of a large manufacturer be similar and different to the operations of a small newsagent?
16. What is meant by ergonomics? How will it help an organization to improve the design of the work-place?
17. 'Production is the process that ensures things get done.' Discuss.
18. Imagine that you have joined an organization that has experienced a number of operational problems. What might these problems be and how would you deal with them?
19. By referring to specific benefits that might be achieved, explain how computerized scheduling could improve an organization's operations.
20. Examine the role of purchasing in the production process. What advice would you provide for a trainee buyer?

Short-answer questions

1. Give two examples of forms of primary production.
2. Name two difficulties an organization's production department might face.
3. What is meant by value analysis?
4. Name two factors affecting a business' location.
5. Provide two recent examples of businesses integrating.
6. Name two diseconomies of scale.
7. A garden furniture manufacturer taking over a sawmill would be an example of what type of integration?
8. Describe two features of flow production.
9. Describe briefly the benefits to a manufacturer of using computer integrated manufacturing.

10. What is meant by standardization?
11. Identify two problems arising from keeping stock levels low.
12. Describe the benefits of Just-in-Time manufacturing.
13. Explain how method study differs from work measurement.
14. Name two motivational techniques that might be used to improve output.
15. Explain briefly how the product life cycle might influence research and development.
16. Name two issues that might be of constant concern to an operations manager.
17. What is meant by tertiary production?
18. Provide two examples of bulk-decreasing industries.
19. Name two techniques an organization might use to evaluate the financial potential of a major investment.
20. Explain the difference between being product-led and being market-led.

Projects

Projects in the field of production or operations can be very practical, involve a great deal of common sense and provide a useful opportunity to both integrate and transfer business skills and disciplines. For example, it may be possible to:

- analyse the operations framework and layout of an organization and suggest changes and improvements, which could involve using financial information and capital appraisal techniques;
- provide some form of analysis of the location or size of an organization;
- look at plant safety;
- provide suggestions on how to improve manufacturing technology.

Production is at the heart of an organization's activities and it is sometimes difficult to understand how all of the different elements fit together. Such projects will increase your understanding of this area.

Suggested reading

Hill, T., *Production/Operations Management* (2nd edn). Prentice Hall, 1991.
Lucey, T., *Management Information Systems* (6th edn). D. P. Publications, 1991.
Stefanou, R., *Understanding Industry Now* (2nd edn). Heinemann, 1991.
Timings, R. L., *Manufacturing Technology*, Volume 1. Longman, 1990.
Wild, R., *Production and Operations Management*. Cassell, 1989.

10

An introduction to the accounting process

Accounting acts as an information system by processing an organization's data in such a way that interested parties such as managers, shareholders, providers of finance and employees will have the means to understand how the organization is performing. Everyday business transactions act as input into the accounting system and the output is valuable financial information, which can then be analysed and contribute to decision-making processes.

The process of financial accounting involves the preparation of final accounts, which are then presented by the stewards or directors of the organization as representing a 'true and fair' view of the organization's activities. From final accounts, ratios and other figures can be extracted that provide fairly precise indicators of a company's performance.

Case Study—IT in accounting

The revolution in IT has had a major impact on the way in which accounting offices function. For example, it has assisted in the capture and identification of information. More rapid capture enables organizations to become more efficient. Another benefit is that data can be processed more quickly and in a range of different ways.

At the heart of the IT revolution in accounting have been improvements in software. Such developments have provided computer-based solutions to traditional financial problems. One company that has generated significant interest in accountancy software has been the Kettering-based Pegasus Group, which supplies software packages covering stock control, invoicing and ledger entries and a wide range of other accounting techniques. Following a boom in software sales, the company has built up to a turnover of around £13m a year and leads a highly competitive UK market in micro-computerized software packages for use on companies' personal computers.

With '1992' having happened, Pegasus believe that their future depends on the successful development of pan-European products. They

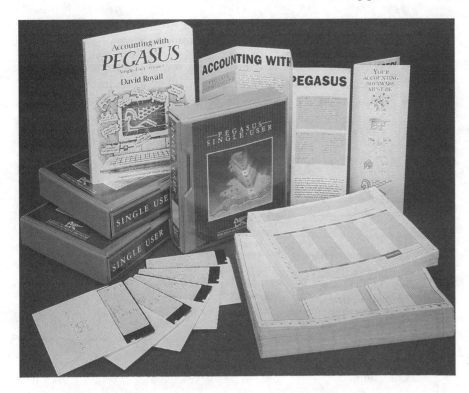

Figure 10.1 Software packages produced by the Pegasus Group. (*Source*: Pegasus Group.)

feel that, although accountancy practices marginally differ from country to country, there are core techniques that make their pan-European approach feasible. For example, variations include:

- three different payment dates on French invoices;
- a system of 'negative debits' rather than credits in Portugal.

To help overcome some of these obstacles, Pegasus have formed a partnership with the French software company Saari to develop truly European products. Such an alliance is now helping Pegasus to broaden its customer base so that it can increase its potential turnover.

Developments in IT at a practical level have provided a system that makes information easier to understand. This means that the wide variety of users who have to deal with such information can respond more quickly with better and more informed judgements.

Questions

1. List the benefits of IT in accounting.
2. Explain what is meant by the following:

- software;
- invoicing;
- stock control;
- ledger entries;

- turnover;
- pan-European;

- negative debits;
- customer base.

3. Why have many UK companies in recent years engaged in joint ventures with other companies from different countries in the EC?
4. What might the dangers be of depending on a system of computerized accounting?

Case Study—Cable & Wireless interim results

Table 10.1. Cable & Wireless interim results 1990–91.
(*Source*: Cable & Wireless)

£m (unaudited results)	6 months to 30 September 1990	6 months to 30 September 1991	% growth
Turnover	1264	1569	24
Profit before taxation	301	351	17
Attributable profit	161	186	16
Earnings per share	15.1p	17.3p	15
Dividend per share	3.7p	4.25p	15

Questions

1. Explain what is meant by 'interim results'.
2. Why do earnings per share differ from dividends per share?
3. How would shareholders calculate dividend yield? What further information would they require?
4. What other profitability ratios might shareholders wish to use?
5. Why might it be inadvisable to make comparisons between the results of Cable & Wireless and those of British Telecom?
6. List the other dangers of using ratios.
7. If you were a shareholder of Cable & Wireless, what information other than accounting information would you like to see?

Case Study—Controlling accounting standards

A new era in the setting of accounting standards began on 1 August 1990 when the Accounting Standards Board (ASB) took over from the Accounting Standards Committee (ASC). Unlike the ASC, which was a joint committee of the six major accounting bodies, the new Board is independent of the professional institutes and its aim is to set accounting standards *in its own right* rather than seek approval from the accountancy bodies.

The creation of the ASB is viewed as a progressive step, designed to establish a better system of accounting practices. Up until the 1960s, the growth of the accounting profession had gone unnoticed. However this quiet progression was rocked in 1967 when AEI was taken over by GEC. AEI had forecast a profit for that year of £10m, but, when the figures were published, they showed a loss of £4.5m. At the time, it was argued that such a diversity of practice brought the accountancy profession into disrepute. How could they bear a 'true and fair' view of a business' activities? In the ensuing controversy, it became clear that the difference arose because of different subjective judgements. This led to the formation of the Accounting Standards Committee and Statements of Standard Accounting Practice (SSAPs).

Though the Accounting Standards Committee marked a major step forward in setting accounting standards and towards ending a multiplicity of accounting practices, throughout the 1980s it was subjected to a number of widely held criticisms. For example, the committee was criticized for:

- failing to respond to emerging issues;
- a lack of timeliness in publishing standards;
- failing to be independent;
- lacking flexibility.

The formation of the ASB in 1990 was felt to provide greater independence as it could issue standards in its own right by acting on its own authority. One important part of the new ASB is the Urgent Issues Task Force, which, as its name implies, is intended to handle issues that need to be dealt with quickly. Another feature of the Board is the quality of the team members, who have come from industry, the practising profession and the City. Its membership of 12 includes a full-time Chairperson and Technical director.

The agenda for the ASB comes from another new accounting group, the Financial Reporting Council (FRC). The membership of the FRC includes the Secretary of State for Trade and Industry and the Governor of the Bank of England. The Council's aim is to guide the ASB on its work programmes and to ensure that its work is properly financed.

In September 1991, the ASB set out their first *Financial Reporting Standard (FRS1)* on cash flow statements, which was to be regarded as standard in respect of financial statements on or after reporting periods from 23 March 1992. This first FRS supersedes SSAP 10 concerning sources and applications of funds.

The FRS1 was designed to create a new financial statement to answer many of the criticisms directed at funds flow statements. Previously, companies drew them up in different ways, they were difficult to compare and they tended to look at funds or profit rather than at cash.

FRS1 represents the first move forward by the ASB to improve the quality of accounting information. Cash flow statements have been designed to provide further valuable information on the connection between profitability and liquidity. As soon as the Board settles into its role, members of the various arms of the accounting profession expect that further standards will be introduced.

Questions

1. Explain why the accounting profession requires accounting standards.
2. Who might accounting standards be designed to protect?
3. Why should the ASB be independent?
4. What is meant by 'a true and fair view' of business activity?
5. Find out about any SSAP or FRS. Explain what it was designed to achieve.
6. Why does the ASB require an Urgent Issues Task Force?
7. How might the ASB be helped by working to an agenda created by a body that includes the Secretary of State for Trade and Industry and the Governor of the Bank of England?
8. Compare and contrast a cash flow statement with a funds flow statement.

Case Study—T Chest Pine Ltd

You have recently been appointed as Accounting Assistant at T Chest Pine Ltd, a small, private limited company that sells pine furniture in and around North Yorkshire. On the day you start your new job, the company Accountant, Sally Webster, is, unfortunately, on holiday. She has, however, left you with the memo shown in Fig. 10.2.

To: The Accounting Assistant   *Date*: 30 April 19—
From: Sally Webster

I apologize for not being able to meet you during your first week with us and I am looking forward to having a chat with you when I return to work. In the meantime, I have listed below a few tasks I would like you to undertake. If you require any specific help this week, ask either Peter Robinson, the Company Secretary, or Mary Foster in the General Office.

Figure 10.2 Memo from the Company Accountant to the Accounting Assistant.

Task 1
I enclose a copy of our year-end final accounts for the end of last

month. Could you please draw up a series of appropriate ratios and place them under the headings of:

- profitability;
- liquidity;
- asset usage;
- capital structure.

Task 2
Could you make brief comments on each of the ratios you have drawn up.

Task 3
Note that we have proposed a 10 per cent dividend for our shareholders. Given the present economic climate, do you think that this is a good return? I would be interested in your comments.

Task 4
We presently value our stocks using the LIFO method of valuation. We do, however, find that this provides a slightly higher valuation than we would like. Could you please suggest an alternative method of valuation and briefly outline your reasons for suggesting that method in a short report which I can present to the directors when I return from my holiday.

Task 5
Our depreciation of fixed assets takes place on a straight-line basis. We are considering moving to either a reducing-balance method or a machine-hour method. Explain which of these two methods of depreciation you would prefer to deal with and why.

T Chest Pine Ltd's final accounts

Profit and loss account for the year ending 31 March 1993

	£	£	£
Sales			350 240
Less Cost of sales			
Opening stock		19 540	
Purchases		195 520	
		215 060	
Less closing stock		23 280	
			191 780
Gross profit			158 460

cont.	£	£	£
Less Overheads			
Wages and salaries		36 743	
Sundry expenses		21 345	
Light and heat		535	
Depreciation—plant	2 000		
—buildings	2 500	4 500	
Bad debts		5 400	
Advertising and distribution		18 998	
			87 521
Net profit			70 939
Less corporation tax			22 000
Profit after taxation			48 939
Less dividends—ordinary 10 per cent			15 000
			33 939
Less transfer to general reserve			20 000
			13 939
Add retained profit brought forward			12 770
Retained profit carried forward			26 709

T Chest Pine Ltd's balance sheet as at 31 March 1993

Fixed assets	£ Cost	£ Provision for depreciation	£ Net book value
Land and buildings	100 000	5 000	95 000
Plant	80 000	4 000	76 000
	180 000	9 000	171 000
Current assets			
Closing stock		43 280	
Debtors		24 320	
Bank		1 555	
		69 155	
Less current liabilities			
Creditors	6 446		
Proposed dividend	15 000		
Taxation payable	22 000	43 446	
Working capital			25 709
			196 709
Financed by:			
Share capital			
Ordinary shares 150 000 £1 shares			150 000
Reserves			
General reserve		20 000	
Retained profit		26 709	
			46 709
			196 709

Case Study—Reading annual reports

Recent research has indicated that private investors, financial journalists and even financial analysts fail to scrutinize companies' annual reports. Instead, most tend to focus on interim and preliminary announcements and then react rapidly to the information they provide. The consequences of this are a flurry of press releases that generate rapidly constructed newspaper reports and unnecessary fluctuations in share prices.

The annual report, therefore, currently tends to be neglected. Mr David Tweedie, Chairman of the ASB, did some research into this when he was Professor of Accounting at Lancaster University. From questionnaires sent to the private shareholders of Scottish and Newcastle Breweries, he showed that the chairperson's report was the most frequently read part of the annual report. Just over half said that they read it thoroughly. At the other extreme, 37 per cent said that they did not even look at the notes to the financial statements.

Another later survey, also by Mr Tweedie, supported these findings. He found that, among institutional investors and stockbrokers, 20 per cent did not read the notes to company accounts thoroughly, while about 10 per cent did not scrutinize the balance sheet and 9 per cent did not study the profit and loss account.

As we have seen, the importance of company announcements regarding the analysis of full accounts is evidenced by the fact that they provoke share price movements. When announcements are made, particularly preliminary statements, shares move sharply, but when the annual reports are released, share prices tend to remain relatively static.

This area is generating a lot of concern among accountants. Mr Graham Ward, a partner with Price Waterhouse, referring to the annual report, recently said that, 'It is depressing that so much effort goes into something that attracts little attention'. Members of the accounting profession today feel that company announcements and preliminary results do not really show the whole picture and fail to provide all of the additional information that the users of reports ought to consider. This whole issue is open to debate for the future as the accounting profession tries to persuade users of accounting information to understand, question and analyse the figures they rely upon.

Questions

1. What is an interim report?
2. Why do many people tend to read the chairperson's report and fail to analyse other parts of the annual report?
3. How important is it to analyse the annual report? Explain why.

4. How will your experience of your business studies course help you as
    an investor?

Activity

Write to a public limited company and ask them to send you a copy of
their most recent annual report and accounts.

What would you consider to be the most important aspect of the report
if you were:

*   a shareholder;
*   an employee;
*   a creditor;
*   a manager?

Analyse the report further under the following headings:

*   sales figures;
*   profitability;
*   liquidity;
*   share capital;
*   other important areas.

Activity

One aspect of your work that integrates many business disciplines
together in a very practical way is the formation of a *mini-company*.

Allocate a specified time period for this activity. Go through the procedures of setting up a mini-company either by means of a kit, Young
Enterprise or by producing your own materials. Involve yourself fully in
the recording procedures.

At the end of the exercise, produce a company report with a set of final
accounts. Provide an analysis of the final accounts, together with a series
of notes designed to help shareholders and other interested parties to
understand your figures.

Activity

Find out more about the accounting profession. Obtain information from:

*   your careers adviser;
*   the relevant Chartered body;
*   a local library;
*   friends, relatives or other contacts who work as or with accountants.

Comment on:

- the nature of the job;
- the diversity of work undertaken;
- the career progression;
- the examinations that have to be taken.

Essay title 1 — To what extent does ratio analysis enable users of financial information to draw meaningful conclusions about the performance of public companies?

The emphasis in this question is on 'to what extent' and the examiner would expect you to show a good knowledge of ratio analysis and its pitfalls as well as a basic knowledge of alternative indicators of the performance of public companies. The introduction should, therefore, attempt to show that you have a sound understanding of the question, explain what final accounts are, define ratio analysis, indicate generally why it is needed and comment briefly that it would be dangerous to depend upon ratios.

Ratios can be divided into four broad areas:

- profitability;
- liquidity;
- asset usage;
- capital structure.

The body of the answer should indicate why ratios are used in such areas. The benefits of using at least one ratio from each area should be stated to show how useful ratios can be for the end user. It is also important to show how different types of users can benefit from the different types of information produced. A shareholder, for example, may be more interested in profitability, while a manager is likely to be more interested in asset usage.

However, accounting is only an information system and, as with any system, only as good as the information put into it. For example:

- it reflects information from the past and only enables predictions to be made about the future;
- accounting systems may be unmanageably large and this may influence the quality of information they produce;
- it is difficult to make comparisons with other firms or industries using ratios;
- ratios cloud events with generalizations;
- many positive factors about an organization may be ignored by ratios;
- events may be distorted by outside influences, such as inflation.

It would be wrong for any user of financial information, creditor, share-holder or whatever, to base their decisions *solely* upon an analysis of ratios. Other indicators, both within the organization and those in the external business environment, would also be important. For example:

- *internal factors*, such as market share/growth/indicators; new product development; mergers/takeovers; quality of staff; industrial relations; image/health and safety and so on;
- *external factors*, such as state of the economy; business environment; trade wars; concern over social costs and so on.

In conclusion, ratios are important for a variety of users, but they do not provide the whole picture. Other factors must be taken into consideration to put such figures into perspective.

Essay title 2—Discuss the importance of the profit and loss account. Why do profit margins vary from industry to industry?

A good introduction will show what a profit and loss account is, that essentially it is an income statement that matches income against the cost of buying goods or the costs directly incurred in making the goods as well as overheads or expenses and then it indicates how any surplus or profit has been allocated or how a loss has been funded.

A profit and loss account has three sections:

- the trading account;
- the profit and loss section;
- the appropriation account.

Though a candidate would not be expected to draw up a full profit and loss account, it would be useful if they made the distinction between each of the three sections and discussed the ingredients and importance of each part.

The trading account is important because:

- it shows the profit on trading;
- it matches direct costs with sales;
- it provides a gross margin on activities;
- it indicates how much profit is indicated on each level of sales;
- through ratio analysis, it provides an indicator that might show stock losses, changes in prices and so on.

The profit and loss section is important because:

- it provides a final profit figure;
- it takes into account overheads;
- it shows non-trading income, such as the sale of assets;

- through ratio analysis it can indicate what is happening to overheads and so on.

The appropriation section is important because:

- it allocates profits;
- it shows where they go;
- indicates to shareholders what the directors or stewards are doing with their investment.

Overall, the profit and loss account is a valuable source for a variety of users of accounting information.

Now to the second part of the question. Explain briefly what a profit margin is. Such margins may vary for a variety of reasons, for example:

- risk;
- research and development;
- economic factors;
- nature of the industry;
- changes in the external environment;
- structural reasons;
- based on the wishes of the shareholders;
- dependent on the objectives of the shareholders.

Any plausible reason must be supported with an explanation and, if possible, an example.

In conclusion, the profit and loss account is just *one* financial statement for users of financial information. It provides information for analysis and thus provides a basis for the making of decisions and forecasts.

Essay title 3—Comment on the items that might appear as assets in the balance sheet of a company. Why might it be necessary to adjust the values of assets from time to time?

The introduction should first define a balance sheet as a 'snapshot' of what a firm owes and owns on a particular date and then assets as items owned by a business or anything owed to it.

Assets vary considerably in nature, for example:

- some may be redeemed for cash very quickly;
- others may be difficult to redeem for cash;
- some may be more certain than others in value;
- many assets constantly change value.

For these reasons, balance sheets show assets in an inverse order of liquidity and assets are broken down into fixed and current.

Fixed assets should be defined. They could be broken down into:

- intangible fixed assets, such as goodwill, brands;
- tangible fixed assets, such as land and buildings;
- investments, such as shares in other companies.

Current assets are sometimes called circulating assets because they are constantly changing. For example, through the cash cycle from stocks to debtors to cash. They might also include prepayments and short-term investments.

Assets constantly change in value. For example, fixed assets wear out. Depreciation reflects this wear and tear, consumption or reduction in the useful life of an asset. On the other hand, some assets, such as property, might appreciate, increasing in value, or depreciate, decreasing in value, from one time period to another. Therefore, for a balance sheet to show an accurate valuation, it must be adjusted to incorporate these changes between periods so that a true net book valuation appears in the assets.

Intangible fixed assets will also have valuations that vary from time to time. For example, a lot of discussion has taken place in recent years about brand accounting. It has been said that if brands are not included in the balance sheet or are constantly revalued, organizations are undervaluing their assets and leaving themselves open for a possible takeover. Investments also change in value *between* time periods, according to market influences.

Current assets are constantly changing and will have to be revalued every time a balance sheet is drawn up. For example, stocks have to be valued by taking a physical stock check using some method of stock valuation.

In conclusion, then, assets provide vital information for shareholders on their investment and, using efficiency ratios, on how it has been used.

Essay titles

1. Final accounts provide a range of information for a variety of users. Who uses final accounts, how do they use them and what do they look for?
2. 'Accounting standards help to ensure that accounting statements depict a "true and fair" view of a business' activities.' Discuss.
3. The asset side of a balance sheet normally appears in an inverse order of liquidity. Explain why. Explain, too, why fixed assets are often depreciated.
4. Describe two contrasting methods of stock valuation. Then show how the method of stock valuation used will influence profits.
5. Using examples, show how ratios might be used to assess a business' liquidity. What strengths or weaknesses might liquidity ratios identify?

6. What is ratio analysis? How useful is it for making comparisons between:

   - different companies;
   - different years?

7. A friend has approached you for advice about setting up a system of accounting for a newly formed small business. Advise your friend about:

   - how accounting records should be kept;
   - the information your friend requires;
   - the sort of final accounts your friend should present.

   What other financial advice might you provide?

8. 'Profit is only one point of comparison between a number of different companies.' Discuss.

9. Explain what is meant by inflation accounting. What are the benefits of using such a system?

10. Company A is a highly geared company and its activities are in sharp contrast to Company B, which is low geared. What is meant by gearing? What are the benefits of being:

    - highly geared;
    - low geared?

11. Explain the nature of information that can be extracted from financial statements. Who might be interested in such information and why?

12. Wolfgang Ltd is concerned about its liquidity. What information could be drawn from its accounts and what immediate action could be taken to improve its situation?

13. 'Inflation distorts accounting information.' Discuss.

14. Explain why current assets are usually called circulating assets. Why do many liquidity ratios not include stocks?

15. Explain how companies share and allocate their profits. What benefits might they gain from creating reserves?

16. Examine the importance of the balance sheet. How might information extracted from the balance sheet be interpreted?

17. How might a business control its assets if balance sheets are only drawn up at the end of each accounting period?

18. Examine the differences between financial and management accounting.

19. Why do accountants require accounting standards? What are the arguments for and against them?

20. 'Accounting is merely another information system.' Discuss.

Short-answer questions

1. Name three users of accounting information.
2. What is a trial balance?
3. Provide the equation that applies to horizontal balance sheets.
4. Define goodwill.
5. What is the cash cycle?
6. Explain why stocks are valued at cost.
7. If the gross profit of a business is £3000, the cost of sales £5950, the closing stock value £4100 and the purchases £5000, what are the opening stock value and the sales?
8. Describe one liquidity ratio.
9. What are SSAPs? Using one example, explain what it is trying to achieve.
10. Name two areas to which profit might be allocated in an appropriation account.
11. Explain what a gross profit to sales ratio might indicate.
12. If the debtors figure is £18 300 and the annual sales £187 000, what is the debt collection period?
13. What are the benefits of calculating stock turnover?
14. Why might a company's gearing be of interest to a bank manager?
15. What is meant by 'historical cost'?
16. Explain briefly the difference between FIFO and LIFO.
17. Explain why the reducing balance method of depreciation meets many of the criticisms levelled at the straight-line method.
18. Define accounting.
19. What is the name of the ratio that divides net profit by sales?
20. Describe what is meant by ROCE.

Projects

There are almost endless numbers of projects that you could work on in this area, but here are just a few ideas. It might be:

- interesting to analyse and then make comparisons between a series of accounting statements for companies in the same industry;
- possible to coordinate a period of work experience in either an accountant's office or in the accounts department of a large organization while undertaking the project;
- useful to assess the impact of IT on accounting in the working environment;
- possible to find out how the company you work for or college you attend records, presents and analyses financial information.

One of the problems you may come across is that many accounting systems are different and sometimes it is difficult to understand how each works.

Suggested reading

Cassidy, Peter, *Financial Accounting*. Stanley Thornes, 1990.
Giles, Richard, *A Foundation in Business Accounting*. Stanley Thornes, 1991.
Holden, Philip, *BTEC Accounting*. Heinemann Educational, 1988.
Pizzey, Alan, *Accounting and Finance* (3rd edn). Cassell, 1990.
Wood, Frank, *Business Accounting I* (5th edn). Pitman, 1989.

Glossary of accounting terminology

Note: items in italics are defined elsewhere in the Glossary.

Accountant: prepares accounts.

Accounts clerk: assists *accountant*.

Accrual concept: recording a transaction in the period to which it relates, not when it is paid.

Acid-test ratio: tests for the ability of a company to pay its debts soon. The formula is *liquid assets* over *current liabilities*.

Appropriation account: describes how profit is used. The funds are paid out as *dividends* or retained as *reserves*.

Assets: items that continue to have value for the business—a valuable resource.

Audit: external check of *financial accounts* to report whether they are true and fair.

Bad debts: sales of goods or services that have occurred on credit but where the customer is thought to be unlikely to pay for them.

Balance sheet: summary of *assets*, *liabilities* and *capital* at a particular point in time.

Bank loan: money lent by a bank on which it charges *interest*.

Bank overdraft: amount of money taken out of current account that is in excess of that paid in.

Budget: a forecast of the future. It may include such items as a *profit and loss account*, *balance sheet* and so on.

Capital: the total stock of wealth owed to the shareholders.

Capital employed: share capital and long-term *liabilities* and/or *total net current assets*.

Capital expenditure: money spent on *fixed assets*.

Cash flow statement: describes where money comes in from and where it is paid out to for a period.

Consistency concept: similar items should be treated consistently from one period to another.

Corporation tax: tax on company profits.

Cost of sales: the direct cost of goods sold (inclusive of materials and other direct costs).

Creditors: suppliers who have sent goods but not yet received payment for them.

Current assets: cash or any other *asset* that will be converted into cash during the next year.

Current liabilities: overdraft and other amounts owed that are repayable in the next 12 months.

Debentures: long-term loans with fixed repayment dates. The *interest* is usually paid annually.

Debtors: customers who have bought on credit but who have not yet paid their debts.

Declining balance method: *depreciation* on *fixed assets* calculated as a percentage of their declining *net book value*.

Depreciation: process of *writing off* the value of a *fixed asset* over its economic life.

Dividend: amount of profits distributed to the shareholders.

Dividend cover: *dividend* over net profit after tax.

Dividend yield: *dividend* per share over *market price per share*.

Earnings per share: net profit after tax over number of ordinary shares.

Expenses: costs incurred on goods or services that are no longer of value.

FIFO (First In First Out):   method of stock valuation where stock bought first is charged to the *profit and loss account*.

Finance director: head of the finance department who also sits on the company's board of directors.

Financial accounts: prepared to satisfy legal reporting requirements for 'published accounts'.

Finished goods stock: *stock* that production has transformed from the raw materials into a company product ready for selling.

Fixed assets: *assets* that are not for resale but are used over a long period to enable the company to perform business.

Freehold land and buildings: those owned by the company.

Furniture, fixtures and fittings: miscellaneous *fixed assets*, such as desks, shelving and electrical tools.

Gearing ratio: long-term *liabilities* (may include an overdraft) over *capital employed*.

Going concern concept: the company will continue trading in the foreseeable future.

Gross profit: *sales* less *cost of sales*.

Hire purchase: purchase where the title to the goods does not pass to the buyer until the final instalment is paid.

Historical cost: stated at cost value.

Inflation accounting: adjustments are made to the accounts to reflect changes in price levels.

Intangible assets: valuable items that have no physical form, such as patents, goodwill, leases and so on.

Interest: payment made to compensate lender for loss of use, risk and inflation.

Invoice: document showing goods sold. Used by both sellers and buyers for their records.

Lease: contract to allow the lessee to use an asset leased from a lessor.

Leasehold land and buildings: property rented under a lease contract from the freeholder.

Liabilities: amounts owed to others.

LIFO (Last In First Out):   method of stock valuation where the *cost of sales* is calculated on a last in first out basis.

Liquid assets: cash and debtors.

Liquidity: the extent to which *liquid assets* are available to pay debts.

Long-term capital: sources of finance not repayable in the next year.

Long-term liabilities: *liabilities* due for settlement over one year from *balance sheet* date.

Management accounts: accounting information prepared for managers.

Market price per share: the price *shares* in a company are currently being bought and sold at.

Net book value: the difference between the cost of a *fixed asset* and its accumulated *depreciation*.

Net current assets: *current assets* less *current liabilities* (that is, working capital).

Net loss: *Cost of sales* plus *expenses* when this is greater than the revenue generated.

Net profit after tax: *gross profit* less *expenses* less tax.

Net profit to sales ratio: net profit over *sales*.

Net realizable value: *sales* value less the costs of selling.

Nominal share value: par value of a share unrelated to its market value.

Operating profit: also called net profit (before interest) and trading profit.

Ordinary share capital: consists of issued shares to the owners of the company.

Plant and machinery: equipment usually used in the direct production of the business' goods.

Preference shares: give their owners fixed rates of *dividend*, limited voting rights but preference on the winding up of the company.

Prepayments: amounts paid in advance of the period during which the benefit will arise.

Price earnings ratio: *market price per share* over *earnings per share* (after tax).

Profit and loss account: accounting statement showing the net profit for the period.

Profit margin: net profit (before interest and tax) over *sales*.

Provision: created in anticipation of a future *asset write off* or a potential *liability*.

Prudence concept: principle of accountants: recognize a profit when it is realized but a loss as soon as possible.

Ratio analysis: expressing one variable in relation to another and comparing the result with other firms, years, budget and so on.

Raw materials: they are still in the state in which they were bought from the suppliers.

Reserves: generally, amount of profits *not* paid out to shareholders as *dividends*.

Residual value: estimated value of a *fixed asset* at the end of its economic life, for instance scrap.

Return on capital employed: net profit (before tax) over *capital employed*.

Revaluation reserve: amount by which *assets* are revalued over historical cost.

Sales: *turnover* or revenue obtained as a result of a company selling its goods or services.

Secured loan: the lender has the legal right to be repaid out of the proceeds of the *asset* on which the loan is secured.

Share: ownership of a company is split into a certain number of issued shares.

Share premium account: proceeds of a share issue in excess of the *nominal share value*.

Shareholders' funds: *nominal share value* shares plus *reserves*.

Stock: goods bought (whether worked on or not) for resale, that is normal trade.

Stock turnover: cost of sales (per annum) over *stock* value.

Straight-line method: the principle that a *fixed asset* depreciates equally over a number of years.

Trading account: part of the *profit and loss account—sales* to *gross profit*.

Trading profit: also called net profit (before interest) and *operating profit*.

Turnover: same as revenue or *sales*.

Value added tax (VAT): customs and excise levy this for each sale/purchase.

Vertical format: modern format of *balance sheet* with shareholders funds vertical, not horizontal to *net current assets*.

Work-in-progress (WIP):   materials partly processed.

Working capital: *net current assets*.

Working capital ratio: *current assets* over *current liabilities*.

Write off: to charge as an *expense* in the *profit and loss account* rather than an *asset*.

11

Finance and decision making

In business, the successful management of finance is vital. All companies have to engage in a planning process to carefully consider where their financial needs lie and how they are going to meet them. This process of financial planning involves looking at the resources that are available, forecasting changes in needs for the future and then ensuring that all financial objectives and contingencies are catered for and met.

In many markets, the stakes are high and risks are taken. Whereas a good decision will bring in a high return, a poor decision may have dire consequences. Companies must carefully analyse investment alternatives to ensure that decisions provide shareholders with the best possible return.

Case Study—Late payments damage company health

The recent UK recession claimed a record number of victims. Many of them blamed their demise on more than just high interest rates and overall economic downturn. They claim that, having supplied goods and/or services, particularly to large companies, late payment by those customers frequently dealt the final blow.

It is difficult to establish the number of cases where late payment has contributed to business collapse, but one indication is a near doubling of county court judgments in 1991 used to demand payments.

Many organizations today deliberately delay payments to creditors in order to improve their cash flow position but, in so doing, they often cause serious problems with their suppliers. Suppliers find it very difficult to fight back and always risk losing vital business if they do so. A recent survey by accountants Pannell Kerr Foster finds that 70 per cent of small- and medium-sized companies believe that late payments made the recession worse and that an overwhelming 96 per cent believe that it adds to business problems. For example:

- 76 per cent of firms have to wait three months or more for their bills to be paid;
- only 14 per cent receive their money within the contractual limit of 30 days;
- manufacturers fare worst as eight out of ten of them have to wait up to three months for payment;
- 96 per cent say it adds to their business' problems and 30 per cent say it seriously affects their business.

Many feel that small businesses face a 'Catch 22' position. Businesses need to sell goods and/or services but do not want to take their largest customers to court. Some of the largest British companies are subjected to the greatest criticism. Many of these companies generate up to a third of their profits from their large cash reserves, instead of using such reserves to pay suppliers on time.

Delaying payment seems to have become part of the British business culture. Many organizations have become aware of the benefits of holding on to money as long as they can and feel that it is only common sense to do so. Large companies not only have the resources for monitoring credit, but also have easier access to funds. Whereas a small business requiring cash might go to a bank and be charged interest at base plus from day one, a PLC will be able to go to the Stock Market, float a rights issue and then not have to pay shareholders until the first dividend some six months later.

There is general agreement that imposing interest on overdue debts might improve the situation. Of companies that already charge interest on delayed payments, nine out of ten feel that they have not lost customers as a result and that the system has encouraged prompt payment.

Another solution seems to lie in the Courts and Legal Services Act 1990. This provides for most debt cases to be handled by county courts rather than the High Court. It also provides for the client to be represented by a debt-collecting agent rather than a barrister and for the debt-collector's fee or commission to be recoverable by the court.

A surprising package of measures designed to improve prompt payment appeared in the 1992 Budget. These measures today mean that large companies will have to reveal in their accounts the length of time they take to pay bills. Companies awarded government contracts will also have to commit themselves to paying their sub-contractors promptly— normally within 30 days. The Department of Employment has agreed to provide up to £90 000 to small business associations to set up support services for their members in areas where the problem of late payments is severe and will also provide them with advice on how to pursue offenders.

Whether the above measures work remains to be seen. Late payments are hardly likely to disappear overnight. However, as long as large businesses continue to borrow, in effect, from their suppliers' banks instead of their own banks, they will continue to place their suppliers at a severe competitive disadvantage.

Questions

1. Explain why many organizations deliberately delay the payment of bills.
2. How might delayed payments improve working capital?
3. Why is it difficult for suppliers to take action against delayed payments?
4. What would you consider to be a reasonable credit period. Explain why.
5. How have delayed payments contributed to the recent recession?
6. What liquidity ratios refer to payment periods? How useful might they be?
7. Why might large organizations be less likely to suffer from working capital problems than small organizations?
8. What are the solutions to delayed payment?
9. Describe other steps an organization might take to improve its working capital.

Case Study—British Gas accounts for 1991

Look at Table 11.1, which gives a five-year financial summary of the balance sheets of British Gas, and then answer the questions that follow.

1. Using ratio analysis to support your answer, comment briefly on British Gas' working capital position between 1987 and 1991.
2. If you wanted to make a more detailed analysis of their working capital, what further information might be of use to you?
3. Creditors (falling due after more than one year) have increased. Provide possible reasons for such an increase.
4. What might intangible assets be?
5. The British Gas debtors figure has risen between 1987 and 1991. Imagine that you are a credit controller. How might you attempt to reduce the size of this debtors figure?

Table 11.1. British Gas accounts summary for 1987–91 (*Source: Directors' Report and Accounts*, British Gas PLC, 1991.)

	1987 £M	1988 £M	1989 £M	1990 £M	1991 £M
CURRENT COST BALANCE SHEET					
Intangible fixed assets	43	145	301	558	686
Tangible fixed assets and fixed asset investments	17 060	16 989	18 495	19 934	21 807
Total fixed assets	17 103	17 134	18 796	20 492	22 493
Current assets					
Stocks	199	252	333	338	366
Debtors	2 048	1 788	1 876	2 374	3 147
Investments	959	2 076	1 214	623	838
Cash at bank and in hand	40	29	47	32	61
	3 246	4 145	3 470	3 367	4 412
Creditors (falling due within one year)	(2 096)	(3 039)	(3 104)	(3 220)	(3 790)
Net current assets	1 150	1 106	366	147	622
Total assets less current liabilities	18 253	18 240	19 162	20 639	23 115
Creditors (falling due after more than one year)	(1 831)	(1 721)	(1 369)	(1 442)	(2 763)
Provisions for liabilities and charges	(41)	(61)	(91)	(132)	(191)
	16 381	16 458	17 702	19 065	20 161
Called up share capital	1 038	1 038	1 065	1 065	1 065
Share premium account	—	—	33	33	34
Current cost reserve	14 114	13 722	14 598	15 732	16 452
Profit and loss account	1 229	1 411	1 688	1 912	2 253
British Gas shareholders' interest	16 381	16 171	17 384	18 742	19 804
Minority shareholders' interest	—	287	318	323	357
	16 381	16 458	17 702	19 065	20 161

Case Study—What happens when companies fail?

Many companies in the 1990s have found themselves caught between falling demand for their products and high interest rates on debts incurred in the boom years. High gearing, late payments from debtors and tougher terms from banks have added to their predicament. There have been some notable corporate victims, including Stormseal and Polly Peck, but these have been dwarfed by the more spectacular falls of BCCI and the Maxwell empire.

The early signs of a company in difficulty appear a long time before they crash. Falling profits, increased gearing and then reported losses indicate that something is amiss. Temporary share suspension 'pending confirmation of the company's financial position' might then follow.

Liquidation is the next stage. If the directors feel that the company can no longer pay its debts, it is therefore insolvent and, under the provisions of the Insolvency Act 1986, must be liquidated. Liquidation may be voluntary or compulsory if it is ordered by a court, usually on behalf of a creditor.

Receivership involves the appointment of someone outside the company, who might be an accountant from a firm that specializes in receiverships. The receiver then supervises the sale of the company, which might either be sold as a complete unit or involve the breaking up of the company and the disposal of its assets. The receiver will attempt to extract the highest prices for assets to meet the demands of creditors as fully as possible. Secured creditors are paid initially and, once they have been paid, any unsecured creditors will be paid. Once the needs of creditors have been met, any remaining funds will be distributed to shareholders.

There are two situations that may stave off liquidation. First, a company may resort to an *Administration Order*. This will again involve the appointment of someone outside the company to supervise the company's activities. This will stop a company being forced into receivership by its creditors and may provide it with a welcome opportunity to get its affairs sorted out. Second, when a company is encountering difficulties, there is always the possibility of a *white knight* appearing on the scene in the form of another company willing to mount a rescue.

No matter what happens, nearly all bankruptcies cause confusion, particularly if a company has assets and creditors spread across several countries.

Questions

1. Explain why the business failure rate increased so dramatically in the early 1990s.
2. How could businesses have tried to avoid the crisis?
3. What starts to happen when a business experiences difficulty?
4. Explain the difference between liquidation and receivership.
5. Study the press. Try to find a recent example of a white knight.

Case Study—A partnership in overseas investment

Manufacturing through a joint venture overseas has been the aim of Bromsgrove Power Supplies Ltd, the Midland engineering company that has the stated aim of contributing to environmental energy production. It has developed a system that recovers heat from electricity generation and then reuses it to generate further electricity. The recovery rate is nearly 99 per cent. Energy is stopped from being unnecessarily wasted. Their techniques have been widely acclaimed by British electricity companies across the UK, but, looking to the future, Bromsgrove Power Supplies have been reviewing opportunities in Europe.

A major Dutch company has approached Bromsgrove Power Supplies Ltd for a joint manufacturing project in Europe. At about the same time, Bromsgrove has also been negotiating with a German company.

The Dutch project involves an investment of £100 000. Profits are expected to be:

- £28 000 in Year 1;
- £35 000 in Year 2;
- £48 000 in Year 3;
- £46 000 in Year 4;
- £38 000 in Year 5.

The German project involves an investment of £145 000. Profits are expected to be:

- £40 000 in Year 1;
- £42 000 in Year 2;
- £67 000 in Year 3;
- £69 000 in Year 4;
- £60 000 in Year 5.

You have been asked to act as a consultant to Bromsgrove Power Supplies Ltd.

Questions

1. Advise them on the financial merits of each project. Comment on:

   - average rate of return;
   - payback;
   - net present value (with a discount factor of 8 percent).

2. What other considerations would you take into account before making a decision about the project?

Table 11.2. DCF tables from 1 per cent to 10 per cent over 6 years – per cent rate of discount

Future years	1	2	3	4	5	6	7	8	9	10
1	0.990	0.980	0.971	0.962	0.952	0.943	0.935	0.926	0.917	0.909
2	0.980	0.961	0.943	0.925	0.907	0.890	0.873	0.857	0.842	0.826
3	0.971	0.942	0.915	0.889	0.864	0.840	0.816	0.794	0.772	0.751
4	0.961	0.924	0.888	0.855	0.823	0.792	0.763	0.735	0.708	0.683
5	0.951	0.906	0.863	0.822	0.784	0.747	0.713	0.681	0.650	0.621
6	0.942	0.888	0.837	0.790	0.746	0.705	0.666	0.630	0.596	0.564

3. One adviser has suggested that any project should take into account the wider costs and benefits of each proposal with a cost–benefit framework. What is this and what areas might it include?

Case Study—Investment capital from 3i

The British motor trade has been subject to vast structural changes over the last few years. Though many big groups have been divesting themselves of individual businesses, some small companies have become larger, even during the recession. One reason for this has been that long-term capital has been available for the well-managed business. For example, 3i invested £14m in the motor trade during 1990–91. Much of this involved helping small businesses to grow.

As a large investment institution, 3i has access to massive resources but, as well as engaging in multimillion-pound transactions, it is also willing to provide capital to smaller investors. Roughly half of its investments are for less than £200 000. The purposes of the funding vary quite widely—it may be to enter a new market, launch a new product, expand or install a new plant. 3i state that they are not always concerned about the size of any venture, but are often more interested in the quality of management and the prospects for growth.

3i considers itself to be a 'hands off' investor that takes a long-term view rather than a short-term investor that might wish to see quick returns. Their investment usually involves the provision of equity or venture capital rather than loan capital. Thus, 3i becomes a part-owner of a business, usually as a minority shareholder. The great benefit of this is that share capital strengthens the balance sheet by reducing the level of gearing. An organization can thus raise loans in the future if they are required. Many of the businesses hit badly by the recession were too highly geared.

Packages from 3i for the motor trade have enabled businesses to take a more strategic view towards financing. Long-term capital has been provided for long-term growth, allowing businesses to then raise short-term capital for short-term needs.

Questions

1. What is venture capital?
2. Distinguish between long-term capital and short-term capital. What might each be used for?
3. What are the benefits of including an institutional investor such as 3i as a minority shareholder?
4. Explain what is meant by the following terms:

- structural changes;
- hands-off investor;
- equity;

- gearing;
- highly geared;
- strategic view.

Activity

Examine the financial press. Search for signs of organizations that are experiencing the early stages of financial difficulty or for articles which refer to such situations.

From the information you have managed to amass and using a report format, explain why you feel that the company you have chosen is experiencing such problems.

Activity

Obtain a small business pack from a bank. Assess:

- the different forms of finance available for small businesses;
- the services the bank provides for small businesses;
- the requirements for a business plan;
- the advice and literature provided by the bank.

Activity

Examine a construction project taking place in your local community. Comment on the likely:

- private costs;
- private benefits;
- social costs;
- social benefits.

Try to assess the risks involved in this project. Given the current economic climate and the attendant risks, if you were managing the project, what level of payback and average rate of return might you be looking for?

Essay title 1—How might a small business assess its financial requirements? What sources of finance might be available and what are the implications of using each source?

In your introduction, say that the successful management of finance is essential for all businesses. For example, bad financial management could seriously damage a good business. Businesses therefore have to pay close attention to managing their finances by closely controlling, monitoring and assessing their requirements.

Small businesses will have:

- different requirements to those of large businesses;
- short-term needs and long-term needs.

Examples should be given of each type of need.

Assessing requirements over the next six months or year might be done using a cash flow forecast. The answer should, possibly using a brief example, show what this is, how it is used and the benefits it provides. The forecast might be part of an overall business plan that coordinates the strategic, tactical and operational elements of the business.

Long-term financial needs are much more difficult to assess. To do so would require a strategic audit. If such needs involve a major investment proposal, then capital appraisal techniques would be required. Capital appraisal should be briefly explained and the various techniques mentioned.

Sources of finance might include:

- *capital*—through various forms of ownership. Examples should be mentioned; the implications are that it would involve expense, loss of control, sharing profits among larger numbers of shareholders, risks of securities market and so on;
- *profit retention*—keeping funds available for reinvestment, which might involve satisficing, but it creates reserves, is cheap and enables funds to be spread among assets;
- *borrowing*—this might involve debentures or loans from banks. The problems associated with source are that it might lead to excessive gearing, lack of flexibility and will definitely involve meeting interest and capital repayments;
- *leasing and hiring*—a variety of schemes is available, but essentially enables an asset to be used, can be charged to a profit and loss account, enables equipment to be changed frequently and tax allowances to be claimed by the lessor;
- *overdraft*—is short-term finance to ease cash flow problems and is expensive but flexible;
- *factoring*—can be used to obtain immediate payment against debtors and is an immediate way of improving liquidity;
- *trade credit*—delaying the payment of bills improves cash flow but may penalize suppliers, involve loss of discounts and goodwill;
- *enterprise allowance schemes, grants and others*—these are often discretionary and may depend on fulfilling certain criteria.

In conclusion, financial requirements have to be carefully assessed and then matched to sources of finance that provide the broadest range of benefits.

Essay title 2—Explain the importance of managing working capital. Why is it possible for a profitable firm to run out of cash?

In the introduction, mention that at the heart of an organization are its operational activities. For these to take place cash, liquid assets, the cash cycle and the effective management of working capital need to be in place to enable the business to engage in value-adding activities that may ultimately lead to profitability.

The body of the answer should:

- define working capital;
- explain what it does and how it works;
- refer to the credit and cash cycles.

A firm that does not manage its working capital effectively may:

- not be able to buy in bulk and so miss out on trade discounts;
- lose cash discounts;
- not be able to offer credit facilities;
- be unable to innovate;
- may lose its reputation;
- may suffer action from creditors;
- may have overtraded by overextending itself.

Working capital may be managed by:

- reducing the credit and cash cycles;
- utilizing fixed assets more effectively;
- reviewing stock levels or improving stock management;
- employing a credit controller;
- improved use of budgeting;
- use of short-term solutions.

If a firm is profitable it does not necessarily mean that it is managing its working capital effectively. Profit should be defined. Profit may be gross and then net but does not refer to cash. Profit will be spread among the assets generated from the activities that have taken place over the financial period. Some of these might be liquid and others illiquid. If the firm has not been managed properly, it may be possible for large profits to be made but for the firm to suffer working capital problems (a numerical example could be given to illustrate this point).

In conclusion, working capital oils the wheels of an organization. Without effective management of liquid funds, firms would find themselves in a financial straitjacket.

Essay title 3—A large company is considering whether or not to build a factory on the outskirts of a market town in the Thames Valley. What factors should be taken into account before making such a major investment decision?

Introduce the essay by saying that any major investment involves risking funds now in the hope of securing returns later. In order to minimize the risk element, the project must be carefully appraised beforehand.

Each capital appraisal technique should be carefully analysed and may include:

- the average rate of return method;
- the payback method;
- discounted cash flow—net present value;
- discounted cash flow—internal rate of return.

Simple numerical examples may be used to highlight the above.
Other factors might include:

- locational factors combined with the overall aim of building on the lowest cost site, such as integration with group companies, labour, housing, amenities, land, regional advantages, safety, communications, government influences and others;
- wider influences that not only take into account the organization but also the community in which it intends to locate, for example, by means of cost–benefit analysis, it would be possible to consider:
  —private costs;
  —private benefits;
  —social costs;
  —social benefits;
- marketing factors—the strengths, weaknesses, opportunities and threats (SWOT) of products or markets in which the organization intends to compete would have to be considered;
- environmental factors—political, economic, social and technological (PEST) must also be considered, together with the overall stability of the business environment.

An organization must never make a decision without first carefully analysing not just the financial factors but also a host of other factors that might influence the outcome of the project.

Essay titles

1. 'Larger businesses will have a wider range of sources of finance available at lower cost than those available to smaller businesses.' Examine this statement. How can small businesses hope to compete with larger businesses?

2. Examine how and why a company would carefully balance its capital requirements between risk capital and loan capital.

3. Explain how a public company might finance an investment project. What would be the dangers of becoming too highly geared?

4. A company in Reading urgently requires short-term finance. What advice would you give?

5. Explain the difference between cash and profit. Why is it possible for a cash-rich firm to be unprofitable and for a firm that has very few liquid assets to be profitable?

6. Explain why many businesses fail. How might they avoid such failure?

7. 'When businesses grow they leave themselves open to a whole host of problems.' What might these be and how might they take steps to avoid such problems?

8. Examine closely the various techniques for appraising an investment. What are the benefits of each technique and what information do they each provide?

9. 'Whenever a firm grows it puts strains upon its working capital.' Discuss.

10. What is cost–benefit analysis? Explain why social costs ought to be considered when making an investment decision?

11. You have been asked to advise a small company about the sources of finance available to develop a programme of expansion. Outline the issues you would highlight and advice you would give.

12. Explain the actions that a highly geared company with working capital problems might have to take. What are the benefits (if any) and dangers of being highly geared?

13. What is a cash budget? How useful is it for predicting a company's cash flow?

14. What techniques would you use if you were responsible for managing a firm's trade credit? How might such techniques improve their working capital?

15. What is leasing? How might leasing alter the structure of a firm's final accounts?

16. What are the dangers of insufficient working capital? How should the credit cycle be managed?

17. You have been asked to advise on an investment decision. What information would you require and how would you undertake the task?

18. Analyse a major investment with which you are familiar. What are the major costs and benefits of the project?

19. Explain how a recession might affect the ways in which a business manages its assets.

20. What is venture capital? What are the advantages of using venture capital instead of loan capital?

Short-answer questions

1. Explain how interest rates might affect the demand for loans.
2. What is risk capital?
3. Give two reasons for a company wishing to go public.
4. Explain how ordinary shares differ from preference shares.
5. Name two dangers of issuing too much risk capital.
6. Name the tax charged on company profits.
7. What is a debenture?
8. Name two advantages of using loan capital.
9. Explain why many businesses might frequently use overdraft facilities.
10. Describe why an organization should not hold too much cash.
11. How might ratio analysis help an organization to manage its working capital?
12. Name two techniques for appraising capital.
13. What are externalities?
14. How does a social benefit differ from a social cost?
15. What is meant by factoring?
16. What are the benefits of using a discounted cash flow method of investment appraisal?
17. How does a debtor differ from a creditor?
18. Name four areas that should appear in a business plan.
19. What is collateral?
20. Why might a company raise a rights issue?

Projects

Managing finance and making sound investment decisions are important activities for all organizations. Though many of these decisions are routine and commonplace, they have to be carefully researched and managed. A bad decision could, and often does, place a firm in crisis. Two key areas instantly spring to mind for project work. These are:

- to liaise with a small local business, produce a cash flow forecast for its activities and amend and monitor the forecast over a period of time;
- to undertake a period of work experience with a business that wishes to take an investment decision in the forthcoming months, then appraise the decision they wish to take and find out about the most appropriate form of finance for the project.

One of the problems of working in this area is that factors influencing either a cash flow forecast or an investment decision are constantly subject to change and therefore both areas require extensive research.

Suggested reading

Bendry, M., R. Hussey and C. West, *Accounting and Finance for Business Students—An Active-Learning Approach*. D.P. Publications, 1992.

Hines, T., *Foundation Accounting*. Checkmate Arnold, 1987.

Millichamp, A. H., *Finance for Non-financial Managers—An Active-Learning Approach*. D.P. Publications, 1992.

Weston, J. Fred, and Thomas E. Copeland, (UK adapters Alan F. Fox and Robin Limmack). *Managerial Finance* (2nd edn). Cassell, 1988.

Wood, Frank, and Joe Townsley, *Finance*. Pitman Polytech, 1986.

12

The management of costs

In order to develop a business strategy, managers must use financial information to plan, control and monitor their activities. Management accounting involves extracting data and then processing it in such a way that it can provide the maximum benefits for operational decision making.

At the heart of controlling activities is the importance of costs. Nearly all business activities involve some form of cost and this knowledge is fundamental, particularly when making decisions that influence products, prices and profitability. The great benefit of this process is that, though it will never actually eliminate uncertainty, it may well help to reduce it.

Case Study—Distinguishing between costs

The two broad areas fundamental to all costing and management accounting are *fixed costs* and *variable costs*.

Variable costs are those that increase as output increases. They therefore increase in direct proportion to the number of units produced. If, when you manufacture 10 units you expend £50 on variable costs, when you manufacture 100 units you will incur £500 of variable costs.

Fixed costs are those that are independent of the numbers of units produced. They will not change over a range of output.

So what might these costs include? Imagine that you want to distinguish between variable and fixed costs in a clothing factory, so that you could later use this information for costing purposes.

To find the variable costs you would have to look at the organization's operational activities and analyse what goes into producing each unit of production. The cost of *direct materials*, such as fabrics, would probably be the first variable cost you would identify. *Direct labour* or shop floor labour, which can be directly identified with the production process, is also a clear variable cost. Other variable costs would include *variable overheads*. These are other costs that vary with output. Variable overheads might include the cost of electricity or power used to make each extra unit, as well as other materials and costs, such as lubricants for the sewing machines, labels, cotton, packaging and adhesives that are used in direct proportion to output.

Fixed costs are more likely to be found in the office at the clothes factory. They might include rent, rates, insurance, depreciation and administrative costs. Remember that fixed costs are fixed in the short term, but may vary over a longer period.

In practice, measuring variable costs is quite easy. You go to the factory floor and measure the materials that go into an item and the time taken to produce it. You then add variable overheads. The total of the variable cost is then known as the *marginal cost*, because it represents the costs incurred from the manufacture of one more unit, which in this case is a garment. Remember that marginal costs only take into account variable costs, not fixed costs.

Fixed costs are not as easy to measure. It is not possible to relate these to each unit. For example, how much insurance or rent is required for one unit? It is not possible to say. All you can do with fixed costs is carefully analyse what each is and then total them.

Once you have identified the above costs, they are then available for decision making in the hope that they can be used to improve the way in which the clothes factory is managed.

Questions

1. Explain the difference between fixed and variable costs.
2. Identify both the fixed and variable costs in the company or college in which you work or attend.
3. Explain what will happen to both fixed and variable costs if output is increased.
4. How will fixed and variable costs appear on a graph that relates costs to output?
5. Where would total costs appear on the above graph?
6. Explain what is meant by marginal cost.
7. Why is it useful to know information about marginal costs? How might this information be used?

Case Study—Stake Out Ltd

Stake Out Ltd is a private company, manufacturing small, high-quality canvas tents for hillwalkers and campers. Business has been healthy over the last two years as the recession has encouraged people to invest in lower-budget holidays and because of increasing growth in the leisure market for camping equipment.

The company is managed and owned by Rachel Hunter, who is the Managing Director, and Kuldip Gill, who supervises operations. They have a small factory unit on a trading estate and they employ 15 full-time employees—a foreman, 12 machine operators who cut out canvas for part-time workers and 2 dispatchers. The part-time workers are employed as contractors, using their own sewing machines at home to make up the tents from the cut-out pieces that have been sent to them.

The foreman is paid £250 per week, the machine operators £200 per week and the dispatchers £180 per week. The part-timers are paid £50 for each tent they produce.

Other business costs include:

- electricity at £120 per week;
- rent and rates at £560 per week;
- loan repayments, including interest, at £220 per week;
- other fixed costs at £100 per week;
- directors' salaries for Rachel and Kuldip at £400 each per week;
- material costs for each tent at £15.

The existing capacity for Stake Out is 160 tents per calendar week. If it needs to produce more than this, it has to pay higher rates to cover overtime put in by the part-time workers, which results in an increase in part-time costs from £50 for each tent to £65 for each tent, up to and including a capacity of 180 tents, and from £65 to £95 for each tent up to a maximum capacity of 200 tents. At present, tents are priced at £105 and Stake Out Ltd has a consistent weekly turnover of 140 tents.

On 20 October, Stake Out is approached by two major retail Army and Navy chains that have tested samples and wish to purchase some tents. Fosters wish to purchase 40 tents per week and are willing to pay £100 per tent. N&M wish to purchase 20 tents per week and are willing to pay £98 per tent.

As a personal friend of the directors and an adviser on their business activities, these figures have been left with you for further analysis.

Questions

1. Construct a table to show the fixed, variable and total weekly costs at each rate of production up to the maximum capacity of 200 units.
2. Present the fixed, variable and total costs in a graphic form for the week.
3. Calculate the profit the company is generating at its present level of sales of 140 tents per week.
4. Explain why the variable cost per unit increases as output moves towards maximum capacity.

5.   Advise the directors as to whether they should accept:

- the Fosters order;
- the N&M order;
- both;
- neither.

Support your answers with figures and explanations.

Case Study—Using management information

Those who rise to senior positions in the manufacturing sector in Japan will usually have worked for several years in every area of the organization before their appointment, including manufacturing and accounting. The net result is a breadth and depth of expertise, experience and understanding that those in the West just cannot match.

So, who reads *and* fully understands management accounts in a British manufacturing business? Attention is usually focused on the monthly management accounts prepared using traditional costing techniques. These reports will tend to dominate monthly review meetings and consist of complex schedules and summaries that typical non-financial executives will probably be too embarrassed to admit that they do not really understand.

To overcome this problem, manufacturing managers should be provided with some sort of financial education that should be viewed as an extra manufacturing tool. At the same time, management accountants should spend more time at the sharp end of manufacturing so that they can learn more precisely how the information they provide contributes to decision making.

The next step would be to develop performance measures and data that is analysed in such a way it is focused precisely according to the organization's needs. The key to the exercise would be to keep measures simple and flexible and presented in a form that all at a meeting will understand. The management accountant's role in this would be to coordinate the collection and presentation of data and then become more involved in the decision-making process based on it. After a short period of time, the gulf of understanding between accounting and manufacturing will diminish and any former conflicts will soon be replaced by harmony.

Questions

1.   What benefits arise if financial managers work in a variety of areas in an organization?
2.   Why may costing techniques be complex?

3. Explain why all senior managers should have a basic knowledge of management accounting techniques.
4. What is a performance measure?

Case Studies—The Disney attraction

Theme Holidays Ltd is a private company that specializes in providing holidays for adults and children alike who require a unique form of entertainment. All of their holidays involve overseas packages based on a theme. With the opening of EuroDisney in 1992, they are finding that half of the packages they now provide are based on this one resort, while the other half are to theme destinations in the United States.

Theme Holidays is currently reviewing its profitability for 1994. They anticipate that their fixed overheads will be £450 000 for the year. With the EuroDisney packages, a quarter of the variable costs go in travel costs, at an average of £30 per package. They anticipate selling EuroDisney packages at an average of £160 per holiday for 1992.

The American holidays are sold at an average price of £650 per holiday. Travel costs of £200 for the American holidays comprise half of the variable costs of the holiday.

Market research has revealed that, during 1994, Theme Holidays expect to sell 4000 holidays.

Questions

1. Work out the contribution for both the European and American holidays.
2. Calculate the company's profit for the year before tax and interest.
3. Market research also revealed that if Theme Holidays reduced their prices by 10 per cent, they could sell 300 more holidays per year. Calculate how this would affect profitability and advise accordingly.
4. Theme Holidays are aware of the size of their fixed overheads. How would a 10 per cent reduction in fixed overheads through cost-cutting measures affect both of the above?
5. Explain briefly how variations in exchange rates, particularly against the dollar, could affect the profitability of the packages.
6. Suggest two alternative strategies that Theme Holidays could use to increase profitability.

Case Study—CleanEasy Ltd

Insolvency specialists, it seems, are not the only type of business to flourish during a recession. As many companies drive to improve efficiency and cut costs without compromising quality, many have turned to contracted business services in an effort to hive off non-core activities.

CleanEasy has benefited enormously from this process. They claim that conditions are booming as many companies wake up to the benefits of utilizing professionally managed external support services. CleanEasy have noted the rapid growth of the contracted services sector with pleasure and feel confident that this area will continue to grow. They have responded rapidly to this growth by undertaking an expansion programme that has resulted in an increase in their fixed costs so that they are now as follows:

	£
• loan repayment and interest	230 000
• rent and rates	95 000
• insurance	980
• staff salaries	325 000
• other fixed overheads	100 000
• promotion	5 000

The average contract size for CleanEasy is £24 000 per annum and they currently expect to increase their number of contracts for the forthcoming year to 130. Each contract will cost them at least £12 000 in direct labour and at least £4000 in direct materials. Other variable overheads will be about £1000.

Questions

1. Work out the break-even point for CleanEasy in terms of value and volume (to the nearest contract).
2. Draw a break-even chart to illustrate the above.
3. How much profit will they make with 130 contracts?
4. Given the nature of their investment, CleanEasy wish to make £300 000 profit for the year. How many contracts would they require to achieve this?
5. One strategy CleanEasy are proposing to adopt is to increase their promotional budget. If they increase this budget to £50 000, research has indicated that they will achieve at least 35 more contracts. How will this affect profitability?
6. Another strategy they are considering is to decrease price. Further research has revealed that if the average contract price fell to £22 000, they could expect to gain at least 45 new contracts. How will this affect profitability.

Activity

Working in a small group:

- decide on a product you feel you could produce;
- decide on a pricing strategy and agree a price;
- calculate your fixed overheads;
- calculate your variable costs;
- estimate how many of these products you might be able to sell.

Work out a break-even point, in terms of both volume and value, and assess the potential profitability of the project. Using various forms of visual aids, make a presentation to other members of your class or group outlining the possibilities for your venture.

Activity

Find out about the financial information generated in your institution and its use for managers. Arrange an interview with the bursar, accountant or administrator or ask them to come and speak to the group.

Prepare a series of questions to ask in readiness for the interview or meeting. For example:

- What financial information is generated by the accounting system?
- How is decision making influenced by IT?
- Are any activities costed and, if so, how?
- Is break-even analysis ever used?

Activity

Find out about accounting software packages and what they do by writing to a selection of software companies. From the promotional information you receive, try to analyse how such packages improve the quality of information available to managers using them.

Essay title 1—To what extent is break-even analysis an important managerial tool?

The key to answering this question is responding to the 'to what extent?' element. To do this effectively, you must constantly refer to how break-even analysis is used as well as the dangers or flaws associated with each use.

In your introduction, say how management today is a far more scientific and analytical process than it ever used to be. In the modern, competitive world, decisions have to be based on hard information extracted using a range of techniques. At the heart of management accounting is the knowledge of costing and costing techniques. One such technique is marginal costing. Break-even analysis is a widely accepted marginal costing technique.

The early part of the answer must show that you know what break-even analysis is. You must therefore:

- define marginal costing;
- show how it overcomes the problems of allocating fixed costs;
- show how contribution is calculated;
- define breaking even and the break-even point;
- show, briefly and with a basic numerical example, how it is calculated.

So, how is break-even analysis used as a managerial tool? It may be used as a simple device to:

- forecast profits/losses at different levels of sales activity;
- help with pricing decisions, so that different outcomes at different prices may be assessed;
- be used to assess how changes in production/sales may affect profit;
- be used to establish profit and production targets with a built-in margin of safety;
- analyse the effects of different strategies.

The great benefit of break-even analysis is that it is a simple tool that is easily understood and capable of being used by managers with a range of business backgrounds.

There are, however, a number of dangers in using a simple tool such as break-even analysis for many of the above mentioned managerial decisions. To a large extent it over-simplifies business behaviour and then completely ignores the external environment in which a business is operating. A proposal might be perfectly feasible in *theory* but completely impractical in *practice*. Break-even analysis just reduces business activities to an equation (try to give an example here).

Other factors that might affect the quality of decisions made on the basis of break-even analysis might be that:

- it can be argued that fixed costs are, in reality, stepped and likely to change at different levels of activity;
- break-even analysis does not take into account the physical capabilities of the organization, such as that at a certain output attractive profits may be made, but the problem is that you might not have the ability to achieve that output;
- variable costs and sales are unlikely to be linear;
- break-even analysis only depicts short-term relationships;
- it is dependent on the accuracy of forecasts.

In conclusion, then, break-even analysis is clearly an important managerial tool, but its use must be further qualified. It is a simple tool and many decisions are complex. It may be better viewed as part of a range or package of other tools, forecasts and techniques of analysis.

Essay Title 2—Explain briefly the various types of costs and describe the importance of each. How may a knowledge of costs and costing techniques help a business to price its products?

There are two significant elements to this question. First, the description of costs and the importance of the various types and second, the applied element, illustrating how costs are used in practice to price products. The second area should show some understanding of the usefulness of costing for marketing purposes.

In the introduction to your essay, explain that it is difficult to make any sort of informed business decision without an accurate knowledge and assessment of costs. Such knowledge allows alternatives to be considered and compared, for example, when considering which products to continue to produce, decisions about departments and so on. Costs relate closely to organizational objectives. For businesses to pursue profitability, they have to be efficient. A knowledge of costs and the importance of each helps them to be so.

Your answer should then analyse each type of cost and comment on the importance of each. For example:

- *fixed costs*—costs that do not increase as output increases in the short term, which provide a knowledge of overheads, can be used for break-even analysis and provide an idea of how much output an organization's resources may be able to cope with;
- *variable costs*—costs that increase as output increases, as more variable costs have to be used as input to increase output, which are useful for break-even analysis, can be directly attributed to each product, are easy to identify and can be controlled and varied easily in the short term;
- *semi-variable costs*—sometimes considered as a more accurate way of assessing many costs, for example, as output increases telephone bills and office electricity may increase, therefore, this is a more realistic way of assessing overheads;
- *average costs*—these are total costs divided by the total quantity produced and provide a quick and easy unit cost, relate costs to items produced and provide a basis for a margin;
- *marginal costs*—the cost of producing extra units of output, which is very useful as it enables the contribution for each product to be identified and then allocated to cover fixed costs; both marginal costs

and marginal costing techniques provide the basis for break-even analysis, allowing forecasts to be made and used as a basis for decision making.

Pricing is one of the four Ps of the marketing mix and has an important bearing on the success of any product. Costs and costing techniques are an essential element of the pricing process as they will determine margins and profitability. The two commonly used costing techniques to set prices are:

- *cost-plus pricing*—many firms use no other basis to price other than a simple mark-up on the cost to themselves—information is simply pieced together to provide a unit cost and then a margin is added; higher turnover goods for which there is more competition may have a smaller margin than more inelastic products that may be kept in stock for longer;
- *contribution pricing*—this involves separating out the different products that make up a company's portfolio in order to charge individual prices appropriate to a product's share towards total costs and is based on the marginal costing approach (give a brief description of marginal costing and break-even analysis, together with a numerical example).

In conclusion, no business in the modern world could survive for long without a knowledge of costs and costing techniques. If such techniques were not used for pricing products, they would be neither profitable nor competitive.

Essay title 3—Explain the purpose of budgeting. How useful is it for controlling an organization's activities?

In your introduction mention that all organizations require some form of direction. Having established objectives and developed a business strategy, budgets provide a basis for making things happen. It places an onus on budgeted areas to perform in a way that has been outlined for them.

What, therefore, is a budget? A budget is a device used to determine something we wish to do. For example, we may budget in order to afford our holiday, change cars or whatever. This is essentially a financial plan. We may have a short-term financial plan, to pay our car insurance, or a long-term financial plan, to save for a deposit to buy a house, for example.

The purpose of budgeting is to:

- give everybody something to work towards and that matches organizational objectives;
- increase cooperation between departments;

- enable non-accountants to become aware of costs;
- provide direction;
- create a system of financial planning that is integrated throughout the organization;
- provide a system of control;
- enable all employees to identify how they contribute towards corporate objectives;
- provide a basis for variance analysis and to take action to improve efficiency and improve profitability.

The question then asks 'how useful' is budgeting. Answering this part must involve looking at both sides of the coin.

Budgeting is useful for:

- enabling organizations to achieve objectives;
- coordination;
- planning;
- making decisions;
- controlling all areas.

The problem with budgeting, however, is that:

- if actual results are widely different, budgets lose their significance as a form of control;
- following budgets too rigidly may restrict the organization;
- budgets may be ignored if they do not have support.

In conclusion, budgeting is an important way of planning for the future, making decisions and controlling activities. They need to be introduced with the support, understanding and commitment of all concerned for them to be effective.

Essay titles

1. Explain the importance of management accounting. Using examples of different techniques, show how and why it might help an organization to plan for the future.
2. Examine the differences between financial accounting and management accounting. Using examples, explain how information from each type of accounting might be used.
3. A business wishes to introduce a system of financial planning. Advise them about the measures available for it to do so.
4. Examine the nature of costs. Show how a knowledge of costs might aid decision making.
5. What is budgetary control? How might it help an organization to achieve its objectives?

6. Using examples, examine the process of budgeting. How does variance analysis support budgetary control?
7. Explain the difference between absorption costing and marginal costing. How does marginal costing meet some of the criticisms of absorption costing?
8. Describe how costing might influence decision making. Refer to specific examples in your answer.
9. 'The value of break-even analysis is in its simplicity.' Discuss.
10. Using a numerical example, show how break-even analysis might be useful for decision-making purposes. What would be the dangers of relying too heavily on the break-even process?
11. Explain how accounting information might be used to aid decision making. Why will such information never be able to eliminate risks?
12. 'Accounting supports the decision-making process.' Discuss. What other areas also support the decision-making process.
13. Examine the usefulness of costing for marketing purposes.
14. Using specific examples, examine the areas of accounting with which non-accountants should be familiar.
15. Describe the objectives of budgeting. How might such a system work in practice?
16. You have been asked to report to management on a proposal to implement a system of budgeting. Use a report format to present your answer.
17. What is a management information system? How will it improve the quality of decision making?
18. You have been asked to advise an organization about the likely profitability of product X. It is expected:

    - to sell for either £8 or £12;
    - that variable costs will be £6 per unit;
    - that sales are likely to be either 8000 at £8 or 3000 at £12;
    - that fixed overheads will be £14 000 per annum.

What other influences should affect the pricing decision?

19. Describe how to draw a break-even chart. How should the chart be used?
20. Examine the importance of budgeting. How might such a process provide a business with genuine competitive advantages?

Short-answer questions

1. Explain the difference between fixed costs and variable costs.
2. Give one example of a semi-variable cost and explain briefly *why* it might be a semi-variable cost.

3. What are marginal costs?
4. Describe how average costs are calculated.
5. Name two benefits of a system of budgetary control.
6. Explain what is meant by variance analysis.
7. What is absorption costing?
8. Explain how contribution is calculated.
9. Define the term 'break even'.
10. What is the margin of safety?
11. Name two uses for break-even analysis.
12. Suggest two dangers of relying solely on break-even analysis.
13. Name three factors external to the accounting system that will affect the quality of decisions made.
14. What is a cost centre?
15. Explain what happens when sales exceed the break-even point?
16. What is an adverse variance?
17. Name two dangers of relying on a system of budgetary control.
18. Explain why average fixed costs will fall as output increases.
19. Provide two examples of direct costs.
20. What is a flexible budget?

Projects

Management accounting is fundamentally concerned with providing information for decision makers to use. The better the quality of information, the better the quality of decisions made. In order to utilize and manage the information resource, many organizations have set up management information systems that many claim are the major difference between successful and unsuccessful organizations.

Some interesting areas for project work might involve:

- finding out more about information systems, the benefits they provide and the people they involve;
- assessing the effectiveness of such a system;
- finding out how much a system benefits management accountants.

Suggested reading

Chilver, Dr Joseph, *Finance*. Stanley Thornes, 1990.
Duff, Trevor, *Cost and Management Accounting*. Pitman, 1988.
Hussey, Roger, *Cost and Management Accounting*. Macmillan, 1989.
Izhar, Riad, *Accounting, Costing, and Management*. Oxford University Press. 1991.
Knott, Geoffrey, *Financial Management*. Macmillan, 1991.

13

People at work

It is now widely recognized that people are the most valuable resource that any organization has. It is therefore the responsibility of all decision makers in a company to look after its human resource. In particular, of course, the personnel function has an overriding responsibility to look after the employees of a company from the time they apply for, and are offered, a position until their working contract is terminated.

An understanding of the factors that motivate or demotivate people at work is essential to any student of business studies. There are many ways of rewarding and recognizing effort.

People at work are represented by official and unofficial organizations in a wide number of ways—from pay bargaining to the organization of the works outing. Trade unions still play an important part in representing employees in bargaining with their members' organizations.

Case Study—Irish and UK unemployment

Geographic proximity, cultural and linguistic similarities and a long tradition of movement between the two countries mean that Ireland shares a common labour market with the UK. When times are good in the UK and/or when times are particularly hard in Ireland, emigration tends to siphon off excess labour from Ireland. Conversely, when the UK economy contracts, returning labour forces up unemployment in Ireland.

The 'common labour market' theory is strongly supported by recent trends. Unemployment in Ireland commenced its latest rise at precisely the same time as unemployment in the UK (see Fig. 13.1).

In both countries, the rate of increase has accelerated in the intervening period and at a similar pace. Of the 750 000 increase in unemployment in the UK in the March 1990–July 1991 period, almost 70 per cent has occurred since December; of the 42 000 increase in Ireland, 78 per cent has taken place since December.

If history can be relied on as a guide, unemployment in Ireland will stop

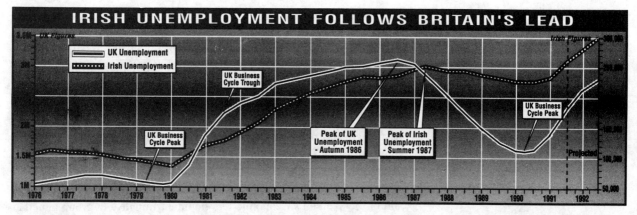

rising *only* when it has peaked in the UK and, even then, probably after a delay of about six months.

Figure 13.1 Irish unemployment follows Britain's lead. (*Source*: Irish Press.)

Questions

1. What is the relationship between unemployment in the two countries highlighted by the text and graph shown in Fig. 13.1?
2. Why is this a problem for the Irish economy?
3. Is it possible for the Irish government to do anything to reduce this problem?

Case Study—Do equal opportunities really exist?

Do we really live in a world of equal opportunity? Women represent 43 per cent of the British work-force but only 11 per cent of them occupy managerial positions, 9 per cent of them senior management positions, 5 per cent of them directors and less than 1 per cent of them chief executives. The Hansard Society Commission's recent report stated that, 'If boardrooms are where power and influence reside, then women are clearly excluded'.

The careers of women have, for so long, suffered from two perennial problems. First, the age-old view of many male colleagues that the advancement of women challenges their narrow 'male-as-breadwinner' view of roles. Second, many employers' inability to accept and cater for female career interruptions without considerable prejudice or adequately catering for women to do so. Hanson company secretary Yve Newbold was confronted with this dilemma when one of her own staff became pregnant and put off her decision whether or not to return to work until after the birth. She commented that, 'When you face it yourself, all the theoretical stuff goes and you're brought back to basics with a crunch. Do you train somebody else? Do you regret you didn't employ a man in the first place?' Such views have too often meant that, purely because of their biology, the careers of women have been set back, on average, about seven years and in order to recoup lost ground they have frequently to choose between having a career and having a family and, either way, had to work much harder than their counterparts to play the predominantly male career game.

Many feel, however, that though this was certainly the position in the past, there has been a change in attitude towards women in the board-rooms of Britain in more recent years. Some of Britain's most influential chairmen have begun to recognize the need to attract women at the most senior level in order to improve competitiveness. Lady Howe is chairper-son of the Women's Economic Development Initiative (a group aimed at making industry more aware of the changing economic role of women) for its umbrella group Business in the Community. She feels that it is the heads of companies who should take a lead in this area and has influenced many of them. She expresses enthusiasm about how female employee policy is evolving and predicts 'considerable change' over the next ten years.

For example, recent changes have taken place at Tesco where Sir Ian MacLaurin instigated research to find out why only 2 out of the 387 store managers were women. As a result, more women have taken up senior positions. At ICI, the number of women moving into middle and senior management positions has trebled in the last five years and Sir Denys Henderson has recently appointed a woman to his Board as a non-executive director. Sainsbury have completely revised their management structure to accommodate more women so now a third of their retail managers are women and 340 line managers are able to work part-time.

Unilever UK chairman Mike Heron recently suggested that men and women actually work better together, as opposed to a majority male or majority female working environment. He feels strongly that more com-panies should take account of this. Though this is almost certainly the case, it is probably a long way off. In the top 1000 UK companies, there is 1 female general manager, Jann Westfall of Levi UK, and one managing director, Anita Roddick of the Body Shop. It would seem that British companies have, for too long, ignored a very important resource.

Questions

1. Discuss why so few women occupy senior managerial positions in British industries.
2. Mike Heron of Unilever suggested that men and women actually work better together. This has become a popularly held view. Explain why this might be so.

3. Comment briefly on how the two problems that women have had to cope with mentioned in the text might have affected their careers. If you were the chief executive of a large organization and were concerned about these problems, how would you deal with them?
4. Comment briefly on other equal opportunity issues likely to be of concern for company chairpersons.

Case Study—The Standard Occupational Classification

In 1990, a new Standard Occupational Classification (SOC) was introduced. When deciding on the format and structure of the SOC, it was agreed that the basic concept to be classified should be that of 'a job', seen as a set of employment tasks. This would be indicated by the job title or description and would not require any ancillary information on the status in employment. SOC has been designed with a hierarchical structure with three main levels (Major, Minor and Unit Groups), each lower level aggregating to the level above.

Unit groups   → Minor groups   → Major groups
(374 categories)   (77 categories)   (9 categories)

Two examples of how the hierarchical structure of the SOC works are:

- *a dentist*—who would be found in Unit Group 223—Dental Practitioners—that links with Minor Group 22—Health Professionals and Major Group 2—Professional Occupations;
- *a lorry driver*—who would be found in Unit Group 872—Drivers of road goods vehicles—that links with Minor Group 87—Road transport operatives and Major Group 8—plant and machine operatives.

How the classifications are organized can be seen from Table 13.1.

Questions

1. How might the SOC be of use to the government Employment Service and as a tool for use with the Census of Population?
2. How might the SOC be of use in market research?
3. Carry out a survey of people's occupations in your area. Try to classify them into major groups. Present your findings in charts and tables.
4. What effect is improved education and training likely to have on the distribution of the population into major groups?
5. How can the SOC help government bodies to more accurately plan training provisions?

Table 13.1. Basic structure of the Standard Occupational Classification

Major Group	General nature of qualifications, training and experience for occupations in the Major Group	Sub-major Group
1. Managers and administrators	A significant amount of knowledge and experience of the production processes, administrative procedures or service requirements associated with the efficient functioning of organizations and businesses.	a Corporate managers and administrators b Managers/proprietors in agriculture and services
2. Professional occupations	A degree or equivalent qualification, with some occupations requiring post-graduate qualifications and/or a formal period of experience-related training.	a Science and engineering professions b Health professions c Education professions d Other professions
3. Associate professional and technical occupations	An associated high-level vocational qualification often involving a substantial period of full-time training or further study. Some additional task-related training is usually provided by means of a formal period of induction.	a Science and engineering professions b Health associate professions c Other associate professions
4. Clerical and secretarial occupations	A good standard of general education. Certain occupations will require further additional vocational training to a well-defined standard (say, typing or shorthand).	a Clerical occupations b Secretarial occupations
5. Craft and related occupations	A substantial period of training, often provided by means of a work-based training programme.	a Skilled construction trades b Skilled engineering trades c Other skilled trades
6. Personal and protective services occupations	A good standard of general education. Certain occupations will require further additional vocational training, often provided by means of a work-based training programme.	a Protective service occupations b Personal service occupations
7. Sales occupations	A general education and a programme of work-based training related to sales procedures. Some occupations require technical knowledge but are included in this major group because the primary task involves selling.	a Buyers, brokers and sales representatives b Other sales occupations
8. Plant and machine operatives	The knowledge and expertise necessary to operate vehicles and other mobile and stationary machinery; to operate and monitor industrial plant and equipment; to assemble products from component parts according to strict rules and procedures and subject assembled parts to routine tests. Most occupations in this major group will specify a minimum standard of competence that must be attained for satisfactory performance of the associated tasks and will usually have an associated period of formal experience-related training.	a Industrial plant stationary machine operators and assemblers b Drivers and mobile machine operators
9. Other occupations	The knowledge and expertise necessary to perform mostly simple and routine tasks often involving the use of hand-held tools and, in some cases, requiring a degree of physical effort. Most tasks in these occupations have limited scope for personal initiative and judgement, and may not require formal educational qualifications, but will usually have an associated short period of formal experience-related training. All non-managerial farming occupations are included in this major group, primarily because of the difficulty of distinguishing between those occupations that require only a limited knowledge of agricultural techniques from those which require specific training and experience in these areas.	a Other occupations in agriculture, forestry and fishing b Other elementary occupations

Case Study—Lean production

The Japanese have revolutionized many working practices. They invented 'lean' production. The decision-making process is lean and planning is lean and both are carried out with the direct and total involvement of the workers. The Toyota company was one of the founders of 'lean' production immediately after the World War II. This system supplanted 'fat' production with its excess of bureaucratic decision-making processes and top-level company decisions. The advantage of lean production is, among other things, that it combines the advantages of artisan manufacture (taken as attention to detail) with the advantages of mass production. It has undoubted advantages in terms of cost reduction. Judging the speed with which American corporations are installing 'lean' production, it is certainly regarded as a winning formula.

Moving from production centred on traditional, large assembly lines to more technologically sophisticated processes that are no smaller, but are organized differently—using equipment such as robots—entails a reduction in staff. This can have considerable social and economic consequences.

Questions

1. Why might 'lean' production improve human relations in the work-place?
2. What are the implications of 'lean' production for working practices?
3. What harmful social and economic consequences may result from 'lean' production?
4. Is 'lean' production appropriate for all industrial sectors?

Case Study—Food safety

In all industries, health and safety are key ingredients of working practice. This is nowhere more true than in food preparation where very high standards must be met to ensure that the health and safety of employees as well as safety of the products that will be sold to consumers are of a high standard.

Study the following information regarding Fenland Foods and then answer the questions.

Fenland Foods specializes in making cook-chill meals. These are ready prepared restaurant menu dishes that are:

- assembled from ingredients such as vegetables and meat;
- cooked on a large scale;
- packed;

- chilled and stored;
- transported to Marks and Spencer shops;
- sold to shoppers;
- re-heated ready for eating.

Walk into any Marks and Spencer food section and you will find a selection of these dishes. A busy person can buy a meal after work, take it home and quickly re-heat the dish for eating.

Cook-chill meals now account for a third of Britain's annual turnover of ready meals. Around 400 000 packs are sold every day. People who do not have the time to spend on cooking still want to eat well.

The cook-chill method is simple and cheaper in energy terms than deep-freezing.

Fenland's central kitchen prepares the meals. These are then chilled to between 0°C and 3°C and kept refrigerated until they are needed. For the next five days, according to the label, they can be heated up to 70°C for serving.

The giant kitchen of Fenland Foods goes on chopping, mixing, steaming, boiling and baking 24 hours a day, 6 days a week. It is only on Saturday that the plant stops producing and maintenance work is carried out.

Hygiene and cleanliness is of great importance in the food industry. All staff must be trained in safe working practices before they can start. Though it is hot in the cookhouse, other work areas are cool and the fridges icy cold. Hygiene and safety standards are rigidly enforced and cleaning is continuous in all areas.

From the moment Fenland employees enter the factory they must follow food safety rules. Here are some examples of the rules:

- do not smoke on the site;
- wash your hands properly;
  - —before starting work;
  - —after every break;
  - —after wiping your nose;
  - —after sneezing;
  - —after using hoses;
  - —after cleaning down;
  - —after touching the floor or anything that has been on the floor;
  - —before touching products;
  - —after using the lavatory;
- all cuts, grazes and burns must be covered with the correct blue detectable waterproof dressings;
- do not take cigarettes, matches, purses, wallets and sweets into the work-place;

Outdoor changing room
All employees remove coats/hats,
lock away large bags, personal
possessions and umbrellas.

Go to

Indoor changing room
1. Remove wellingtons, hat and
   hair net from personal locker

2. Lock shoes and valuables, i.e.
   jewellery, wallets, purses in locker.

3. Put hair net and hat on.

4. Put wellingtons on.

5. Wash hands.

6. Put coat on and fasten properly.

7. Walk downstairs into Production
   Area and walk through foot bath.

8. Wash hands and rub on debac
   solution (an ointment that
   kills germs).

9. Enter Production Area.

Figure 13.2 Fenland Foods' rules
for changing for work.

- do not take pins, needles or staples into the work-place;
- do not put your hands in your pockets;
- do not eat in the work-place unless it is your job to do so;
- use a disposable tissue to wipe your nose, then place it in a waste bin and wash your hands;
- do not put your fingers in your nose, mouth or ears while working.

These are just a few of the many rules that all employees at Fenland must know and put into practice.

The flow chart in Fig. 13.2 shows the stages involved in changing for work.

Questions

1. How can management at the plant ensure that all personal working practices are strictly followed through? Answer in detail, exploring areas such as induction, training, monitoring of standards, penalties and so on.
2. Why is it essential to involve employees in the decision-making process related to Health and Safety?
3. What are the penalties for a company failing to meet Health and Safety and Food Safety requirements?
4. How would you go about making sure that changing routines are strictly adhered to at all times?
5. Why is it important to retain an existing labour force in food processing firms?
6. In what other industries does safety come at a premium?

Activity

Try to relate Maslow's hierarchy of needs to a working environment with which you are familiar—perhaps a part-time job or study life at your school or college. To what extent does the organization that you work for or college that you attend meet your needs? What suggestions can you make for improvements? How feasible would it be to implement your proposals?

Activity

The graph shown in Fig. 13.3 shows trade union membership in the UK up to 1990. Study books and journals to try and find an explanation for the trends, peaks and troughs shown in the graph.

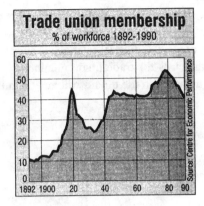

Trade union membership
% of workforce 1892-1990

Source: Centre for Economic Performance

Figure 13.3 Trade union membership (*Source*: Centre for Economic Performance.)

Activity

In early 1992, government ministers, employers and the TUC pledged their commitment to a set of national targets for vocational training. These included:

- to ensure that, by 1997, four out of five young people are qualified with four GCSEs or equivalent in NVQs and GNVQs;
- entitle young people who can benefit to study to A level standard or NVQ equivalent;
- structure and design all education and training to develop 'self-reliance, flexibility and broad competence', as well as specific skills;
- provide 'training and development' for all employees by 1996;
- award 'Investors in People' status by 1996 to half of Britain's organizations employing 200 or more people, the award to stand for the achievement of a minimum standard of training.

Investigate how far we have progressed in meeting these targets.

Essay title 1—Unions and management need to work together towards common goals. Discuss.

In this essay you will need to look at the changing relationship between unions and management, the growing emphasis on human resource management and to identify the goals of unions and management. You should take examples from a variety of countries.

Industrial relations are concerned with communication between representatives of employers and representatives of employees. Successful industrial relations involve striking a balance between the various interests.

From the employer's point of view, industrial relations is about having the right to manage—the ability to plan for the future so that a company can continue to be a success, to make profits for its shareholders and to keep its employees motivated.

From the employee's point of view, industrial relations is about securing the best possible living standards for trade union members.

Representatives of management and trade unions will meet regularly to discuss such issues as:

- pay;
- bonuses;
- the working environment;
- disputes;
- work schedules;
- grievances;
- health and safety at work;
- hours;
- production targets.

As well as local bargaining that concerns small-scale industrial relations, larger issues may be thrashed out on an industry-wide scale. Pay for state employees, for example, is normally agreed on at an annual pay award. The parties involved will normally be the central executive of a union and employers' leaders.

It has become increasingly recognized that managers and employees need to work together to share common interests. The use of the phrase 'human resource management' is recognition that the human resource is the most valuable to any organization and that good working conditions will lead to the best results. Under good human resource management, people will be valued at work and the emphasis will be placed on common approaches to common problems.

Within Europe, the trade unions of Sweden are probably the most 'integrated' into the political system and the economic-industrial system. The unions have always been represented at board level, in management committees and management bodies of any sort and play an active role in the decision-making process. Germany has also introduced a system of worker co-management.

In Japan, a trade union is simply a body for voicing the opinions of employees for, as soon as they begin to work for a company, they take an oath of loyalty to the company. In a number of companies in Japan the daily ceremony of flag-hoisting and reciting the company prayer is still adhered to. Workers in many companies wear achievement armbands that are given to the worker in each group who has the best productivity record and these are worn with pride. There is also a tradition of handing down a job from father to son.

In Japan, many employees are given considerable responsibilities in the work-place. 'Production islands', for example, are individual production units staffed by several workers, an engineer and a manager. The employees have absolute responsibility for a certain sector of work. It is probably an exaggeration to say that everyone does everything, but certainly within the 'island' there is a continuous exchange of all duties. Also, all employees of any rank may change 'islands' when they wish to and when they consider it advisable in respect of the general aims of the company. This system of organizing work into 'islands' is at the root of Japanese success in all sectors of industry, but particularly in the automobile sector.

In other countries, such as Italy, France and the United Kingdom, there is a stronger tradition of conflict between management and unions. This stems from the early years of unionism in the late nineteenth and early twentieth centuries as the unions were actually set up to combat the worst excesses of management, such as low wages, inhumane working conditions and to provide benefits for members in times of hardship. Because unions were the product of conflict, confrontational attitudes became the norm for a long time. Western economies have been characterized by booms and slumps in the economy throughout the twentieth century. It is in times of recession that working people are likely to suffer most.

However, more recently relations throughout the industrialized world are undergoing a profound transformation. In many ways this is a response to the human resources school of thought among managers— the need to enhance the contribution of the individual at every stage of manufacture.

A good example of how relations are changing comes from Italy. The big Italian labour confederation the CGIL is the most powerful trade union body in Europe. In 1991 it changed its policy, accepting the need for worker participation in management, a rejection of the old principle that company policy decisions are the bosses' problem. The unions now accept that *everyone* should have a say in the future. The second policy change implied recognition of the importance of each individual in a company.

In the United Kingdom the decline in the power of unions has been reinforced by legislation that made pre-strike ballots compulsory and severely limited the ability of unions to mount sympathy action. Under laws introduced by Mrs Thatcher, union funds have also became vulnerable to litigation.

One union has sought to carve out a niche for itself by being politically moderate and mounting a campaign to sell itself to employers as much as to workers. The Electrical, Electronic, Telecommunications and Plumbing Union (EETPU) sought to mitigate the increasing anti-unionism by signing 'no strike' deals, largely with incoming Japanese companies. The agreements seek to replace the traditional confrontational nature of British industrial relations with a framework of consultative processes in which workers participate in decision making. Other unions, such as the General Municipal Boilermakers, are beginning to draw up similar packages.

The EETPU's strategy seeks to participate in the new 'human resource' approach of modern management. Many managers, however, argue that British companies still have a long way to go to match the quality and productivity achieved by the Japanese.

Today, the trade union movement is facing the challenge of a rapidly changing world of work. Many traditional jobs are disappearing, to be replaced by ones requiring new skills and working practices. White-collar occupations have increasingly replaced blue-collar jobs and women and part-timers play an increasingly important role in the labour market.

It would be unrealistic to say that managers and trade unions today share a commonality of interests; there are still many old-fashioned employers exploiting poorly paid labour in poor working conditions. At the turn of 1990 it looked as if there would be a resurgence of union militancy and, in particular, increasingly large pay claims. However, the ensuing recession soon stopped this trend and union members were forced to concentrate on saving jobs. A continued form of frustration for employees is disagreement about salaries and wages between one occupation and another and the proliferation of unions in some work-places. The historical patterns of union growth show long upward and downward swings. Despite the wider adoption of human resource management, it is possible that factors such as European integration may help the unions confront the globalization of production and company power.

Essay title 2—How can managers ensure that employees needs are met in the working environment?

Employees have a wide variety of needs. Different individuals will have different requirements when seeking work. It is therefore not a simple task to meet employee needs. For example, one person may seek a part-time job that is close to home which pays a modest income. Another person may seek a highly rewarding job anywhere in the world.

Work is about feeling valued as well as about receiving a pay packet. As the American writer Studs Terkel suggests in his book *Working*, 'It is about a search, too, for daily meaning as well as daily bread, for recognition as well as for cash, for astonishment rather than torpor; in short, for a sort of life rather than a Monday-through-Friday sort of dying'.

In looking at needs, it is important to describe the findings of Abraham Maslow. He built up a picture of a hierarchical set of needs.

Basic needs include a reasonable standard of food, shelter and clothing. These are obviously of prime importance. Only when these essential needs are met, can we look to fulfilling higher needs. In the work-place, employers can meet these basic needs by providing such facilities as toilets, a reasonable temperature to work in, reasonable lighting, acceptable pay and other basic requirements.

Security needs relate to the basic need of individuals to feel safe. Quite clearly everyone needs to feel safe at the place of work from being bullied or intimidated, from being the butt of prejudice, from working with dangerous machinery and equipment, from being able to be sacked with no warning or notice served and so on.

Group needs concern an individual's needs for love and affection. The majority of people want to feel part of a group. In the work-place, this can be organized by arranging induction programmes, so that new trainees meet other people at work, social outings, meetings, clubs and football teams and the opportunity to talk to others in the working environment (such as is possible in an open plan office).

Self-esteem needs are those of an individual for self-respect and the respect of others. This can be achieved by promoting people and rewarding them for good work, by granting them privileges, by giving them opportunities to represent the organization at functions and so on.

Maslow placed self-fulfilment at the top of his hierarchy of needs. This is because self-fulfilment means full personal development and creativity. In many organizations today employees go through an appraisal procedure, allowing them to identify their own targets and goals. They can be encouraged to develop their own specialist skills and interests. They can be given the opportunity to be creative and do things in their own way. By working in small Quality Circle groups, individuals can play a major part in constructing their own working pattern.

Today 'human resource management' involves recognizing the need to build each of the above elements into job descriptions.

In the end, however, it is not just the nature of the job that is important in meeting individual needs, but individual attitudes to work and expectations of the job. Some employees may simply be looking for a 9 to 5 routine job. They may feel that they have enough responsibility in their everyday lives and that they simply want pay for work delivered.

Following on from Maslow, Herzberg identified five 'satisfiers' that can increase motivation at work. These are:

1. recognition of effort and performance;
2. the nature of the job—how challenging it is;
3. sense of achievement;
4. responsibility;

5.   opportunities for promotion and improvement.

On the basis of his research, Herzberg went on to suggest that jobs could be given more meaning if they incorporated elements of responsibility, a more creative use of abilities and opportunities for a sense of achievement.

Vroom developed a theory that what people required from a job should be related to their estimation of the likelihood of achieving it to give a better measure of motivation.

Most researchers stress the importance of the work-place as one of shared goals and aspirations rather than of conflict.

You could conclude your essay by looking at possible ways of motivating employees apart from pay. These methods could include:

- *job enrichment*—the aim of job enrichment is to upgrade the contribution of employees in work tasks so that they feel more highly appreciated;
- *job enlargement*—this involves giving employees a greater range of responsibilities;
- *employee participation*—the flattened organogram in which decisions can be made at all levels of an organization helps employees to feel important and valued for their contributions to the decision-making process;
- *Quality Circles*—in the UK these typically consist of small groups of seven to eight people who voluntarily meet on a regular basis to identify, investigate, analyse and resolve quality-related matters or other work-related arrangements using problem-solving techniques, (the members tend to be from the same work area or do similar work).

In today's economy, employees have higher expectations than ever before. No longer is it acceptable (if it ever was) simply to meet lower-level needs. Today's education system seeks to develop the whole person, so, if industry is to attract quality employees, it will have to employ quality human resource management.

Essay title 1—Why are women returners likely to be an important part of the labour force in the next decade? What factors would encourage women to return to work?

There is no standard definition of a woman returner. For most people, the term probably brings to mind the woman who has left work to have children, has remained at home for several years to care for them and is unlikely to return to exactly the same post as the one she left. However, some women in other situations can also be regarded as returners, such as those caring for elderly or sick relatives, returning to work part-time for the same or different employers or training for a different occupation before returning. This group also contains many single parents, for whom the problems of staying at work, or returning to it can be particularly acute. All of these constitute a large group of potential employees who have a range of different needs that employers should be aware of and bear in mind.

Women returners are expected to be a major source of addition to the labour force in the next decade and are regarded as being particularly important because of the reduction in the numbers of younger people. In 1994 there will be 1 million fewer 16–19-year-olds in the population than in 1984, a fall of 29 per cent. Similar trends are projected in most countries in the European Community. British companies must, therefore, make fuller use of the work-force that is available—and women returners in particular, if they are to remain competitive with their European counterparts.

About half a million women a year are currently returning to work in the United Kingdom. This should be seen in the context of the total number of women who are economically active or inactive. In Great Britain, 16.1 million women were aged 16–59 in 1989. Of these, 11.2 million (nearly 70 per cent) were economically active, including almost a million who were unemployed, so a major pool of potential workers does exist.

In a Labour Force Survey that was carried out in 1989, it was found that over 800 000 economically inactive women said that they would like to have had a regular paid job, but were unable to take one at that time because of home or family responsibilities. Half of these had children under five.

Around 1.2 million women with youngest children under 5 said that they would not like to work at present, compared to under 350 000 of those with children from 5–9 years. On this basis it seems reasonable to assume that a large number of those currently caring for under fives will, in fact, return when their children are of school age.

Women are in demand in many of the rapidly growing sectors of the economy. Clearly part-time work has become a more important feature of current working patterns, but, in addition, the boom sectors of the economy, including banking, financial services and leisure all need workers. The old heavy industries, such as mining and shipbuilding, which were traditional male preserves, are in decline. In industries like engineering, extensive changes are taking place. For example, the Henley Centre for Forecasting stated in September 1989 that, by the end of the 1990s, there will be over 700 000 electronics engineers in Britain, more than half of whom will be women. The female-dominated occupations of catering, caring and cleaning are labour-intensive industries and are thus resistant to technological advances.

What would enable more women to return to work? In a Gallup survey carried out in 1989 of women who were not economically active and had full-time caring commitments, 64 per cent said that they would like to work and 51 per cent said that they could not work because of children at home. If suitable arrangements could be made for their dependants, 32 per cent of women said that they would return to work now and a further 21 per cent within the next two years.

Suitable hours of work were seen as a necessary complement to care arrangements. Over 80 per cent expressed a preference for either part-time or school-term working, although their choice might have been influenced by perceptions of likely care facilities.

Other factors felt to be important in a job were a friendly and supportive atmosphere, interesting and varied work, help with childcare and an opportunity to use their abilities.

The survey also showed that this group has useful experience and potential. Over 60 per cent had worked full-time (more than 30 hours), 12 per cent had worked in a professional capacity and 29 per cent in clerical or office occupations.

Most women who return to work make their own arrangements for childcare. Most relied on members of their family, followed by childminders.

More employers are now exploring ways of retaining or attracting this group of women. Practices to retain and attract women returners could include: greater flexibility of working hours, such as optional part-time working, flexitime and special time off to cope with family sickness. Childcare assistance is still a fairly uncommon practice with under 5 per cent of all employers offering this benefit.

Some employers have moved towards allowing extended maternity leave or 'career breaks'.

Much more will need to be done however, to attract women back to work and retain them.

Essay titles

1. What are the main challenges facing trade unions today?
2. What methods, apart from pay, can be used to motivate employees?
3. 'Training is the biggest challenge facing companies in the 1990s.' Discuss.
4. How can a company maximize its return on its human resource?
5. 'People are an organization's most important resource.' Discuss.
6. What are the main functions of the personnel department?
7. Why is it important for a company to devise an effective equal opportunities policy?

8. 'Employees do not always require a rewarding job.' Discuss this assertion.
9. 'There is one best way of carrying out a work task.' Discuss.
10. In their book *In Search of Excellence*, Peters and Waterman asserted that shared values lie at the heart of a successful operation. Discuss this, drawing on practical examples.
11. Do the objectives of trade unions always clash with those of management?
12. What are the main problems encountered by women at work? How can these difficulties be minimized?
13. 'There is no such thing as equal opportunities!' Discuss.
14. How effective are the various forms of industrial action available to trade unions?
15. Are trade unions today more or less important than in the past?
16. 'The greatest challenge to trade unions is that of recruitment.' Discuss this assertion.
17. Is the Single Union Deal the way forward for industrial relations?
18. What are the most effective ways of recruiting skilled employees?
19. Why is appraisal important to individual employees and organizations?
20. How might Quality Circles help to improve employee motivation? What are the other benefits of Quality Circles?

Short-answer questions

1. What is the basic principle of scientific management?
2. What do you understand by the term 'Hawthorne effect'?
3. What is job enrichment?
4. What is a flat rate of pay?
5. What is a commission?
6. What is job analysis?
7. What is a job description?
8. Describe the stages in the employment procession.
9. What are the advantages of internal as opposed to external recruitment?
10. Describe the role of a private employment agency.
11. What is meant by induction?
12. Why is it important to make job applicants aware of the conditions in which they will be working?
13. How can ratios be used to monitor the effectiveness of a selection process?
14. Give a simple definition of redundancy.
15. What do the terms work to rule and blacking mean?

16. What is a general union?
17. What is the job of a shop steward?
18. What are the main aims of trade unions?
19. What is collective bargaining?
20. Why have white-collar unions grown faster than other unions?

Projects

There are a range of project titles that can be explored in relation to the human resource. Interesting examples would be:

- looking at what the impact of Japanese working practices has been on British industry—perhaps you could investigate some British companies that have introduced Japanese-style practices;
- investigate the techniques that are used to motivate employees— carrying out a survey of a number of companies and seeing how the techniques employed relate to Maslow's hierarchy;
- seeing how a trade union is organized and how its organization has altered in recent years;
- studying the way in which the personnel department organizes the employment in a local company.

Suggested reading

Cole, G. A., *Personnel Management*. D. P. Publications, 1988.
Drucker, Peter F., *The Practice of Management*. Butterworth Heinemann, 1989.
Farnham, David, and John Pimlott, *Understanding Industrial Relations* (4th edn). Cassell, 1990.
Graham, H. T., *M + E Human Resources Management* (7th edn). Pitman, 1992.
Lanz, Karen, *NatWest Business Handbook—Employing and Managing People*. Pitman, 1991.
Peters, Thomas J., and Robert H. Waterman, *In Search of Excellence: Lessons from America's Best-run Companies*, Harper & Row, 1984.

14

Communication

At the centre of all business activities, and of management in particular, lies the fundamental requirement of being able to communicate effectively. Communication involves the passing on of ideas and information. In a modern business environment, this not only involves basic communication skills, such as listening, speaking, reading and writing, but also an ability to use business technology.

Effective communication provides a medium through which people can achieve their own and corporate goals. Knowing how to use technical and specialist jargon and technology helps in the solution of problems and avoids misunderstanding. Effective communication, then, enables people to present their ideas, avoid misunderstandings, save time and resolve conflicts.

Internal communication is communication within an organization. This may involve clarifying understanding, initiating action, negotiation or providing the basis for employee motivation and teamwork and so on.

External communication is concerned with communications emanating from an organization and these will, ultimately, determine how the organization is viewed by others.

Case Study—Business television

At 11 a.m. all over Britain every Tuesday, BMW sales staff congregate in their showrooms to watch a message from the management. BMW are among the pioneers in the field of *business television*. This involves organizations transmitting words and pictures to their own employees. BMW has been transmitting messages to nearly all of their dealerships in the UK. Staff typically view a 20- to 30-minute broadcast that is broken down into 4 or 5 segments. Items tend to involve a wide variety of areas and may include sales and marketing details, product information, details of competitors and so on. Though parts of the broadcast are recorded, other parts have live segments that enable employees to phone up, question executives and obtain feedback.

Peter Walker, BMW's marketing communications manager, says that

'The primary advantage is immediacy'. He feels that, 'TV has more impact than sending documents or video tapes. I wouldn't say we have saved a fortune yet, but we may end up reducing the number of conferences and meetings we hold. I think you end up communicating more'.

Business television first found favour among the large dispersed companies of North America and pioneers in the field included the electronics giant Hewlett-Packard and the brokerage house Merrill Lynch. Research in the early 1990's revealed that US industry is spending about £200m in private business networks. Gillian Greening, European marketing communications manager for Amdahl, the American computer manufacturer, recently decided to extend the company's broadcasts into Europe. Eight times each month employees in North America, and now Europe, gather to watch an hour-long programme, which concludes with a live question and answer session with senior staff. She feels that, 'The spoken word is so much more effective than print. Business TV gives us the ability to communicate directly without the message becoming diluted down the management chain'.

Rockwell International also use business television. They feel that the main advantage of broadcasts is to spread information to sales staff. In a company with more than 10 000 products and sometimes several dozen new ones every month, they feel that business TV has become vital. They argue that it acts to bind together a large company, to create a culture or bond that makes staff feel closer to each other.

Assessing the real value of business TV is very difficult. A questionnaire in 1991, however, suggested that business TV would help at least 40 per cent of those watching the broadcasts to perform their jobs better.

Questions

1. What is business television?
2. How might business television improve communications in a large organization?
3. What communication skills are necessary for those involved in the broadcasts?
4. What are the dangers of using business television?
5. Why might business television improve the ways in which employees work?
6. How might business television cut down on paperwork?
7. Suggest several alternatives to business television.

Case Study—Developing an edge with E-Mail

Though the insurance industry is often perceived as being conservative, it has always been highly competitive. For example, IT has been viewed by many providers of insurance as a weapon with which to outwit opposition by reducing in-house administration costs.

At the heart of Sun Alliance International's strategy is the use of electronic mail, or, E-Mail as it is commonly known. It is essentially a software product run on networked PCs or mainframe systems where the user can communicate with anyone on the system through defined groups and often on pre-formatted screen layouts. At Sun Alliance, there is a belief that E-Mail will give their organization a strong edge over competitors and also strengthen its relationships with brokers.

The reason behind this move by Sun Alliance was that cost studies had indicated that something had to be done to control the increasing expense of conducting insurance business for both insurers and brokers. The traditional method of placing business was based on paper form-filling. Typically a broker would approach a number of companies and it would take between one and two weeks to gather the replies. Sun Alliance's aim was to make their business more attractive for brokers by speeding it up and making it easier to process. They viewed E-Mail as a way forward in developing business partnerships.

Sun Alliance opted for Verimation's Memo electronic mail product. Initially it was used for internal messaging and then its use was spread throughout the group. Many felt that the system meant that employees were not restricted to office hours or limited by their secretary's hours. After initial in-house success, Sun Alliance decided to try out the scheme with some of their larger brokers.

The Verimation Memo forms facility allows each broker to adapt a basic screen format to their own design. The great advantage of electronic screen-filling over paper form-filling is speed. Brokers quickly discovered that they could bulk-process routine tasks such as claims notification without the usual phone call or posting of forms. They found that with E-Mail claims notifications could be sent in on the same day.

With E-Mail brokers also found that messages could be free of telephone and postal charges. Time was saved in filling in forms and responses were swift. At the same time, E-Mail allowed work to be directed at specific people at Sun Alliance so that close ties with individuals could be maintained. Brokers have become enthusiastic about the system as they have watched their paperwork shrink. They claim that the system has been quick and easy to use and saves them both time and money. E-Mail has supported their business relationship and made Sun Alliance an attractive partner. (See questions, page 193.)

Editorial

The world's food markets are changing, and so is United Biscuits. Today we are a leading food manufacturer with sales of almost £3 billion, employing 40,000 people worldwide – no mean achievement for a business that was created by the amalgamation of a handful of British regional biscuit companies. Over and above this, however, we are now truly European, and truly international.

We've achieved this by developing down routes that our Scottish founders most likely never contemplated. But they would, I think, have approved. For as group chief executive Eric Nicoli says in our current annual report, 'We're doing more of what we do best, in ever more dynamic and disciplined ways, in more of the world's most promising market-places.' These are the keys to our success and our growth, and our global reach will, moreover, increase in the years to come.

*Here, then, is **UB Journal**, a new publication to reflect the scope and scale of United Biscuits today. It will be published three times a year. Its aim is to give everyone who works for UB a feel for what goes on across our group of companies and perhaps a sense of pride in being a part of it.*

*You will know that specific divisional news and factory topics are now being covered in individual company newspapers. **UB Journal** has a company news round-up, but it aims to give the UB group overview. Write to us here at West Drayton with your views and comments on the **Journal** and on any other topic of business interest or concern. We aim to start a regular letters page based on what we receive.*

*Above all, we hope that you will find **UB Journal** a good read.*

Figure 14.1 *UB Journal's* editorial. (*Source*: *UB Journal*, magazine of the United Biscuits Group, issue 1, 1992.)

Alan Riley
Managing Editor

Questions

1. Explain briefly what is meant by electronic mail.
2. How might E-Mail improve communications?
3. What are the other benefits of E-Mail?
4. Explain why IT and E-Mail may provide Sun Alliance with a competitive advantage.
5. Explain what is meant by the following:

   - IT;
   - networked PCs;
   - broker;
   - conservative;
   - in-house;
   - mainframe systems;
   - claims notification;
   - software product.

Case Study—United Biscuits

The editorial in Fig. 14.1 appeared in the first copy of the new *UB Journal*.

Questions

1. Why do United Biscuits use a journal to communicate with their employees?
2. What sort of articles and contents might they put into this journal?
3. What is the aim of the journal? Explain why they have this aim.
4. What items might appear in a news round-up?
5. Explain what is meant by global reach.
6. Examine other methods available to a large organization that may be used for communicating information of common interest to all employees.

Case Study—Designing an information system

You work in an administration department of a medium-size organization in Cheshire. Your role is wide and varied and, since having worked for this company, you have undertaken a variety of tasks and worked on a range of projects. You have just received the following memo from the Company Secretary.

MEMO

To:
From: Company Secretary *Date*: 10 April 19—

We are soon going to review our requirements and needs for our information system with the stated aim of updating our facilities within the next 12 months.

I would like you to undertake some preliminary research into the range of factors that might influence our choice of information system. In order to undertake such research, I realize that you will have to audit our existing information technology facilities, indicate the criteria that might influence future decisions and also make some recommendations.

Figure 14.2 Memo regarding designing and information system.

Questions

1. Assume that the memo in Fig. 14.2 is actually based on the company you work for or the college you attend. Undertake some preliminary research, auditing your IT facilities. Consider the factors that might influence your choice of system in the future and piece together some recommendations. Present your findings in a *formal report* entitled, 'Meeting our information needs in the future'.

2. Write a memo back to the Company Secretary indicating that you have completed the report.

3. You have been asked to speak to a meeting of senior executives about the above report. What skills might you require in order to do so effectively? How would you use them? What visual aids might you require?

4. Having taken the above into consideration, present your speech about the report to other members of your group, answering any questions where appropriate.

Case Study—Technology on the road

The mission statement of the Automobile Association (AA) puts priority on people and service. It aims to 'make AA membership truly irresistible' and 'to be the UK's leading and most successful motoring and personal assistance organization'. The key to the AA's success is, therefore, the extent to which it manages to achieve its mission. In order to be able to do this, the AA has to manage a huge amount of information efficiently. It feels that effective information management is the vital component in providing a quality service.

Figure 14.3 An AA shop.

If we consider the nature of the organization, we can understand its needs for information management. For example, there are some 25m telephone calls to the AA each year, of which 8m calls are to its 0800 number. The AA also has to phone out and has some 8000 handsets. The AA's principal businesses are services to members and membership, which employs 7000 staff and runs 3600 patrols. Its services operations include insurance and financial services, which employ 4500 staff, as well as retail, travel services, the AA's own driving school and, of course, publishing—the AA is the UK's biggest publisher of maps and guides.

ICL has 16 mainframe computers installed with the AA, 8 of which are at the AA's corporate centre outside Basingstoke. The AA uses an IT system based on internationally recognized standards. They have chosen an open system approach that allows information systems to be developed in a coherent manner so that they can pursue new commercial opportunities. Their system also allows for information to be accessed between systems so that opportunities for cross-selling services can be utilized. The implementation of the computer systems at the AA is so effective that it has become part of the DTI's open systems demonstrator programme.

The AA's annual expenditure on IT is over £40m. This high cost is partly due to the fact that the AA group is opening a new shop every 13 days and installing networked terminals in its shops and offices at the rate of 2 to 3 a day. Investment in computer technology is, therefore, running at £1m per month and computer usage is growing at an annual compound rate of 25 per cent. All of this is part of a tactical plan that covers aspects of hardware, software and communications.

The applications of the IT being installed at the AA are based on the fact that it is a service business. Key performance indicators are linked to response times for telephone answering, portfolio retention and break-down times. IT helps them to measure and improve these areas and, further, create an environment that attracts, develops and responds to customers.

Questions

1. Examine the IT needs of the AA.
2. To what extent will IT influence how well the AA manages to implement its mission?
3. What sort of IT products, software packages and services are the AA likely to use?
4. Explain what is meant by the cross-selling of services.
5. How does the AA assess the effectiveness of its IT systems?

Activity

Try out the following simple communication activities:

- form small groups and let each member of the group talk, without notes, about some interest for a minute;
- analyse the problems for both the receiver and the transmitter—see if there were any barriers affecting the communication of the message and comment briefly on the posture and body language of each speaker;
- in the same groups, make up a statement, such as 'When Jackie went to the station she bought a newspaper', then get each member of the group in turn to add an item of information to the statement after having first repeated all of the previous statements and see how much information each person can remember.

Activity

Load a word processing package into the computer, then:

- open and name a file;
- type in a letter;
- correct any mistakes;
- save and print it.

Comment briefly on the package you are using and how easy, or otherwise, it is to use. Find out, list and then, if possible, try to undertake some of the other functions provided by the package.

Activity

Obtain a range of external communications from a number of companies. These could include:

- advertisements;
- in-house magazines;
- annual reports and accounts;
- other publicity materials or organizational literature.

Comment briefly on what each type of material is designed to achieve and its effectiveness in doing so.

Essay title 1—Examine the four basic communication skills and then indicate, briefly, how they may be used for both internal and external communications.

The area covered by this particular question is so broad that a good candidate may become carried away and write too much or examine just one aspect of the answer instead of responding to all of the requirements of the question. Structuring the answer to this question logically and planning the structure beforehand is, therefore, essential if an effective response is to be given.

In the introduction you need to respond to the requirements of the question. The four basic communication skills are listening, speaking, reading and writing. Indeed, many would add that the use of IT skills is now a fifth. Such skills are necessary for a wide range of communication requirements, both internally, within the organization and externally, outside the organization, influencing the way it is viewed by others.

The four basic communication skills in more detail are:

- *listening*—which involves hearing a message, has an element of interpretation and may involve evaluation and then action;
- *speaking*—which enables direct contact to take place, can involve questioning and feedback and can be used to remove ambiguity;
- *reading*—which covers a wide range of communication, the audience and technical nature of the information being important in this area;
- *writing*—which is used when the receiver is remote from the sender, can be used to transmit very complex information and can be kept to refer to later.

The use of each of these communication skills in internal communications may be:

- to present facts and information;
- to give instructions;
- to provide a basis for negotiation;
- to present findings;
- to motivate employees;
- to provide teamwork.

Spoken communications may be useful for face-to-face exchanges, meetings and internal telephone calls. Written internal communications may involve memos, reports (both informal and formal), the writing of agendas and minutes for meetings, notices and in-house journals and newspapers. Brief examples of how the skills could be used should be given.

External communications may be used to:

- communicate with customers, shareholders, suppliers, competitors, governments, communities and so on;
- answer queries;
- reassure;
- provide and support an image by means of public relations activities and so on.

External communications may be:

- *verbal*—by telephone, face-to-face, interviews and conferences;
- *written*—in business letters, advertising, annual report and accounts, magazines and literature;
- *visual*—in corporate videotapes, exhibitions, demonstrations and so on.

Brief examples of how skills could be used should be provided.

In conclusion, the success of every organization will be determined by how well it communicates with others. Though there may be an increasing number of methods of transmitting information today both internally and externally, its quality will continue to be determined by the four basic communication skills.

Essay title 2—'IT is the lifeblood of the modern organization.' Discuss.

This is another question that requires the answer to be carefully structured. Though the answer should examine various uses of IT, a good answer should use extensive analysis to respond to the question. For example, what are the benefits of the different IT applications? How does it help overall competitiveness? What are the dangers of relying too heavily on IT?

In the introduction, the answer should examine the need for information management. For example, for decision making, gathering, communicating, processing and storing data. The answer should then define IT.

It should then refer to some of its operations such as:

- capturing data;
- verifying data;
- classifying data;
- sorting data;
- summarizing data;
- calculating and using data;
- storing data;
- retrieving data;
- reproducing data;
- communicating.

An organization benefits from the use of IT because it:

- improves competitiveness;
- enhances communications;
- makes information available for decision making;
- links plants and offices;
- improves their response to the market.

Each of the points above should be extensively supported by examples of specific uses of IT.

So, what are the modern tools of IT and how are they used? What benefits do they provide? This section of your answer would briefly analyse the various functions of:

- computers, for example, for word processing, databases, spreadsheets, DTPs, expert systems, accounting, etc. and so on;
- direct communications, for example, electronic mail, networking, homeworking and so on;
- manufacturing, for example, CADCAM, CIM, robotics, expert systems and others;
- telecommunications, for example, datel, fax, confravision and such.

IT has enabled modern organizations to become much more flexible, responsive and efficiently managed, market-orientated units. There are, however, some dangers to relying heavily on IT. Though organizations gain many benefits and may reduce costs, these may be at the expense of skills. There is also the danger of losing information. Also, operators may understand the software but not the system and there is always, of course, the danger of computer fraud.

In conclusion, then IT has contributed to a general transformation in the ways companies operate. Even compared to the way things were just

10 years ago, we can see just how much things have changed and that we are now in a new era for business.

Essay title 3—Your friend has recently set up a small business acting as an agency for a number of large organizations. Advise her on her probable IT requirements.

The introduction should say that all businesses in a competitive environment will have a range of IT requirements. The extent to which a small business meets its customers' needs will depend on the quality of service provided. The service may be enhanced, improved and made more efficient by means of a variety of IT applications.

IT should be defined. The IT requirements for a small business will depend on:

- the industry in which they operate—the question mentions an agency but not the type and travel, insurance, financial and other agencies would all involve the use of specialist types of IT common to all in that particular industry;
- the scale of the organization;
- the use of IT by customers, that is, if the customer has a fax and wishes to communicate quickly, then the agency must respond to this need;
- competition from other agencies and the IT facilities they use;
- the rate of technological change in that industry;
- the amount of information processing that will need to be done.

Planning an effective information system will, therefore, require an evaluation of the resources available and the information requirements of the agency. Cost, performance, reliability, flexibility and the expected life cycle of the system will be important considerations, as well as the specific uses to which the technology will be put.

The agency will possibly, if not certainly, require the following:

- a PC with a range of applications, which might include spreadsheets, databases, word processing, an accounts package and desktop publishing (a brief description of each type of package and why it would probably be useful for the agency should be provided);
- some form of direct communication system between computers, such as networking or E-Mail.
- a fax machine.

In conclusion, as the business grows, technologies change and competitors emerge, so its IT requirements will change and will need to be monitored constantly.

Essay titles

1. Comment on the four basic communication skills and, using examples, emphasize their importance in business.
2. Name three different types of internal business communications. Examine the uses and importance of each.
3. What structure should a formal report take? What areas of business are reports suitable for?
4. Examine the benefits of holding meetings. Explain how meetings might delay or improve the decision-making process.
5. What is meant by the term 'IT'? How might it be used to improve the performance of a business?
6. Outline three IT applications and then indicate how such applications might improve the performance of a small business.
7. What is a personal computer? Examine the purposes, functions, features and benefits of the standard application packages available for a PC.
8. Explain how spreadsheets might be used in a business context. What benefits might they provide?
9. What is a database? How might it be used and what controls restrict the type of data held?
10. Why might an organization wish to use a desktop publishing package? What benefits might such a package provide?
11. 'Could an expert system ever replace an expert?' Discuss.
12. Outline the benefits of E-Mail. Does this mean that organizations will ever achieve a paperless environment?
13. Discuss the benefits of technology in manufacturing. How will such technology change the roles of those working in the manufacturing sector?
14. Why do organizations require systems analysis? How does such analysis affect the design of systems?
15. Assess the impact of recent changes in telecommunications on business activities.
16. What are external business communications? Why might they indirectly influence a business' activities?
17. Examine the role of telecommunications in a modern organization. To what extent have recent changes improved the ways in which organizations operate?
18. Assess the role of IT in a modern office.
19. Analyse both the internal and external communications systems of an organization with which you are familiar.
20. Explain how and why IT acts as an aid to communication.

Short-answer questions

1. Name the four basic communication skills.
2. Suggest two uses for memos.
3. Name three elements that should appear in a formal report.
4. What is a PC?
5. What is a spreadsheet and how might it be used?
6. Describe two benefits of using databases.
7. What is DTP?
8. Describe briefly two uses of a word processing package.
9. Explain how an expert system might improve the operation of a system.
10. How is a network used?
11. Outline three benefits of E-Mail for a large manufacturer with worldwide operations.
12. Explain what is meant by systems analysis.
13. Describe two telecommunications services that would be of use for a self-employed business person who travels extensively.
14. Explain how a fax machine works.
15. What is meant by confravision?
16. Name two business uses of satellites.
17. Why is homeworking becoming more common?
18. Explain how a project planning package works.
19. Describe briefly how a software package with which you are familiar works.
20. Name two dangers of depending solely on IT.

Projects

With the use of IT rapidly developing in the business environment and a far greater awareness of its importance for competitive advantage, this area of communications would be a useful one to research. It might be possible to:

- perform an audit of IT facilities and then make recommendations about some changes or improvements;
- assess the viability of a variety of projects, such as the introduction of a system of E-Mail or the introduction of homeworking.
- compare the cost-effectiveness and performance of a range of software packages.

Suggested reading

Davies, Dick, *Information Technology at Work*. Heinemann Educational, 1986.

Kingsley-Jones, Philip, and Martyn Wilson, *Examining Information Technology*. Longman, 1988.

Pepperell, Don, *Who says so? Communication skills: A Thematic Approach*. Stanley Thornes, 1988.

Smith, Norman, and Hilary Vigor, *People in Organizations*. Oxford University Press, 1992.

Stafford, Christopher E., *People in Business*. Cambridge University Press, 1991.

15

The influence of the economy on companies

Business life does not take place in books; it takes place in the real world and many outside influences affect the ways in which companies behave and act. The environment in which organizations exist is in a constant state of change and one of the most dynamic external factors influencing a company's fortunes is that of the economy, especially during recession. If organizations are to respond to economic changes with effective and appropriate measures, they must be aware of such influences.

The study of economics is concerned with how society decides to allocate its resources. Choices are made by individuals, groups, businesses, national organizations and governments, and agreements are made at an international level. Such decisions cover a broad spectrum of ideologies, patterns of behaviour, cultures, incomes and political beliefs and will influence the behaviour of all companies within each economy.

Case Study—The business community in Thailand

In 1989, Thailand's economy seemed to defy gravity—economic projections assumed growth rates of at least 9 or 10 per cent. Such projections, however, proved unrealistic and in 1992, growth rates were just 5 per cent, half the government's estimate. The Thai economy is going through recession and many businesses are suffering. The measures Thailand takes to cope with this recession will determine the future of the country. It is a make-or-break period.

Bangkok is the capital of Thailand. The country is virtually a city state so that although Thailand has a population of 56 million, the 6 million population of Bangkok produce half the country's output. In the late 1980s and early 1990s the Thai economy boomed. Its gross domestic product grew at an average rate of 11 per cent. In 1989, their stock market performed better than any other in the world and foreign money flooded in. Tourism flourished and it was described as an economic miracle.

However, the advances made and the confidence they created were all a little premature.

At the heart of the problem was not just the world recession but also overheating of the economy. Inflation rose from 1.9 per cent in 1986 to 6.2 per cent in 1990 and then into double figures. The credit binge put pressures on the money supply and interest rates increased to 19 per cent. Inevitably businesses that had borrowed heavily in the past were the first to suffer. Their desire to achieve Newly Industrialized Country (NIC) status seems to have turned into a nightmare.

The engines of internal growth in Thailand have been Chinese immigrants. In the 1950s, the Chinese poured into Thailand and quickly integrated into Thai society. Today Thai-Chinese families run just about everything worth running. The fuel for these engines has been foreign investment, particularly from Japan, which accounts for about half the total foreign investment and includes all of the big names, such as Sony, Mitsubishi and Nissan.

The meteoric successes of Bangkok businesses have been largely attributed to a business environment created by more favourable factors. Thailand was encouraged by the 1980s recovery in the world economy and boosted by simultaneous reductions in both interest rates and domestic inflation. Exports soared from $5.6bn in 1983 to over $20bn today.

Bangkok is, however, choking on its own success. The ancient transport system is an obstacle for further development, public transport is poor and the phone system is overworked and underfunded—their infrastructure just cannot cope. They are trying to pull away from the brink with a series of projects aimed at infrastructure. These include an agreement between BT and the CP Group to provide 3 million new telephone numbers and also three huge transport projects.

Though such projects will undoubtedly help improve Bangkok's problems, another urgent need is to improve the vast economic and social gulf between Bangkok's prosperous, metropolitan area and the rest of Thailand, where income per head is only a *tenth* that of the capital. The government's seventh economic plan, running from 1992 to 1996, stresses a commitment to encouraging businesses to relocate outside Bangkok. Skills shortages are another problem as training has failed to keep up with growth. There is also labour unrest as a result of the vast gap between managers' pay and that of workers.

Many claim that the slump will not be a problem. Though growth in Thailand might only be 5 per cent and a disappointment by their standards, it would represent a boom anywhere else.

Questions

1. Explain why the Thai economy went through a boom period in the 1980s.
2. How did such a period influence the development of businesses in Bangkok?
3. Comment separately on how rising inflation and rising interest rates would influence businesses.
4. How might rising inflation and rising interest rates affect employment figures?
5. Why is the need to generate and develop exports so important for Thailand?
6. What problems might the business community in Bangkok encounter if the infrastructure is not improved?
7. Are there any parallels to be drawn from this case study between the Thai economy and the UK economy?
8. Explain what is meant by the following:

   - growth;
   - GDP;
   - overheating;
   - skills shortages;
   - recession;
   - stock market;
   - credit binge;
   - labour unrest.

Case Study—The demographic time bomb

In the 1990s, companies have been hit by recession, skills shortages, increasing competition, high interest rates and exchange rates, as well as a number of other factors that have required them to manage their resources more effectively. As the economy picks up and comes out of recession, there is yet another challenge for businesses in the UK—the demographic time bomb.

The demographic time bomb is the name given to changes that are happening in the employment market. It is expected that the numbers of young people entering the employment market will fall dramatically by the end of the century. This event is largely attributed to the end of the Baby Boom of the 1950s and 1960s, caused by a combination of the use of the Pill and also by the numbers of women entering the work-force. Around 62 per cent of married women in the UK now work either part-time or full-time. As a result of what demographers call Period Total Fertility Rate (PTFR), the UK has settled down to about 1.8 children per family, but an average value of 2.1 is required for long-term replacement.

For the UK this means that, by 1999, the number of people between 16 and 19 years of age will fall by 25 per cent, or 850 000. If this continues, the crunch year will come around 2030 when deaths will exceed births and the population will actually start shrinking. By that year, those aged

Figure 15.1 A B&Q Supercentre.

80 and over are projected to number 3.4 million, which is 60 per cent more than today and three and a half times more than in 1961.

These demographic changes would seem to indicate that soon too many companies will be competing for too few people. The only solution to such a problem would seem to be for organizations to completely review their policies of recruitment, retention and training.

One organization that has already done this is B&Q. B&Q is well known for the enthusiasm with which it digests the contents of *Social Trends*, the annual publication from the Central Statistical Office. As far back as 1988, as an experiment, it opened its now famous store in Macclesfield, staffed entirely by workers over the age of 50. The project was an unqualified success. Research showed the store to be 18 per cent more profitable than an average of 5 other stores; to have 39 per cent lower absenteeism, 59 per cent fewer thefts and a staff turnover rate that is 6 times lower than their national average. As a result, B&Q have opened another over-fifties store in Exmouth.

This dearth of youth is not simply an employment problem. Young people are, of course, consumers as well, often with large amounts of disposable income. Many companies that have a youthful image are taking care not to alienate older customers with their promotions. For example, Reebok UK claim that the greater proportion of their sales actually come from older sportspeople than from the rest of the market.

One sector almost certain to suffer is brewing, where all the effort over the last 20 years has been put into developing the drinking habits of the young. They will now have to make licensed premises attractive to families and senior citizens. Another area that will be hit is driving schools. The numbers of young people taking the test are down and waiting lists are falling. By 1995 there will be more consumers over 45 than under 30.

The demographic time bomb will influence the actions of almost every company in the UK. On the employment side, it can be defused by maximizing the contribution from existing employees through effective human resource management that is designed to improve retention and by looking towards other sources of employees, such as the long-term unemployed. On the production side, organizations must become increasingly aware of the changing age structure of customers in their markets and take appropriate action where necessary. It would seem that Grey Power is about to reach its full strength.

Questions

1. Comment on the challenges that companies have had to face in the 1990s and indicate briefly how such challenges might have affected them.
2. What is the 'demographic time bomb'?
3. Explain why companies ought to be aware of economic and social trends.
4. Put yourself in the position of a senior manager of a major High Street clothes retailer. How would you cope with the demographic changes outlined in this Case Study?
5. Comment on how the demographic time bomb might influence any other economic issues, such as unemployment, inflation, savings, investment, balance of payments and so on.
6. What other factors are currently influencing employment and consumption trends?

Case Study—Economic indicators

Look at Table 15.1, then answer the following questions.

Table 15.1. International economic indicators for mid 1992

	Inflation		Interest rates		GNP/GDP growth		Industrial prod'n		Unemployment		Current account	
	annual change, %		3m'th money mkt, %		annual change, %		annual change, %		rate, %		last 12 months, $bn	
	latest	year ago	latest	year ago	latest	year ago	latest	year ago	latest	year ago	latest	year ago
UK	4.0	8.2	10.50	11.94	−1.7	−0.7	−1.6	−2.0	9.4	7.0	−7.9	−24.7
Australia	1.5	6.9	7.10	11.42	−1.1	0.2	−0.7	−1.9	10.5	9.1	−9.8	−13.4
Belgium	2.7	3.3	9.56	9.00	3.4	4.0	−2.4	3.3	8.2	7.5	4.7	3.9
Canada	1.6	6.3	6.88	9.31	−0.2	−1.1	−1.0	−5.4	11.1	10.5	−23.4	−18.8
France	3.2	3.3	10.00	9.25	1.7	1.5	0.4	−1.7	9.8	8.9	−6.3	−10.0
Germany	4.8	2.5	9.70	9.14	0.9	5.3	3.2	3.9	6.2	6.2	−23.2	33.7
Italy	5.6	6.6	12.25	11.75	1.0	1.7	−1.7	0.1	9.9	10.2	−32.6	−35.0
Japan	2.2	3.4	4.75	7.97	3.2	4.7	−4.6	6.8	2.0	2.0	84.9	38.1
Netherlands	4.3	2.7	9.44	9.15	3.9	4.2	3.4	4.3	7.0	7.3	9.8	11.0
Spain	5.9	6.8	12.88	15.15	4.9	5.0	−0.5	−1.1	16.5	15.7	−16.1	−15.8
Sweden	5.1	10.0	11.75	12.35	2.1	2.3	−11.8	−4.4	3.4	1.9	−3.6	−5.7
USA	3.2	4.9	4.13	6.06	−0.0	0.2	2.1	−3.6	7.3	6.7	−8.6	−92.1
OECD	4.2	6.1	—	—	3.5	4.5	−0.8	0.3	7.2	6.4	—	—

Questions

1. To what extent had the performance of the UK economy changed between the date shown and the previous year?
2. In your opinion, at what point in the trade cycle was the UK on the date shown?
3. Comment briefly on both the favourable influences/trends and unfavourable influences/trends in the UK, indicated by the figures from the study.
4. To what extent do the UK indicators show that the UK government policy over the period was achieving its economic goals? Refer briefly to the costs incurred in achieving such goals.
5. Use a variety of presentation techniques to compare the performance of the UK economy with the other countries shown.
6. From your analysis of the table, comment on which country seems to offer the most favourable external economic environment for businesses.

Case Study—Government industrial policy

The measures adopted by governments when they intervene in selected industries or sectors are all part of government industrial policy. Industrial policy is a way in which governments can influence the pace of change, whether it be of growth or decline, by helping to restructure selected industries.

At any moment in time, restructuring is taking place. Some industries are expanding while others may be on their way into absolute decline. Such changes can have profound implications for people in many industries, as well as certain areas of the country. Government industrial policy measures are a way of influencing this economic evolution so that, as restructuring takes place, changes do not harm society.

There are four basic types of industrial policy:

	Accelerative	Decelerative
Concerning one or a few firms	1	3
Concerning an industry	2	4

Accelerative policies are those that are designed to increase the pace of restructuring by means of a series of financial inducements.

Decelerative policies, on the other hand, are those that are designed to slow down the pace of change and assist companies experiencing structural decline.

As the matrix showed, both accelerative and decelerative policies may be applied either to one or a few firms or to a whole industry:

- *1.*—the government in this type of policy will attempt to increase the pace of development for either one or a few selected firms in the hope that such developments will act as a stimulus for growth in other firms and industries;
- *2.*—such a policy will involve a series of industrial policies designed to stimulate growth in a whole industry, for example, the hi-tech sunrise industries or developing other new industries;
- *3.*—this policy may be necessary to slow down the decline of a large business that is floundering and likely to collapse, which, as a result, has been called lame-duck policy and, in the past, has included the bailing-out of many shipyards and Rolls-Royce among others;
- *4.*—this policy will occur where a whole industrial sector requires assistance and led, partly, to many of the nationalizations that occurred in the 1940s.

The main problem with accelerative policies is in their directing action towards organizations that are going to succeed anyway. Equally, it would be wrong to waste taxpayers' money on firms destined to fail, so, with decelerative policies, a government has to take into account the extent to which assistance would be beneficial to the economy as a whole and whether it would be just a temporary measure or become a permanent burden on the taxpayer.

The future direction of industrial policy depends on two areas. First, the political wishes of the British government. The four consecutive Conservative election victories have meant that there has been a steady disengagement from the selective support for industry given by labour governments. Second, the effects of European policies from the EC that aim to harmonize government support programmes so as to minimize distortions of competition within the Single Market. In fact, over the last few years there has been a move away from domestic industrial policies in the UK towards an acceptance of what the EC Commission decide and this instead determines industrial support.

Questions

1. What is government industrial policy?
2. Explain why governments have an industrial policy.
3. Distinguish between accelerative and decelerative industrial policies.

4. Explain why the government may wish to slow down the decline of a large business.
5. What are the dangers of accelerative and decelerative industrial policies?
6. What has happened to UK industrial policy over recent years?

Case Study—The importance of the General Agreement on Tariffs and Trade (GATT) talks

Many of us today overlook that it was not the stockmarket crash of 1929 that caused the worldwide depression of the 1930s, but, rather, the rise of protectionism, which started with the Smoot Hawley Tariff Bill of 1930 when the US became protectionist. This started a chain reaction around the world and, as a result, world trade fell by 40 per cent in the first 3 years of the decade alone. A recession had led to a worldwide slump.

After World War II, there was a determination that there should never again be a great depression. Thus, in 1947 the GATT came into being. The agreements and treaties created by GATT covered mainly manufacturing and agriculture and contributed to the eight-fold expansion of world trade over the following four decades. Every few years the treaties were revised and, by the mid 1980s, GATT was ready for further revisions.

The developed nations then wanted to include intellectual property and services in the round launched in Uruguay. The topic of agriculture, however, came to dominate the talks. The EC's Common Agricultural Policy (CAP) extensively subsidizes the agriculture of member states. This was felt to create unfair competition and the Americans wanted subsidies reduced by 75 per cent. The agriculture ministers of the EC offered 30 per cent. The GATT talks broke up in disarray. There were some attempts to rescue them, but the deadlines were not met.

The Americans are sounding increasingly protectionist after lack of support from both Europe and Japan. As a result, there is little likelihood of important general agreements being established on a range of services. While this has been happening, Europe has been enjoying the benefits of the Single Market. Such benefits will only be short-lived, however, if the continued failure of the GATT talks plunges the world into another great worldwide depression.

Questions

1. Explain why protectionism contributed to the worldwide slump in the 1930s.
2. What is GATT and what was it formed to do?

3. Why does EC agriculture have an unfair advantage in world markets?
4. Why do many European countries not wish subsidies to be removed?
5. Why might the benefits of the Single Market be only short-lived?

Activity

Obtain a copy of the current economic indicators in the UK and then answer the following questions:

- What do the indicators show?
- Which indicators are favourable?
- Which indicators are unfavourable?
- To what extent are the economic indicators a reflection of recent government economic policy?
- How will the economic indicators influence businesses?
- Compare the UK economic indicators with those of at least two other countries and comment on the differences between them.

Activity

Imagine that you are a member of the Government presently in office. Given the economic performance of the UK at the moment, make a list of economic and industrial policies you would like to see introduced, assess their viability and then present your findings to the group. Discuss the comments made and compare your policies with those of others.

Activity

Find out more about the role of the Department of Trade and Industry. If necessary, write to them for information. Comment on:

- the work they undertake;
- the support services they provide;
- any initiatives they are involved in;
- the nature of their literature;
- their help with areas of high unemployment;
- their encouragement of exports;
- their current policies.

Essay title 1 — There is a major revaluation of the exchange rate. Discuss the probable effects of this on the fortunes of British businesses.

This is a classic question covering an important issue for British businesses that it is important for you to fully understand.

In your introduction, say that businesses are affected by a wide range of external factors. Many of these are economic. One particularly important factor, which may have a pivotal influence on business profits and successes, is that of a change in the exchange rate. However, to a large extent this will depend on whether an organization imports, exports, or both, and the amounts involved.

A country's foreign exchange rate is the price at which its own currency exchanges for that of others. Every currency has many rates to reflect all other traded currencies. Movements in the exchange rate will have a direct bearing on profit margins as well as a business' ability to sell overseas (export competitiveness). For example, if the exchange rate is revalued or increases this means that:

- imported goods will become cheaper;
- exports will become more expensive and will, therefore, ensure more income for home companies.

How the above affects a business will depend entirely on their position.

Imagine that a company imports raw materials but has only a domestic market for its products. For example, a regional newspaper may import newsprint from Canada but will only sell newspapers in the domestic economy. When the exchange rate goes up the newsprint becomes cheaper, so this will lower one of their major costs and, hence, improve their profit margin.

Another business, however, such as a white goods manufacturer, may import raw materials/goods from abroad and then export finished products. Though the precise effect of a revaluation will depend on the volume of its imports and exports, we can say that, in general, their import costs will go down and they will receive more for each unit they export. Clearly then, when the exchange rate is revalued, their margin also increases. Though this sounds encouraging, it will only be good if they can maintain the volume of goods they export. With high prices overseas, they may lose their export competitiveness. They may lose sales to other manufacturers of white goods, too, unless, of course, they can convince customers of the value of their products. One way of doing this is to compete on quality and emphasize that their goods are premium products. Note also, however, that high interest rates together with high exchange rates were used as a counter-inflationary policy during the 1980s and early 1990s with dire effects. Although this increases margins, many companies lost their ability to compete overseas.

If a company does not import, just exports, though a revaluation will improve their margin, their ability to succeed will depend on how well they can compete with a higher price.

A revaluation in the exchange rate will, therefore, affect businesses in a variety of different ways depending on whether they import and/or export. For some it will depend on how well they can maintain their volume of exports at a higher price.

Essay title 2—How might a recession affect the fortunes of a small business? What measures might it take to help it to survive this period?

Business studies students are not economics students and, though this question sounds like an economics question, the answer must draw solutions from a range of other business areas.

The opening to this answer must outline what a recession is and what its features are likely to be. For example, an economy is a fluctuating mechanism with high and low points of economic activity, often influenced by a variety of local, national and international activities. The point after a peak is a recession and this is marked by a downturn in economic activity (draw diagram of a trade cycle at this point).

The features of a recession are:

- a downturn in economic activity;
- high interest rates/exchange rates—these will have a bigger impact on businesses that have overextended themselves by borrowing in the past or which have overtraded;
- credit will become tight and it will become more difficult to borrow;
- creditors may extend their payment periods;
- it may be more difficult to obtain credit from suppliers;
- cash flow problems may develop;
- sales may fall, particularly for luxury items;
- margins may have to be cut, prices will fall to entice customers to buy goods;
- cost-cutting exercises may have to take place and this may lead to redundancies;
- organizations that cope badly with the recession may lose their market share;
- falling profits, companies going into liquidation and so on.

Each of the above should be enhanced with an explanation of how they might affect a small business.

A small business might adopt a variety of measures to avoid a period of recession. The measures it chooses will largely depend on the type of business it is, how badly it is likely to be affected by a period of recession and its former activities. They may include:

- *marketing measures*, such as:
  —reappraisal of the market;
  —adjustment of the mix;
  —careful analysis of the actions of its competitors;
  —repositioning strategy;

- *accounting measures*:
  - —assessment of financial requirements;
  - —cancelling of plans for expansion;
  - —reduction of levels of gearing;
  - —improved management of working capital;
  - —improved management of cash flow;
- *employment measures*:
  - —trimming of costs;
  - —reduction in staff;
  - —improved labour productivity;
- *overall*:
  - —improved management/operations;
  - —better response to the market.

Wherever possible examples must be used to support the above.

In conclusion, a recession is rarely something that a business can avoid and it will have a variety of different effects on its operations. Many of the negative effects can be guarded against by adopting a carefully planned strategy.

Essay title 3 —With reference to at least two economic criteria, discuss how each affects the current business environment.

In the introduction, say how business life takes place in an interdependent environment in which many outside factors affect business performance. Many such factors are economic and might include:

- exchange rates;
- inflation;
- recession/recovery;
- interest rates;
- balance of payments;
- international cooperation;
- industrial policy.

It is possible to pursue any of the above but, for the purpose of this answer, refer to inflation and interest rates and, to answer the question well, you must have a good idea of what the current levels of each are.

Inflation occurs when prices are persistently rising upwards. Creeping inflation is a condition experienced by most developing countries. Your answer should then give the current level and indicate any recent changes in it.

Inflation affects the business environment in a variety of ways. These may include:

- distribution of income;

- availability and price of loans;
- expectations;
- labour problems;
- investment;
- lack of competitiveness and so on.

Your answer should make reference to how the current level is influencing each of the above.

Interest rates reflect the price of borrowing. Real interest rates will be the nominal rate less the inflation rate. There is, therefore, a strong link between interest rates and the rate of inflation. The current level should be given as well as any recent changes. Interest rates might affect:

- borrowing;
- business confidence;
- investment plans and so on.

The answer should then say how current levels are influencing the above.

Your conclusion should indicate how the above criteria are currently influencing the business environment.

Essay titles

1. Explain why financial markets may prosper in a period of recession.
2. Examine the influence of high interest rates and high exchange rates on a manufacturing business that depends on its export markets.
3. Analyse the benefits and services provided to businesses by London's financial markets.
4. What is national income? To what extent does rising national income indicate that a nation's businesses are creating and generating wealth?
5. Explain how rising inflation may affect businesses.
6. Examine how a government's policies might encourage business confidence and investment.
7. Comment on both the benefits and dangers of an expanding business developing new markets overseas.
8. Explain how a recession might influence the fortunes of a small business retailing luxury goods.
9. What actions might a business take in an expansionary period of economic activity?
10. Examine the benefits of trading overseas. How might overseas trade be influenced by international trading agreements?
11. Analyse the influence of the Single Market on British businesses. How have many adapted to the new Market?
12. Examine the influence of exchange rates on overseas trade. What

might happen to home markets if a marked fall in the exchange rate took place?

13. Comment on the importance of international cooperation.

14. How might a breakdown of international agreements affect British businesses?

15. Explain how and why the government might try to influence business development.

16. 'Regional policy will result in unnecessary support of lame ducks or unfairly subsidized competition.' Discuss.

17. Examine the current economic conditions for British business and make a brief comment about each.

18. 'Protectionism would destroy the British manufacturing base.' Discuss.

19. Analyse the measures taken in the most recent budget and comment on how it will affect the business environment.

20. Examine the influence of cyclical economic changes on small businesses. How could they protect themselves against adverse influences?

Short-answer questions

1. Using an example to support your answer, what is meant by opportunity cost?

2. Name the four functions of money. Explain how each helps business activity to take place.

3. Explain briefly the relationship between bank lending and interest rates.

4. Describe two government economic objectives.

5. What is a merit good?

6. Name two monopolies.

7. Explain the role of the PSBR.

8. Describe the role of the multiplier.

9. What is structural unemployment?

10. Name two dangers of inflation.

11. Explain the purpose of the GATT.

12. Name three invisible exports from the UK.

13. Indicate one benefit and one danger of a revaluation of the exchange rate.

14. List four benefits of the Single Market.

15. What is fiscal policy?

16. Outline the advantages of international trade.

17. What does a current account deficit mean?

18. When does cost–push inflation occur?

19.   Assess the role of the accelerator on the construction industry.
20.   Using at least two examples, distinguish between direct taxation and indirect taxation.

Projects

The nature of the project work you undertake in this area might depend on the economic conditions at the time. Such a study might, therefore, be topical and difficult to research but it would be very rewarding. Areas could include:

- an analysis of a firm's performance in the Single Market;
- research into how a company fared during a period of recession or recovery;
- a study of how economic factors have affected the performance of either a firm or an industry.

Suggested reading

Begg, David, Stanley Fischer and Rudiger Dornbusch, *Economics* (3rd edn). McGraw-Hill, 1992.

Brimble, Martin, *Economics Explored*. Stanley Thornes, 1990.

Curmen, Peter, *Understanding the UK Economy*. Macmillan, 1992.

Hardwick, P., B. Khan and J. Longmead, *An Introduction to Modern Economics* (3rd edn). Longman, 1990.

Samuelson, Paul, *Economics* (14th edn). McGraw-Hill, 1992.

16

The consequences of business

A business system converts inputs into outputs by means of a series of processes. In so doing, it creates many benefits for a large number of citizens. For example, it provides jobs for employees and managers, products for consumers and dividends for shareholders. However, in making products, it may also create less desirable spin-off effects. Some of its activities may cause nuisance, such as lorries rumbling through populated areas in the middle of the night. Some of its products may have undesirable side-effects, such as tobacco helping to cause cancers. Some of its processes may be dangerous and unhealthy for employees, such as lung diseases suffered by people working with wood. The list of spillover effects can, therefore, be a very long one.

These consequences of business are very important. Industry can transform society and the lives that we live to the good or bad. The emphasis in business studies needs to be on creating a greater awareness of possible negative effects and a commitment among business people to maximize benefits and minimize all costs (particularly ones that affect a large number of citizens). Social responsibility needs to be a key business aim.

Case Study—Pollution in the former Soviet Union

In January 1992, Andrei Yablokov, the Russian government's adviser on the environment, made the first official attempt to chart environmental problems in the 15 republics of the former Soviet Union. He reported that the Communist Party's attitude to pollution had been near catastrophic and that the Soviet military–industrial complex had simply no regard for anything except its goal—Soviet power.

Because of pollution, life expectancy in Russia had declined from 70.4 years in 1964 to 69.3 in 1990. In some badly polluted cities it had diminished to just 44 years.

Some of the disasters are as yet unseen—or exist to become future shocks. They are known as technogenic emergencies—ruptures of pipelines or earthquakes caused by the excessive pumping of oil or water from deep wells. According to the report, in 20 years' time, the city of Moscow will be badly threatened by underground water flooding because of a past disregard for geological structures. Pipeline ruptures account for between 7 and 20 per cent of the oil extracted, with the losses totalling millions of tons.

Radioactive lakes, created over the years by waste from the Soviet nuclear weapons programme that was, are at risk from earth tremors that may send the polluted waters into the Caspian Sea and cause an environmental disaster comparable to Chernobyl.

Aluminium factories in Uzbekistan have produced uncontrolled wastes that are now affecting fruit-growing areas. Lakes around the Urals city of Chelyabinsk, the centre of what was the Soviet nuclear industry, are oozing with plutonium. Heavy use of pesticides has poisoned the rivers.

The Dioxins are present in mothers' milk in Moscow and the Chernobyl accident has rendered much of the Ukrainian and Belorussian countryside uncultivable.

Questions

1. What is the cause of the environmental pollution in the former Soviet Union?
2. Who is responsible for this problem today? Explain.
3. What measures should be carried out to deal with this pollution and the on-going creation of pollution?
4. Who should be responsible for paying for these measures?
5. What are the implications of your answers for the United Kingdom?

Case Study—Energy taxes

In October 1991, the European Commission unveiled a plan to impose an environmental tax on energy. These plans suggested the creation of an energy tax equivalent to $10 on a barrel of oil by the year 2000. Many businesses believe that energy taxation is inevitable throughout the industrialized world and that the EC should use this debate to boost development of energy-saving technology, gaining an advantage in a massive and growing global market.

The European Association for the Conservation of Energy (EuroACE) believes that investment in measures to control emissions of carbon dioxide, the main cause of the greenhouse effect, could be worth $550bn over the next decade. This would involve the installing of insulants, energy management systems and thermostats. Once again it is a question of beating the North-American and Japanese challenge.

The EC is falling behind agreed energy efficiency improvement targets. Between 1974 and 1984, efficiency improved by 20 per cent across the EC. Japan improved by 35 per cent. Now a new target of a further 20 per cent improvement in the decade to 1995 is also slipping. However, tighter controls are on the way. Plans to label the energy efficiency of household goods—from dishwashers to freezers—are being developed, as well as plans to label the energy value of buildings (which make up 42 per cent of the EC's energy demand).

Questions

1. What double gain can EC firms achieve from developing energy-efficient technology?
2. What are the likely consequences of failing to develop such technology in the EC?
3. Should such developments come from the private sector, the public sector or both?
4. Why is it that many people now recognize the need to develop taxes on energy?
5. What are the economic implications of such a tax for society and for particular individuals and groups?

Case Study—Unit trust hopes to clean up the environment

Environmental concern and the financial world do not always go hand in hand. Investors have tended to be more concerned about a company's profitability than about the pollution it might create.

Now, the pressure of public opinion and tougher environmental controls are making environmental concern big business. British businesses involved in the control of pollution today have turnovers of many billions of pounds.

Merlin Fund Management, a small unit trust company, was the first to launch its Merlin Ecology Fund in 1987 (today there are many imitators). The Merlin Fund's aim is to 'invest in companies engaged in pollution control or which demonstrate a commitment to the long-term protection and wise use of the environment'.

The Fund aims to invest in shares that will yield good profits as well as those with a safe record of profitability, such as water supply and waste management.

Questions

1. What sorts of individuals and groups are likely to invest with Merlin? What would be their motive for investment?

2. What effect will the setting up of environmentally concerned investment trusts have on business practice?
3. What measures might companies employ to show that they are environmentally sound?
4. How could the government encourage investors and companies to invest in the environment?

Case Study—Ashworth bypass

The Department of Transport is considering building a bypass around the town of Ashworth. The town currently has one major road running through its centre.

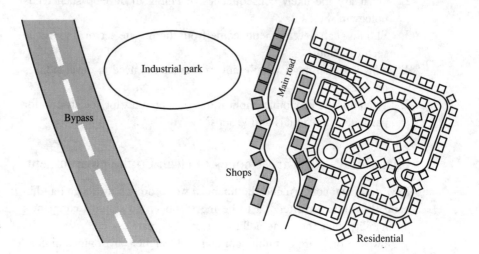

Figure 16.1 The planned Ashworth bypass.

The cost of the new bypass is estimated at £1m and it will take approximately a year to complete. Ashworth has, for a number of years, been a town with high unemployment. There is some industrial expansion in the area and an industrial park is currently being developed. The surrounding area is mainly farmland.

The Department of Transport asked several local people to give their views on the bypass:

*   Mrs A Smith, shopkeeper: 'I am not happy with the bypass. If traffic doesn't keep coming through the centre of town, my number of customers will fall and so will my profits';
*   Mr F Marris, farmer: 'I have land on both sides of the suggested route for the bypass. Think of the disruption this is going to cause the farm';
*   Mr P Jennings, Managing Director of local haulage company: 'I am

looking forward to a new bypass. It will mean I don't have to send my lorries through the town delivering goods';

- Mrs J Ward, resident: 'I am pleased there is going to be a bypass. It means I won't have to look at lorries going by my window every five minutes'.

Questions

1. Suggest one reason that would explain why the shopkeeper is unhappy about the bypass.
2. Suggest two reasons that would explain why the farmer is unhappy about the bypass.
3. Suggest one reason that would explain why Mr Jennings does not like sending his lorries through the town and three benefits his company might receive as a result of the bypass.
4. If you were a resident in Ashworth, give two reasons that you might give for liking the idea of building a bypass.
5. Name four other factors, not mentioned above, that you think the Department of Transport might consider when deciding whether or not to build the bypass.
6. Would you recommend that the Department of Transport build the bypass or not? Justify your answer.

Case Study—Consumer rights

Mrs Tan bought a bathing costume in a sale. She went off on her winter holiday to the Costa Packet. However, when she ventured into the sea, the colours in her costume ran.

As soon as she got back home, she went to the shop and complained, but the response of the shop assistant, Ivor Problem was decidedly unhelpful: 'You haven't been swimming in this have you?' he said, 'It's much too expensive to get wet—it's only for sunbathing. And you haven't got your receipt? A cheque stub isn't good enough as proof of purchase. Moreover we do not give refunds for sale goods, but we can give you a credit note'.

Questions

1. Why was Mr Problem wrong? What were Mrs Tan's rights in this case?
2. How could Mrs Tan have given herself more protection?
3. What was wrong with the product? Why would this have been a problem for the manufacturer and the retailer?

4. What morals can be drawn from this story?
5. What are the implications for business activity?

Activity

No one would design a service station nowadays without making certain, as far as humanly possible, that the local environment would not be damaged in the process. If anyone *did* design a station that might harm the environment, it would simply never be given planning permission.

There are many ways in which a service station can affect the environment. First, there is the choice of site, then the type of buildings, their size and colour, then the type of equipment. When the station is operational, what kind of noise is created? If it is going to be open all night, how will that affect people living nearby? What about the litter? Is the storage area kept tidy? Are there fumes and smells? Are the posters and other advertising overly obtrusive?

Imagine that you are designing a service station:

- make a list of ten requirements, in order of importance, that must be met by a service station if it is to have the least adverse impact on the environment;
- prepare a plan of action for developing a control system for service station operations to limit or prevent harmful environmental effects (for example, that staff collect all litter in the service station area regularly).

Activity

Investigate a local planning issue. Who is involved? Study press reports and other media coverage? Try to identify the costs and benefits that are being discussed. Perhaps you could carry out some of your own survey work. How are costs and benefits being quantified. Who is going to make the ultimate decision? What sorts of evidence will they draw on? How much of this evidence is quantitative and how much of it is qualitative? What decision-making tool will be used to make the final decision? How effective is the decision-making process involved?

Activity

Study the organization of a local pressure group. What particular event caused the pressure group to set up? Who were the founder members? Try to interview them. What sort of organization did they set up? How has the organization been sustained? Does the group have formal rules? What sorts of informal rules does it have? What are the main channels of communication that it uses with members, with the public and with the organization it is putting pressure on? How is the group financed? What are the strengths and weaknesses of the organization? What opportunities and threats face it? What have been the main achievements of the group? What tactics does it employ? Does it have clearly stated objectives? Then think of your own questions to answer.

Essay title 1—Suppose that a new urban motorway is to be built around the centre of a large city. This centre contains both commercial development and housing for low- to middle-income families. They will be affected by the motorway. First, list the costs and benefits of such a proposal. Second, how will the desirability of this project differ for the following groups:

- private motorists;
- commercial vehicle operators;
- shoppers;
- local residents.

A useful introduction to this essay would be a brief explanation of cost–benefit analysis. When deciding on the quantity of a particular good that should be produced, it is necessary to consider the way that both costs and benefits vary at different levels of output. In general, benefits are desirable and costs are to be avoided, so it would seem logical to try to select that output at which the excess of benefits over costs—called the net benefit—is largest. When society has selected this level of output and has allocated its resources accordingly, we say that there is an efficient allocation of resources or, alternatively, an efficient level of output.

Members of a society reap *benefits* when they consume goods and services. This process of consumption enables people to satisfy their wants. The quantity of benefits enjoyed by society will increase as consumption increases. However, resources that go into production are scarce; consumption does not take place free of charge. Production of particular commodities will therefore incur *costs* in the form of the other goods that could have been produced with the resources it uses up.

Production and consumption decisions, therefore, involve trading off costs and benefits. Costs and benefits to individuals are known as *private costs* and *private benefits*. Costs and benefits to society are known as *social costs* and *benefits* (and obviously include all private costs and benefits).

While it is relatively easy to measure many private costs and benefits in money terms, it is not easy to do so with social costs and benefits. Cost–benefit analysis has frequently been used to weigh up government-sponsored projects, for example, the building of a new London Underground line, the siting of the third London airport, subsidies to firms in depressed regions, even the building of fences to stop sheep from straying into the streets of Merthyr Tydfil.

There are many techniques for carrying out a cost–benefit analysis. For example, in carrying out a cost–benefit analysis for the building of a new urban motorway around a city centre, you would measure the money costs and returns of the project, find out all the spillover benefit effects (who would benefit and by how much) and all the spillover costs. All costs and benefits would be measured in money terms. You would obtain figures by asking someone who would benefit from the motorway, how much he or she would be prepared to pay to see the project go ahead. Then you would ask someone who would lose out what would be the minimum sum he or she would be prepared to accept as compensation for the project taking place. You then add up all the gains and losses. If the gains outweigh the losses, the project passes the test.

Inevitably there are problems with such a cost–benefit analysis. You first need to decide who would be affected by the urban motorway and the resulting list would, obviously, be quite extensive.

You would then need to calculate the sorts of questions to ask to obtain a true reflection of the costs and the benefits. For example, suppose you ask a pensioner 'How much compensation would you regard as fair if your house were to be knocked down?' and he or she replied 'Not at any price!' You could then look at what the market value of the house would be, but this would be affected by the prospect that an urban motorway was going to be built there!

Maybe you would decide to use some process of removing rogue answers from your survey, but then which answers would you include and which would you reject?

These are just some of the initial problems inherent in cost–benefit analysis. The shadow prices that you establish to reflect costs and benefits are often quite subjective. Perhaps, though, these better reflect the *real* costs and benefits of projects that affect society than do market prices.

The essay title asks you to first list the costs and benefits of the proposal. You can do this by mentioning private and social costs and benefits. To the bus company, the private costs would include re-routing and re-timetabling; private benefits might include a lower chance of accidents, shorter bus routes, fewer hold-ups. To the person living near the new motorway, the private costs could include noise, while the private benefits would include the increased speed with which he or she could get into town. The social costs and benefits could include:

Social costs	Social benefits
Delays during building operation	Long-term easing of congestion
Money used to carry out the project that could be spent on other projects	Employment created to construct road
Perhaps other traffic would be attracted to use the new motorway, creating more pollution, noise and so on	Spin-offs in building the project—building contracts and building workers spending more in the locality, being just two.

Clearly there are many items that you could add to both sides.

In the second part of the essay title you are expected to focus on different groups. The impact will vary widely for different individuals and groups and for sub-groups:

- private motorists may lose out in the short term as there would be delays, higher petrol bills and so on, but in the longer term, they may be able to make faster journeys, use less fuel and so on;
- commercial vehicle operators may benefit substantially, reducing business costs and increasing profit margins and perhaps they will be able to expand, although some businesses will experience more intense competition as goods will be able to be transported in and out of the area more easily;
- shoppers may have shorter, and cheaper, journeys, so they might, therefore, make their purchases in other areas, which might be a real benefit, but in some areas where local shops might close, pensioners and others would suffer;
- local residents will clearly bear many costs but also gain many benefits, such as loss of property, loss of community, increased noise and so on, but on the other hand, receive compensation for properties, found new communities, increase employment, provide faster routes and so on.

As with any proposal, a new urban motorway involves many costs and benefits. We need to highlight who these costs and benefits relate to and how large they are. We also need to try to weigh up the aggregate effects and look for a net result that will indicate whether or not to go ahead with the plan.

Essay title 2—How will recent environmental legislation affect businesses in the UK?

Increasing public awareness of so-called 'green' issues, such as global warming, water contamination and acid rain among many others, have all put pressure on governments to take action. Inevitably, tighter regulation of the polluters ensues and, in the end, industry must pay. The Government's Environmental Protection Act (1991) is increasingly coming into effect, although many companies are still unaware of its ramifications.

Some companies are barely aware that environmental law exists. The danger is that unwary companies may find themselves vulnerable to substantial liabilities under civil and criminal law. The most graphic example of this occurred in the late 1980s; Shell were fined £1m when there was an oil leak from their Merseyside pipeline.

The Act has introduced several major changes to the law as it affects industry. Integrated Pollution Control, for example, turns the old system of environmental regulation on its head. It affects only certain proscribed sites, which are chosen according to the processes and the substances used there.

In the past companies dealt with a variety of agencies controlling different aspects of pollution, such as the National Rivers Authority regarding discharges into rivers and Her Majesty's Pollution Inspectorate regarding discharges into the air. Under Integrated Pollution Control, however, the Pollution Inspectorate deals with *all* aspects in a particular plant.

Firms need to use an approach called Batneec (Best Available Technology Not Entailing Excessive Costs) for companies failing to do so can be sued in the civil courts. Guidelines have been set up for different industries. For some companies the effects are dramatic. The cost of investing in new, environmentally friendly technology might well put them out of business.

In the 1970s there were many companies that would collect other firms' waste, 'No questions asked' and dump it God knows where. In the 1980s dumpers had to be licensed. Today the responsibility lies firmly with the companies creating the waste under a rule known as 'duty of care'. From now on, companies generating waste have to dispose of it lawfully or ensure anyone handling it for them does so. They must also ensure that any third party taking the waste knows exactly what it contains and is equipped to dispose of it according to the law. Firms that fail to meet their 'duty of care' will be liable to prosecution. As a result, companies will have to keep a strict watch over those they hire to dispose of waste for them.

The Act also covers the control of landfill sites. Anyone running such a site can no longer close it down without proving to the local authority that it is environmentally secure and will cause no harm or damage in the future. In addition to complying with UK laws, companies also have to comply with a range of EC laws that are being enforced more and more severely. Indeed, the UK Government has fallen foul of the European Commission over a number of recent construction projects, including the planned Channel tunnel terminus at Kings Cross, precisely because the company concerned had failed to conduct an efficient environmental audit.

Essay title 3 — Is it possible to carry out the process of wealth creation to the benefit of all members of society?

This is not an easy question to answer because it can be approached from widely differing political perspectives. For example, there are those who think that inequality is a *good* thing and those who think it is a *bad* thing. The answer that follows is an attempt to state the situation in a straightforward unbiased way.

Wealth is the sum total of all the ingredients we have come to value as necessary for our material well-being. Comfortable houses, efficient transport, hospitals, health care and education to help us achieve our full potential, all these contribute to a feeling of well-being, so, in this sense, everyone concerned with providing them is also helping to create our wealth. We all depend on each other, therefore, to create a wealthy society.

Wealth is also a stock, that is a sum of valuables that exist at a given moment in time that are owned by individuals, groups or nations. It is very difficult to measure wealth in this way because it is often hard to ascribe a monetary value to such items as human capital.

Many people involved in business and industry see them as being fundamentally important because they create wealth. They do this by adding value as a result of the process of production, so that people in this country have become substantially better off (see Fig. 16.2).

However, it is also clear that wealth is not evenly distributed. Figure 16.3 shows that, in 1988, the least wealthy, 50 per cent of all citizens in the United Kingdom, owned just 6 per cent of the wealth, while the most wealthy, 1 per cent, owned 17 per cent of the wealth.

There have been countless studies which show that during the years of Conservative government the rich have become richer and the poor have become poorer. Indeed, this is an accepted part of the philosophy of inequality. One of Margaret Thatcher's famous sayings was, 'May all our children grow taller and some grow taller than others'. The context in which she said this was that she was arguing that the improvement in living standards for everyone is a good thing, but that the driving force behind enterprise may be a certain amount of inequality and other incentives that make people want to work harder.

There are many indicators of rising standards of living, such as the number of people who have televisions, dishwashers, phones, cars and so

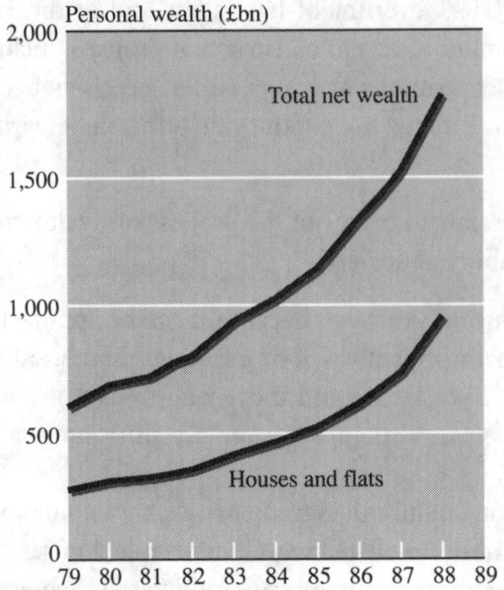

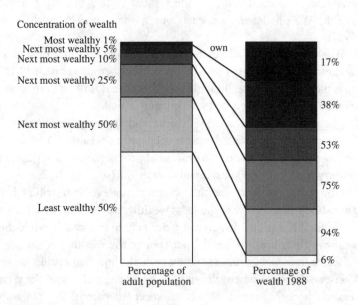

Figure 16.2 The growth of personal wealth in the UK from 1979–89. (*Source*: Family Expenditure Survey.)

Figure 16.3 The concentration of wealth in the UK in 1988. (*Source*: Family Expenditure Survey.)

on and how many of these there are per head. Differential earnings can be an incentive to hard work, particularly if they are coupled with low rates of income tax. In such a situation, people are free to spend their money in the way they see fit. At the same time, many of the poorer members of society can benefit from generally rising living standards. Improved technology, coupled with economies of scale, make a wider range of products available to nearly all at a relatively low cost.

However, such a system also engenders 'relative poverty'. When a person's worth is measured by what they can consume (a point that is frequently rammed home by advertising), whole groups of people begin to feel inadequate—the unemployed, pensioners, the poor. Relative poverty can lead to a strong sense of frustration. It is possible to argue that poorer people become worse off in a time of rising living standards than otherwise because they feel left out. This is a very real problem, not just for this group, but for society as a whole. A society that fails to meet the needs of *all* its citizens can be regarded as being morally impoverished. However, you cannot meet people's needs simply by giving them money and material possessions—you also need to value them and make them feel valued.

It is, therefore, possible for there to be alternative forms of wealth creation if alternative forms of 'equity' are used. For example, the Social Charter of the European Community is all about ways in which we can create a more caring society, a society that values everyone, a society in which emphasis is given to areas like education, health, training and investment in the future for all citizens. There is a considerable difference between wealth creation that provides monetary benefits to nearly all the people and wealth creation that is morally tied to meeting the wider—not purely monetary—needs of *all* people.

Essay titles

1. The concepts of social benefit and social cost involve adding together individual benefits and costs. What problems does this procedure pose?
2. What benefits does industry provide for society? How can the net benefits of industry be maximized?
3. Is pollution mainly a problem for the polluted?
4. How effective are pressure groups in influencing organizational behaviour?
5. Is the consumer king when it comes to the protection of the environment?
6. Compare the relative merits and demerits of various ways of government control of pollution?
7. How should businesses respond to pressure groups?
8. What are business ethics? How evident are they in the 1990s?
9. How can consumers regulate business activity?
10. Should business be made accountable to the local community?
11. 'The "private" can be measured, the "social" is immeasurable.' Discuss.
12. What would be the likely effect of taxes on energy and on pollution?

13. Describe the activities of one major pressure group. How big an impact has this group had on business activity?

14. Should cost–benefit analysis be regarded as an appropriate decision-making tool?

15. What are the major spillover costs and benefits of business activity? Relate your answer to practical examples.

16. Can externalities be measured?

17. 'Voluntary codes of practice will always be more effective than legislation in creating environmental responsibility.' Discuss this assertion.

18. 'Consumers have ultimate responsibility for the environment.'

19. How could the rewards of industrial society be spread out more evenly?

20. 'Economists infuriate deep greens because they insist on trying to calculate the costs and benefits of all change. For example, economists have calculated that when it comes to protecting the environment, people would be prepared to pay $15 (about £8.50) to save the grizzly bear, but only $1 for the whooping crane.' How acceptable do you think the economists' approach is to preserving the environment?

Short-answer questions

1. What is an externality?
2. Define the terms private benefit and private cost.
3. What is a pressure group.
4. List three organized pressure groups?
5. Why are consumers an important pressure group?
6. What is the difference between income and wealth?
7. List four main types of pollution.
8. What is a consumer boycott?
9. What is a non-renewable resource?
10. List three non-renewable resources.
11. What are business ethics?
12. What problems can be caused by the insufficient testing of products?
13. What is the 'duty of care' introduced by the Environmental Protection Act (1991)?
14. What is Integrated Pollution Control?
15. Why is underemployment a problem in some countries?
16. What problems are caused by dereliction?
17. What measures can be introduced to control and reduce pollution?
18. What is meant by the environment?

19. What is acid rain?
20. What are social costs?

Projects

There are several attractive project areas relating to this important area of
the course that you could explore:

- why not look at how a particular company has attempted to develop
  more of a green culture in recent years and see whether the green
  philosophy goes more than skin deep;
- carry out an environmental audit of your school or college, making
  suggestions for improvement;
- find out which industrial sectors are the biggest polluters and do
  some research into this area.

Suggested reading

Cannon, Tom, *Corporate Responsibility*. Pitman, 1992.
Ledgerwood, Grant, and Elizabeth Street, *The Environmental Audit and Business Strategy*.
  Pitman, 1992.
McHugh, Francis P., *Ethics*. Macmillan, 1991.
Porritt, Jonathan, *The Green Index—Directory of Environmental Organisations in Britain and
  Ireland*. Cassell, 1990.
Wilkinson, Margaret, *Equity and Efficiency*. Heinemann Educational, 1992.

17

Integrated case analysis

Case Study 1 — The Paragon Cinema

In the early 1980s it looked as if the cinema industry was dying. Official statistics showed that fewer people were going to cinemas and many were closing down.

It was about this time that Robin Sanders was made redundant from his job as Project Organizer for an engineering company. His work had been to research and determine the most cost-effective ways of carrying out engineering projects.

By chance he heard that *Wogan* had voted Grantham the most boring town in Britain because of its lack of leisure facilities, so Robin decided to use his experience in project investigation (and his own newly acquired leisure) to see if a cinema could be made into a profitable business in Grantham.

One of the first things he researched was the sales figures for a small High Street cinema in neighbouring Newark. His findings were as follows:

	1983	1984	1985
Total sales (£) at current prices	45 624	54 706	62 970
Retail price index	85.6	100	114.9

When Robin looked at the national figures and saw that attendances were falling, he saw something other people had missed. Cinemas were being closed not because films were unpopular, but because the sites the cinemas occupied in the High Street could be used more profitably for supermarkets and multiple stores.

Robin felt he had discovered something important. He worked out his costs and likely takings as part of his business plan, but it took him a year to convince people that the plan was worth financial support.

Figure 17.1 The Paragon cinema.

He estimated that it would cost £55 000 to build his cinema (which he decided to call The Paragon) and he was eventually given a Council loan of £30 000 and a bank overdraft facility of £15 000. He estimated that the cinema would have a lifespan of 10 years before it would need rebuilding and modernizing. (Figs 17.1 and 17.2 show the building and the cinema's projector.)

His first few weeks in business were difficult. He had actually spent more money than he had borrowed and so he needed money to come in straight away in order to break even.

Fortunately, in the cinema business you take in money before you pay out most of your running costs. This helped Robin's business survive. As he now says, though, 'The business had to work in the first few weeks or I would have gone under'.

There are other reasons for his success. Robin sited The Paragon off the High Street, thus halving his rent and rates. He was one of the first cinema owners to computerize all his accounts and paperwork and he was the first in this country to show different films on the same day. By 1990, Robin's net current assets were valued at £100 000.

The Paragon cinema has gone from strength to strength. Over the last four years, the profit arising from the normal activities of the business before taxation and interest payments has stabilized at an annual figure of £25 000. The Paragon is a popular attraction and Robin says, 'I will never work for anyone but myself again. The sense of achievement outweighs

Figure 17.2 Robin Sanders working The Paragon's projector.

everything. Even if I didn't make a large profit, I would have achieved something off my own bat and proved to everyone I can do it'.

In 1990, Robin decided to find out whether there was sufficient demand in the town to justify a second screen. He had seen estimates that the population of Grantham would increase from 30 000 to 50 000 over the next 10 years. In particular, there was an influx into the town of younger people and young couples just starting families. He was also having to turn customers away at one out of five shows due to lack of space.

Robin found out some interesting information—shown in Figs 17.3, 17.4 and 17.5—from a newspaper article based on market research.

Robin currently charges £5 a seat in screen 1 and intends to charge the

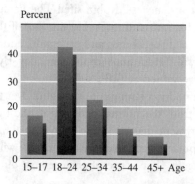

Figure 17.3 Cinema audience by age.

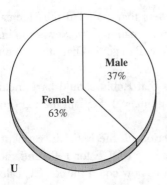
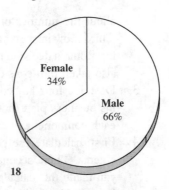

U   18

Figure 17.4 Cinema audience by film certificate.

Trends in cinema admissions

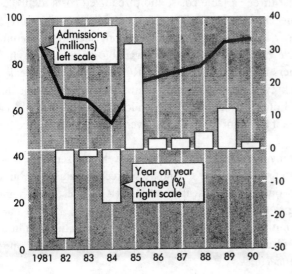

Figure 17.5 Trends in cinema admissions.

same for screen 2. He has calculated that the weekly fixed cost of screen 2 will be £1000. Variable costs of running screen 2 will be £1 per cinema-goer. Robin has estimated that he could run ten performances a week on screen 2. The second screen theatre would be able to accommodate an audience of up to a maximum of 50.

Questions

1. In what ways did Robin Sanders take a risk in setting up The Paragon cinema?

2. First, show how Robin could have calculated the real change in the value of sales at the Newark High Street cinema between 1983 and 1985. Second, assuming that the price of cinema seats at Newark remained constant between 1983 and 1985, what can be deduced

about the number of cinemagoers that attended the cinema there? Third, how important was the information from Newark in influencing Robin's decision to set up The Paragon? What other factors were also taken into consideration?

3. Describe four key components that Robin should have included in his business plan (not including finance). Explain the importance of each component.

4. First, calculate the payback period on the initial investment in the cinema. Then, second, calculate the ROCE for 1990 and show how you made this calculation. Third, how could the ROCE calculation help Robin to know whether or not he has made a worthwhile investment?

5. First, list three variable costs, and three fixed costs incurred in running the cinema. You will need to explain why they are fixed or variable in the case of a cinema operation. Second, how could Robin minimize his fixed costs and his variable costs? Third, how many customers for the screen 2 would Robin require each week in order to break even on this screen? Show how you have calculated this figure. Fourth, describe pricing policies that Robin could adopt for screen 2 if he is not able to break even at the existing price for screen 1?

6. In carrying out market research into developing screen 2, would it be better to use primary or secondary sources of data? If Robin chooses to carry out primary research, what sorts of questions should he be seeking to answer and why?

7. Which indicator of cinema attendance shown in the data in the Case Study gives the best indicator of current trends in cinema attendance?

8. How can Robin make his screen 2 pay? Use data given in the Case Study to support your arguments. What external factors may prevent screen 2 being a success?

Case Study 2—Educational Promotions Ltd

Educational Promotions Ltd (EPL) is a well-established company that has, until recently, specialized in providing a range of educational supplies to schools and colleges wholesale. The company has vast experience in the educational market and has generated considerable goodwill. Its services to this market have included:

- buying in goods, performing a wholesale function and then supplying the goods to schools and colleges;
- receiving a commission on sales by linking manufacturers with educational institutions;

- providing a means whereby the educational services of large organizations may promote their wares.

Recently, the educational market has not been quite as profitable as EPL would have liked and so the company has been consciously changing the emphasis of its business. Though it wishes to retain its share of the educational market, it is looking to the future and to other changes in the external environment, in particular the Single Market, and today has the aim of providing standard wholesale facilities for a wide range of mail-order companies.

These moves, however, are already testing their capacity. It has already proved necessary to take on a short-term lease for extra warehousing facilities close to the company's offices in Oldham and to have had two pre-fabricated extensions added to the business' premises. It employs more than 90 staff in the offices and warehouse and the lack of space is restricting the nature of its operations. It is also becoming acutely aware that, at this present moment in time, though it wishes to retain its offices in the North West, it is not currently the lowest-cost location if the company were to expand. As it wishes to take advantage of opportunities provided by the Single Market, it has researched a number of locations on the eastern side of the country.

An area that particularly interests the directors of EPL is Darlington. The Operations Director has recently been to a seminar in the town and has come back with the following notes about Darlington:

> Darlington was the birthplace of the modern railway and today is the communications gateway to the North-East region. It has a thriving town centre supported by a strong industrial and commercial base. There are a large number of long-standing international companies based in the town and surrounding area, such as DSRM Group PLC, Cleveland Bridge, Whessoe, Millicom, Darchem, Rothmans and Bowater Containers. In addition, there is land available for development north of the existing Faverdale Industrial Estate. Companies that locate in Darlington are able to appreciate the excellent links that Darlington provides to the northern region.
>
> Darlington has excellent communications links, by rail, road, air or sea. The electrified East Coast main line runs directly through Darlington to London King's Cross, providing a high-speed rail link for freight and passengers, who can then change for international destinations.
>
> The A1(M) Durham motorway lies a mile to the west of Darlington, providing superb road access to points throughout the northern region.
>
> Teesside and Newcastle Airports have air links with numerous international destinations, providing regular services for commuters with business abroad.
>
> The ports of Seaham and Teesside offer frequent freight services with facilities for both container and conventional mixed cargo. Sailings to European ports are frequent and freight from world-wide origins is regularly dealt with.
>
> The Darlington Cross Town Route is scheduled for completion by 1995.

Figure 17.6 Darlington town centre.

Current proposals from developers European Land mean that the road could even be completed at an earlier date. When finished, it will provide improved access to the A1(M) and Teesside.

Darlington is situated in a Government-defined Intermediate Area. The Government, therefore, offers financial and other assistance to firms developing or expanding in Darlington, for example, Regional Selective Assistance. These are discretionary grants that may be awarded to enable a project to go ahead. They are based on the amount of capital expenditure to be incurred in a project and the number of jobs to be created or maintained. Almost all manufacturing industries are likely to qualify for grants and some service industries, too, if they have an impact on the national or regional economy rather than just the local area.

Durham County Council also offers a range of financial incentives to help companies in the early stages. The aim is to provide incentives to firms that will create jobs in County Durham rather than elsewhere. Firms renting premises anywhere in Darlington may be able to choose a Rates Equivalent Grant, Small Business Grant or a Relocation Grant. Firms building or buying premises in Darlington may be eligible for a Site Preparation Grant, a Building Improvement Grant, Rates Equivalent Grant, Small Business Grant and a Relocation Grant.

After lengthy deliberations, EPL has decided to seriously consider the Darlington option. The company's main concerns at this early stage are:

- *recruitment*—from the 30 jobs created, at least 4 would have to be supervisory and they would like to recruit these 4 internally as they feel that they need individuals with an inside knowledge of how EPL works, but, if they cannot persuade at least 4 experienced staff to move to Darlington, they might have to develop a detailed training programme;

- *investment*—the cost of the project, taking into consideration the grants offered, would be about £200 000 and, in return they expect profits from the project to be:
  —£75 000 in Year 1;
  —£85 000 in Year 2;
  —£90 000 in Year 3;
  —£95 000 in Year 4;
  —£120 000 in Year 5;

- *the economy*—the directors are concerned that recovery from the slump has been slow and feel that high interest rates and high exchange rates may affect their ability to compete for overseas orders;

- *overtrading*—the Finance Director has pointed out that the proposed plans, which involve holding significantly larger stock levels, may create an imbalance in the working capital ratio;

- *social costs*—there are a number of minor considerations: congestion on the A1M has been a problem in the past, but the site will require good access and will increase traffic locally, which might lead to some opposition, and, depending on the orders taken, there might be considerable waste requirements, and these would have to be investigated beforehand;

- *recent issues*—the directors are concerned about a number of recent issues that they feel might have an effect on their proposals, including public disquiet about the nature of some junk mail, having to comply with new accounting standards, further European Monetary Union and the Single Currency Unit and the demographic time bomb.

Questions

1. Describe, briefly, two functions of a wholesaler.
2. Explain how EPL is likely to benefit from the establishment of the Single Market.

3. EPL has decided to expand their business by diversifying their activities. What is diversification? What further research would you expect them to undertake before finalizing their decision?

4. First, why is the company locating the second warehousing unit away from its centre of operations? Second, make a list of factors that are likely to influence its location decision. Briefly describe the importance of each factor. Third, list four advantages of locating a warehouse in Darlington.

5. First, what inducements could EPL provide to encourage supervisory-level staff to move to Darlington? Second, contrast the benefits of recruiting staff internally with those of external recruitment.

6. First, the cost of the project is £200 000. What sources of finance could EPL use to obtain the necessary capital? Second, using investment appraisal techniques, advise EPL on the financial merits of the project. Comment on the average rate of return, the payback period and the net present value discounted at 9 per cent. Third, what is overtrading? Fourth, how might the proposals affect the working capital? Explain why. What actions could they take to maintain favourable liquidity ratios?

Table 17.1. DCF tables from 1 per cent to 10 per cent over 6 years—per cent rate of discount

Future years	1	2	3	4	5	6	7	8	9	10
1	0.990	0.980	0.971	0.962	0.952	0.943	0.935	0.926	0.917	0.909
2	0.980	0.961	0.943	0.925	0.907	0.890	0.873	0.857	0.842	0.826
3	0.971	0.942	0.915	0.889	0.864	0.840	0.816	0.794	0.772	0.751
4	0.961	0.924	0.888	0.855	0.823	0.792	0.763	0.735	0.708	0.683
5	0.951	0.906	0.863	0.822	0.784	0.747	0.713	0.681	0.650	0.621
6	0.942	0.888	0.837	0.790	0.746	0.705	0.666	0.630	0.596	0.564

7. Explain why high interest rates and high exchange rates might affect the Company's ability to compete overseas?

8. What are social costs? Describe what, if anything, EPL could do about the social costs mentioned in the Case Study.

9. Expand on each of the recent issues mentioned in the study. Which of these might affect their relocation proposals and why?

Case Study—Returning home

Activity

Imagine that, since leaving college, you have been a wanderer. In your twenties you travelled the world as a production engineer, working in Saudi Arabia, Singapore and Hong Kong. At the age of 29 you have returned to the UK with substantial savings and the intention of settling down and setting up your own business. After a tentative discussion with your bank, it supports your ideas but has indicated that, if you wish to raise more than the £12 000 you have saved, you will need to produce a business plan, so that it can evaluate its response to your proposals.

Now carry out the following:

- form small groups to produce a business plan that analyses the following areas and broadly follows many of the guidelines provided:
  —the idea—guidelines: discuss alternative ideas; list these ideas; consider the practicality of each; select one idea and justify the choice as an introduction to the plan; identify the objectives of the business;
  —the market—guidelines: decide what sort of research you should carry out; identify the potential market; how large it is (and whether there is sufficient purchasing power in this part of the market); who the potential customers are; who the competitors are; how much they charge; what differential advantages you might have; how price sensitive the market-place is;
  —the people—guidelines: what expertise the business is likely to require; what you can offer; who you would employ; what wage bill you would expect;
  —ownership and control—guidelines: consider the appropriate legal form for the business; what documentation you would require; what administrative/organizational requirements you would need;
  —resources—guidelines: list the resources required as well as their approximate costs; list the overheads and break them down into variable and fixed;
  —finance—guidelines: prepare a simple cash budget to forecast your income and expenditure for the first three months; produce a break-even analysis and chart to support your plans;
  —presentation—present your plan to the rest of your group.

18

The answers to the short-answer questions and integrated case analyses

Chapter 3

1. Our needs are our basic requirements. They obviously include a minimum standard of food, shelter and clothing. Our wants go well beyond this, however, to include all the things that we would like to have to satisfy our higher needs.

2. Opportunity cost is the next best alternative that is sacrificed when we take a course of action.

3. Money is anything that is generally accepted as a means of exchange.

4. Money should be durable, divisible, portable, easily recognized and it should maintain stability of value over time.

5. Cuba, Mongolia, Laos, Burma, Cambodia, Vietnam, China, North Korea.

6. Production adds value to things so that they become goods or services.

7. De-industrialization is the fall in the relative importance of the manufacturing sector, as measured by output, employment or capital expenditure.

8. Primary: oil extraction, mining, fishing, farming. Secondary: any manufacturing or construction industry. Tertiary: banking, insurance, retailing, wholesaling, hairdressing.

9. A relative definition of poverty relates the condition of the poor to other members of society. An absolute definition sets a standard (usually quantitative) poverty line.

10. Resources are scarce because the uses to which resources can be put are infinite and wants are insatiable.

11. Teleworking usually involves working at home using a computer wired into some form of telephone-linked network.

12. Structural changes involve broad changes in the structure of industry. Some industrial sectors become more important while others contract as a result of changes in demand and supply.

13. A 'third wave' society is one in which the service sector becomes of supreme importance.

14. Conflict theorists believe that society is based on fundamental differences of

interests between different groups, such as landlord and tenant, capitalist and wage labourer. Consensus theorists believe that society is based on fundamental shared interests.

15. Ideology is the ideas, values and justifications of a particular individual or group, such as the dominant ideology of a ruling class.

16. What to produce, how to produce it and who will receive the product.

17. Centrally planned, mixed and free enterprise economies.

18. They 'vote' with money for items they want to be produced, that is, they produce demand.

19. The goods sector is the primary and secondary sectors of the economy combined.

20. Sales maximization is selling as much as possible in a given time period, perhaps to become a brand leader or to maximize sales commissions. Profit maximization is to maximize difference between total revenue and total cost.

Chapter 4

1. How much capital each partner will contribute, how profits and losses will be shared, rules for admitting and expelling partners, voting rights and termination of the partnership.

2. Limited liability gives protection to the shareholders of a company. The maximum they can lose if the company runs into debt is the amount they have contributed by buying the shares.

3. The name of the company, the registered address of the company, the objectives of the company, that is, what types of activities it will engage in, and the capital of the company.

4. The rights of shareholders, the rules and procedures for issuing and transferring shares, the procedures and timing of company meetings, details of how accounts will be set out, powers and responsibilities of directors and details of how company officers will be appointed.

5. Setting-up and running costs can be expensive, the 'red tape', diseconomies of scale, employees and shareholders become distanced from each other, affairs have to be made public and there are heavy penalties for breaking company regulations.

6. Non-executive directors can bring broader experience to a company's board, such as experience of raising capital in financial markets. They may also bring influence and useful contacts.

7. The chairperson will be responsible for acting as a figurehead for the company. He or she will be responsible for chairing all board meetings and for making major public policy statements.

8. Line organization is the typical, hierarchical structure of a company that sets out a clear line of command from superiors to subordinates.

9. Grouping by function occurs when companies are divided into broad sectors,

each with its own particular specialism, such as marketing, accounts and so on. Grouping by process occurs when particular products involve several processes in their manufacture. Each process would then be carried out in a separate department.

10. By Act of Parliament.

11. Public corporations include the Bank of England, British Coal, and the Post Office. Public companies include British Gas, National Westminster Bank and British Telecom.

12. The public sector comprises those organizations that are owned by the government.

13. Privatization is the transference of organizations from the public to the private sector.

14. Day-to-day decision making is carried out by the chairperson and board of managers; major policy making involves consultation with the relevant government minister.

15. Major decisions are approved by the board of directors and carried out by managers.

16. The government owns a public corporation for the people. Shareholders own public companies.

17. The private sector includes cooperatives, partnerships, and franchises. The public sector includes municipal enterprises, local councils, the civil service and the National Health Service.

18. They have a given set of rules that are the same for everybody, they have set patterns of organization, there is a clear chain of command, they can deal with large-scale programmed decisions.

19. The Memorandum and Articles need to be filed with the Registrar of Companies before a Certificate of Incorporation and a Certificate of Trading will be granted.

20. Franchising involves licensing someone to trade under your name in a particular area. The company offering the franchise may provide training and equipment as well as materials and advice.

Chapter 5

1. A shareholder can vote at the Annual General Meeting to appoint a director. He or she can decide whether to retain or sell his or her shares.

    A manager makes many operational decisions and is often responsible for managing a particular division or department of a company. For example, the production manager will decide how to organize the production line, the advertising manager will decide how to spend the advertising budget and so on.

    An employee can decide how many hours of overtime to work, how much effort to put into the work, whether to invest time and effort to gain greater skills through training and so on.

2. Operational decisions will be made by middle and junior managers in an organization. They will be responsible for putting day-to-day policies into effect.

3. Strategic decisions will be made by the senior managers and directors of a company. Strategy concerns the major objectives of the company—the what, how, when and who.

4. The critical path is the series of activities that are most important if a job is to be completed in the time available for the project. It sets out the critical sequence of activities that must be given priority.

5. A→C→F→G

6. A hierarchical organization has a clear chain of command and a hierarchy of offices (setting out who reports to who and the responsibilities of different office holders). A democratic organization is one in which there is far greater equality between its members in terms of decision-making powers. The organizational chart will be much flatter than in a hierarchical structure. Decisions are made by teams of people working together.

7. In a group of five there are enough people to bring a lot of information to decision making, but there are not too many to prevent all views being heard. It is also an odd number, which can help to break an impasse.

8. A decision tree show the options that arise from a decision and sets out the implications of taking particular options. They can be used to trace out all the known outcomes of a particular decision so that a full picture can be created.
   It is also possible to quantify different outcomes.

9. Pick up brush → Wet brush → Add paste → Scrub teeth → Rinse mouth.

10. A programmed decision might involve the re-ordering of toilet rolls or other items of stock, the ringing of bells to mark the ends of lessons, the reading out of instructions to start an examination and so on. Non-programmed decisions might involve the opening of a new course or department, deciding how to react when part of a classroom ceiling is blown off by a gale during lessons or whatever. Many of the decisions made by large organizations are programmed, although many decision makers frequently do their own thing!

11. Evaluation should be seen as an ongoing part of decision making. Evaluation is as much a starting point as a finishing point. The results of decisions will need to be clearly appraised and evaluated to improve the decision-making process. Corrective action can be taken when necessary.

12. Game theory uses mathematical models to study the various strategies that can be employed by individuals and organizations in conflict (competitive) situations.

13. In a closed system, the system will have been programmed to operate in a particular way. A comparator will be used to make sure that the system is complying to the given programme. Adjustments will be made by the com-

parator (such as a thermostat in a central heating system) to ensure that the system works to the values ascribed to its programme.

14. A SWOT analysis is an analysis of the Strengths, Weaknesses, Opportunities and Threats of a product or particular course of action. The analysis is usually of internal strengths and weaknesses and external opportunities and threats.

15. The task is the content of the work, such as would be involved in building a bridge. The process is the interaction between the people working in a group, such as that based on consensus or conflict.

16. An expert system can be used to decide where to prospect for oil. A simulation test on materials can highlight stresses and weaknesses that may occur when products are tested by real conditions, such as are used in car design. A simulation of the economy can indicate the likely macro-economic effects of tax and interest rate changes.

17. Without clear objectives, it is impossible to tell where you are going and to monitor progress.

18. A group is a collection of people with a common purpose who communicate with each other over a period of time.

19. The role of the leader is to make sure that the other members of the group are aware of the group objectives and their individual objectives and to focus the group on working towards these objectives.

20. Participative management is the process of allowing members of an organization to participate in management and decision making.

List of questions for second Activity (page 49)

What are the aims/objectives of the activity?
What is your role in the activity? What will you be expected to do?
When will tasks need to be completed by?
Who will work with you or give you help?
Who will make the decisions?
What resources will be available?
What will other groups be doing? Will you be working together?
What is the importance of this activity relative to other activities?
How will the activity be assessed or judged?
What will be the effect of success or failure?

Chapter 6

1. Statistics means a series of figures. It can also be used to describe a series of devices that can be used to present information and a method for interpreting business data.

2. Primary data is collected by a firm for its own purposes. Secondary data is that collected by somebody else.

3. Techniques of sampling may include:
   - *random*—the advantage is that everybody has an equal chance of being picked; the disadvantage is that it is not very well targeted;
   - *quota*—the advantage is that it is easy to administer; the disadvantage is that it can lead to bias;
   - *systematic*—the advantage is that it is highly structured; the disadvantage is that it is complex to administer;
   - *cluster*—the advantage is that it is well focused; the disadvantage is that it may be difficult to find appropriate respondents.

4. Sources of government statistics may include: the Central Statistical Office, Department of Trade and Industry, Department of Employment, Bank of England, Census data and so on.

5. A tally mark is a quick and useful way of counting totals, displaying them as short vertical lines in groups of five, the fifth crossing through four.

6. Construction of pie chart and bar chart. The pie chart degrees would be:

toothpaste	42
dental floss	21
soap	170
others	127
	——
	360

7. A histogram is a form of bar chart that represents data in the form of the area covered, not necessarily the height of the bar.

8. A frequency polygon is drawn by constructing a histogram, marking off the mid-point at the top of each rectangle and then joining the mid points with straight lines.

9. A Gantt chart is a form of bar or line chart that shows actual with forecast figures.

10. A Lorenz curve is a cumulative frequency curve that is used to demonstrate a disparity of distribution.

11. An arithmetic mean is simply the total of a set of numbers divided by the number of items. The mode is the value that occurs most frequently. The median is the middle number in a distribution or array of figures arranged in order of value. For example, for the series 4, 6, 9, 9, 12, the mean would be 8, the mode 9 and the median 9.

12. A quartile represents one quarter of a range. It enables a distribution to be divided up and analysed.

13. Standard deviation is a measure of dispersion. It is used to analyse how far figures are dispersed from the mean.

14. A normal distribution curve may be used to predict outcomes by means of probability.
15. Index numbers may be used for comparisons and to relate figures to time periods.
16. Weighting enables indices to take into account the relative importance of each factor.
17. Significance testing is designed to test a hypothesis.
18. Two benefits of using IT could be chosen from the following: speed, accuracy, ease of use and so on.
19. A grouped frequency distribution takes into account groups of figures. It may be used to draw histograms, ogives and Lorenz curves.
20. A business may generate marketing data, customer information, purchasing data, accounting data, administrative data and so on.

Chapter 7

1. Increased popularity, rise in price of other meats, rising incomes, falls in the prices of complementary foods, such as rice, changes in population structure, such as more pork-eaters—all might lead to there being an increase in demand for pork.
2. Supplies of camcorders in shops might increase because of a fall in price of camcorder components, improvements in production technology, increase in labour productivity in the industry, increase in demand, shops stocking up for Christmas rush and so on.
3. A pure monopoly exists when there is only one firm in a market.
4. Restrictive practices limit the freedom of trade and production. For example, a supplier may refuse to supply a retailer who does not charge a given price for the items.
5. Petrol retailing, the sale of washing powder, High Street banking are all competitive oligopoly markets.
6. As incomes rise, the demand for most goods will increase. However, there are some inferior goods that become less popular once incomes have reached a certain level. Consumers may actually switch to more expensive substitutes when they can afford to do so.
7. The quantity supplied will increase as price rises because it becomes worthwhile for marginal (new) producers to enter markets and for existing producers to expand output as revenues rise relative to costs.
8. Consumers buy more as prices fall because goods become relatively cheaper and because consumers will buy more at a lower than a higher price.
9. Conditions for perfect competition include many small firms, a homogeneous (identical) product, freedom of entry into the market, consumers are aware of all prices charged by all sellers, there is no inconvenience caused by going to one seller rather than another, many buyers.

10. The external environment is made up of the systems and organizations, individuals and groups that exist outside the firm, such as the social system, competitors, the legal framework, consumers and so on.

11. A merger is the voluntary joining together of two business units.

12. UK, Ireland, France, Belgium, Netherlands, Luxembourg, Denmark, Spain, Portugal, Greece, Italy and Germany.

13. An improvement in technology should reduce the cost of producing a product and, hence, shift the supply curve to the right, leading to a reduction in price.

14. Compact discs and compact disc players, cereals and milk, screwdrivers and screws.

15. Washing powder and washing liquid, pork and beef, tissues and toilet paper.

16. A natural monopoly exists by accident of nature, for example the location of mineral deposits. An artificial monopoly exists where man has created barriers to entry, such as copyright, and patent arrangements, economies of large-scale production and so on.

17. The Monopolies Commission was set up by the Government to examine possible cases of monopoly referred to it by the Government.

18. Monopolistic means tending towards monopoly. In other words, there are likely to be some forms of restrictive practices that may lead to a reduction of output or an increase in price.

19. National standards gave way to European standards in many areas, including food ingredients, labelling and packaging, and this process will simply continue.

20. Taxes are likely to have the effect of reducing supply. They should be seen as a cost of production. The incidence of taxes will affect the use of resources in favour of some lines of production.

Chapter 8

1. Marketing is the anticipation, identification and fulfilment of a consumer need at a profit.

2. Market segmentation is a process of identifying groups of consumers with similar needs and then breaking down the market into parts so that different strategies can be used for different groups of customers.

3. Primary research is obtaining materials first-hand. Secondary research is using materials that have already been published.

4. Low-price, high-price, cost-plus, contribution, demand-orientated, skimming, penetration, destroyer and promotional are all pricing strategies.

5. Marketing goods in the home market rather than overseas involves less paperwork, lower transport costs, a different pricing policy, and so on.

6. There are several bodies that control advertising, including Advertising

Standards Authority, Independent Television Commission, British Code of Advertising Practice and so on.

7. Consumer marketing is selling to consumers; organizational marketing involves selling to businesses and public-sector organizations.

8. Economic determinants of consumer demand may include incomes, prices of substitute products, population size, tastes, habits, government influences and so on.

9. As and Bs would spend more of their incomes on private education and health care, cars, antiques and so on whereas Ds and Es would spend their income on necessities, such as food, rent and so on.

10. Undifferentiated marketing involves offering a single mix to the whole market for a product or service.

11. The phases are development, introduction, growth, maturity, saturation and decline.

12. The functions of a wholesaler include breaking bulk, storage, packing and labelling, advice, credit and so on.

13. Personal selling involves persuasive communication between a seller and a buyer designed to convince the customer to make a purchase.

14. Advertisements are messages sent through the media.

15. Saatchi & Saatchi, J Walter Thompson, BMP DDB Needham, Ogilvy and Mather, BSB Dorland are examples of advertising agencies.

16. Any reasonable strapline is acceptable here, such as 'Once driven, forever smitten'.

17. Dealer loaders are inducements to dealers to make an order. They might include an extra case with every so many bought. For example, 13 for the price of 12 is a 'baker's dozen'.

18. Telemarketing involves using a database to contact prospects and customers by phone.

19. The ASA is an independent body that exercises control over all advertising except TV and radio. It draws up its own codes to ensure that advertisements are legal, decent, honest and truthful.

20. British Standards Institution.

Chapter 9

1. Agriculture, fishing, quarrying, mining, oil extraction and so on are all examples of primary production.

2. An organization's production department may face problems of coordination, labour problems, quality problems, machine breakdowns and so on.

3. Value analysis involves satisfying customers as economically as possible.

4. Transport, raw materials, integration with group, labour, housing, amenities, land, regional influences, safety, communications, government policies and grants and so on all affect location decisions.

5. Any two recent relevant examples are accepted.

6. Diseconomies of scale are human relations, decisions, coordination and external diseconomies.

7. This would be an example of backward vertical integration.

8. Features of flow production are that it is continuous, there is no waiting between batches, there are no leakages from the line and so on.

9. The benefits of CIM in manufacturing include design, ordering of materials, drives CNC tools, control system and so on.

10. Standardization involves controlling variety.

11. Difficulties in satisfying demands, loss of business, loss of goodwill, increased ordering and handling costs are all problems that can arise when stock levels are kept low.

12. JIT reduces holding costs, saves money, is more efficient and so on.

13. Method study involves looking at jobs to find ways of doing them more easily whereas work measurement records the times taken and rates at which jobs are completed under certain conditions.

14. Piece work, measured day work and others are motivational techniques for increasing output.

15. R&D will be influenced by the product life cycle of the product the new item is intended to replace.

16. Costs, quality, safety, productivity, use of plant, inventories and so on are all matters of concern to an operations manager.

17. Tertiary production involves services that are either commercial or direct.

18. Bulk-decreasing industries include those producing steel, beer, oil, chemicals and so on.

19. Investment appraisal, predictions of sales, financial evaluation and so on would be used to evaluate the financial potential of a major investment.

20. Product-led products are developed because costs appear to be low and material use appears to be efficient. Little regard is paid to the requirements of the market.

Chapter 10

1. Users of accounting information include managers, shareholders, suppliers, customers, providers of finance, the Inland Revenue, employees, advisers and brokers.

2. A trial balance is a list of balances extracted from the ledger.

3. Capital + Liabilities = Assets

4. Goodwill is an intangible fixed asset built up over the lifetime of a business, representing its reputation and client base. It is normally only shown in books if a business transfers ownership.

5. The cash cycle reflects the changing nature of current assets. For example,

cash buys stocks, stocks are sold to create debtors and, when debtors pay, they create cash, which can, again, be used to buy stocks.

6. Stocks are valued at cost or net realizable value if this is lower. This is considered prudent as profit is not assumed until a sale has actually taken place.

7. The opening stock value is £5050 and the sales are £8950.

8. Liquidity ratios include the following:

   • current or working capital ratio: ratio of current assets to current liabilities;
   • acid-test ratio/quick ratio/liquidity ratio: ratio of current assets less stocks to current liabilities;
   • debt collection period: debtors over average daily sales;
   • period of credit taken from suppliers: creditors over average daily purchases.

9. SSAPs are Statements of Standard Accounting Practice. SSAP2 refers to the four accounting concepts designed to underlie accounts, such as going concern, consistency, accruals, prudence. The purpose of SSAPs is to provide a true and fair view of a business' position.

10. In an appropriation account, profits may be allocated to taxation, dividends, reserves or kept as a profit and loss balance (retained profit).

11. A gross profit to sales ratio might indicate increases in the costs of raw materials, stock losses, cash losses or a need to review pricing policies.

12. The debt collection period is 36 days.

13. Stock turnover could provide an indication of efficiency. It may enable comparisons to be made with competitors, time periods and other industries.

14. If a company is too highly geared, it may have difficulty meeting interest payments, reduce a business' ability to borrow further, reduce profitability and so on.

15. Historical cost is entry cost that is then reduced over a period by depreciation.

16. FIFO and LIFO are both methods of stock valuation. FIFO makes the assumption that the stocks are valued in the order in which they were delivered, so the stocks that have been held longest will be assumed to have been issued first. This provides a slightly higher valuation than other methods. LIFO assumes that recent deliveries are issued before earlier ones and this tends to undervalue stocks.

17. The reducing balance method allocates higher depreciation costs in the earlier life of the asset.

18. Accounting is an information system that processes business data so that interested parties have the means to understand how well their business is performing. It involves recording, analysing and then interpreting financial

information and providing it in a form that may be used as a basis for decision making.

19. The net profit to sales ratio divides net profit by sales.
20. Return on Capital Employed—the profit made as a result of the capital employed in the business.

Chapter 11

1. There is a direct relationship between interest rates and demand for loans. If rates increase, demand will go down.
2. Risk capital is the investment capital in a project that is designed to generate profit.
3. Further capital-raising opportunities, continuity, economies of scale, the possibility of improving the company's reputation and so on are all good reasons for a company wanting to become a PLC.
4. Ordinary shares, commonly known as equities, are fixed units of ownership. They provide a basis for sharing in the profits and carry voting rights. Preference shares are a less flexible form of share and the rights will vary. Holders have a preferential right to receive dividends and receive their dividends before ordinary shareholders. The dividends may be cumulative, participating or redeemable.
5. Dangers of issuing too much risk capital are that it may not be needed, profits have to be spread among more shareholders, it dilutes the ability to make decisions, it can be expensive to issue shares.
6. Corporation tax is charged on company profits.
7. A debenture is a loan, made at a fixed rate of interest that specifies the repayment period. It is transferable on the Stock Exchange.
8. Advantages of using loan capital can be that it is cheap to raise, inflation will benefit the borrower, interest rates are an expense and this is paid before profits are calculated.
9. Businesses use overdraft facilities for the purpose of short-term borrowing, easing cash flow problems and because it is flexible.
10. An organization should not hold too much cash because it is not generating income, it could be gaining interest elsewhere and, during an inflationary period, it will be falling in value.
11. Using ratios will enable an organization to use sensible liquidity ratios, such as working capital and acid-test. They will also improve the ways in which the cash and credit cycle is managed.
12. Average rate of return, payback, DCF—net present value, DCF—internal rate of return are all techniques for appraising capital.
13. Externalities go beyond the balance sheet and are sometimes known as spillover costs.
14. A social benefit would include benefits created by an organization for the

community, such as jobs, creation of skills and so on. Social costs would include all the negative effects generated by the organization, such as pollution, dereliction and so on.

15. Factoring is the provision of immediate payment against debtors by a specialist company.

16. The benefits of using DCF are that it calculates the return from an investment in real terms by taking into account the changing value of money in future years.

17. A creditor is someone or an organization a business owes money to. A debtor is someone or a company owing money to that organization. A creditor is created when you make a purchase. A debtor is created when you make a sale.

18. A business plan should include a description of the business, personnel, marketing information, cash flow forecasts, break-even information as well as any other information relevant to the future of the business.

19. Collateral is security held against a loan.

20. A rights issue might be raised because it is a cheap way of raising finance quickly, nothing has to be paid for six months and it goes to existing shareholders.

Chapter 12

1. Fixed costs do not vary with output, while variable costs increase in direct relation to output.

2. The telephone is a semi-variable cost as it will increase as more output is generated, but only as a small proportion of the new output. Electricity use in the office is also a semi-variable cost as it may go up when overtime is needed in order to meet an increase in the number of orders.

3. Marginal costs are the costs of producing extra units of output.

4. Average costs are total costs divided by the quantity produced.

5. The benefits of budgetary control include that it provides a way of controlling various parts of the business, it enables predictions to be made about future activities of events, it puts an onus on budgeted areas to perform in a particular way and so on.

6. Variance analysis enables comparisons to be made between actual events and predicted events.

7. Absorption costing involves calculating the unit cost and adding a margin of profit. It bears no relationship to volume or the ability to meet fixed costs.

8. Contribution is calculated by deducting variable costs from the selling price.

9. Break even is the unique point where a business makes no profit or loss.

10. The margin of safety is the difference between the profit and the break-even point.

11. Break-even analysis can be used to enable simple forecasts to be made, for

either the whole organization or for parts of an organization, it shows how each area can contribute towards the payment of fixed costs and so on.

12. Dangers of relying on break-even analysis are that, in reality, many fixed costs are likely to vary, it does not take into account capacity to cope with volume, variable costs and sales are unlikely to be linear, it only depicts short-term relationships and it is dependent on the accuracy of the information used.

13. External factors include economic, political and legal ones, as well as market influences, industrial relations problems and so on.

14. A cost centre is an area of a business that has a responsibility to supervise a budget.

15. Profits are made when sales exceed the break-even point.

16. An adverse variance occurs where the actual exceeds the budgeted figure.

17. The dangers of relying on a system of budgetary control are that it may not meet short-term needs, it may be inflexible, if actual results are too different to those predicted it may lose its significance as a form of control and so on.

18. It means that AFC will be spread over a larger output.

19. Examples of direct costs include direct labour, direct materials and other direct overheads.

20. A flexible budget is one that can be amended to cater for unexpected changes.

Chapter 13

1. Taylor believed that there was a single best way of carrying out a task. The purpose of scientific management was to find this way.

2. When the Hawthorne researchers carried out their work they found that, whatever changes they made, people seemed to work harder. The implication was that the human act of being studied acted as a great motivator for them to perform.

3. Job enrichment involves upgrading and enhancing particular jobs to make them more rewarding.

4. A flat rate of pay is a set amount of pay for a set number of hours.

5. This is a payment made as a percentage of sales made by a salesperson.

6. Job analysis is the process of examining jobs in order to identify the key requirements of each job.

7. A job description sets out how a particular employee will fit into an organization. It sets out what they will do, when and who they are accountable to.

8. The stages in the employment procession are: recruitment, selection, induction, training, transfers/promotion termination.

9. The advantages of internal recruitment rather than external recruitment are that it can be cheaper, saves time, you at least know what you are getting and the person involved knows how the organization works.

10. A private employment agency acts for both companies and jobseekers. It interviews and takes details of a large number of applicants. It then places these applicants with firms on its books requiring labour (often on a part-time basis) that the applicant is suited to. It takes commission from the companies.

11. Induction is the process of preparing a new recruit for work, 'showing them the ropes'.

12. It is important to make applicants aware of what a job entails because you do not want to lose recruits as soon as they are faced with the reality of their tasks after the expense you have gone to in recruiting them.

13. Ratios can be used to monitor the effectiveness of a selection process by controlling the cost of interviewing and monitoring the effectiveness of recruitment procedures.

14. Redundancy is the laying off of employees and the arrangements concerning this form of termination of employment, such as ensuring that redundancy pay and pension arrangements are adhered to.

15. Working strictly to the rule book often means implementing slowing down procedures. Blacking is refusing to handle or deal with particular operations, products or other groups of workers.

16. A general union is one that consists of groups from different industrial sectors and industries.

17. The shop steward represents shopfloor workers in plant bargaining with employers.

18. The main aims of trade unions are to secure improvements in pay, conditions, benefits, hours and holidays for their members and to resolve grievances.

19. Collective bargaining is the negotiation process that takes place between representatives of groups of employers and employees.

20. White-collar unions have grown faster than other unions because the service sector is the most rapidly growing part of the economy, while manufacturing employs far fewer people. Also, in the last 20 years, it has become widely acceptable for white-collar employees to join trade unions whereas previously they were considered to be for factory workers, labourers and so on.

Chapter 14

1. The four basic communication skills are listening, speaking, reading and writing.

2. Memos may be used as reminders, to send short messages, to communicate with selected people, to provide technical instructions and so on.

3. A formal report should include a title page, a table of contents, terms of

reference, procedure, findings, conclusion, recommendations, signature and index.

4. A PC is a personal computer, normally compatible with a wide variety of software.

5. A spreadsheet is a computer program for a large grid or matrix of cells that may be used for mathematical solutions. It is a financial tool and may be used to generate graphics, to organize cash flow, to look at 'what might happen if' situations and so on.

6. The benefits of using databases include, storage of information, sorting of information and easy retrieval of information, among others.

7. DTP is a Desktop publishing package.

8. The uses of word processing include inserting text, amending text, searching for words, producing different type styles, saving text and so on.

9. An expert system would use all available human knowledge and provide a sound basis for decision making.

10. A network will link a number of personal computers so that access to information and software may be shared.

11. The benefits of E-Mail include that there is access wherever there is a telephone line, that it can be used to communicate quickly with different levels of employees, its low cost, that it may be quicker than traditional services, that it saves on paper generation and it may be considered more secure.

12. Systems analysis is the process of investigating ways in which computers might best be used to benefit their users.

13. The services someone who travels extensively may require are radiophones, telephone credit cards, business information services, fax machines and so on.

14. A fax machine works rather like a photocopier but transmits diagrams, pictures and documents in the form of digital signals via the telephone network.

15. Confravision links selected places with sound and vision.

16. Satellites may be used for in-house satellite employee television systems; transferring data between different parts of the world; transmission of voice, pictures, text and so on.

17. Homeworking is now possible because of the tools of IT. It saves on time spent travelling, saves on travel costs. Individuals may be able to access information and communicate as easily from their homes as from an office.

18. Project planning packages can be used to plan and monitor a project consisting of a number of activities.

19. Any relevant software package and description is acceptable.

20. The dangers of depending on IT include the possibility of losing information, breakdowns, repairs, it may be expensive to keep up to date and so on.

Chapter 15

1. Opportunity cost is the cost of an alternative forfeited. Any reasonable answer accepted.

2. The four functions of money are as a medium of exchange, unit of account, store of value and a standard for deferred payments.

3. High interest rates squeeze credit and cause a fall in bank lending. Low rates will lead to an increase in bank lending.

4. Government economic objectives may include growth, stable prices, full employment, balance of payments equilibrium and balanced economic growth.

5. Merit goods, such as education and roads, benefit those who use them as well as other members of society.

6. British Gas and British Rail are monopolies.

7. The Public Sector Borrowing Requirement exists where there is a budget deficit and is the amount the government must borrow to finance planned expenditure.

8. The multiplier will reflect the impact of an injection into the economic system. For example, if £20m is injected and, through various periods, £100m of spending is generated, the multiplier will be 5.

9. Structural unemployment results from the long-term decline of a particular industry.

10. The dangers of inflation can be changes in the distribution of income, effects on expectations, pay claims, investment and international competitiveness.

11. The General Agreement on Tariffs and Trade was founded to promote and develop trade worldwide without any barriers or restrictions.

12. Invisible exports from the UK are tourism, dividends, banking services, insurance services, transfers and so on.

13. Benefits of revaluation are more received for each unit exported and that it will stop prices of imports going up. The danger is that it may reduce international competitiveness and indirectly cause balance of payments problems.

14. The benefits of the Single Market include free trade, larger home market, no bureaucratic restrictions, that it is easier to trade, there are the same conditions in all the markets and so on.

15. Fiscal policy is government policy using the budget as a prime instrument of influence.

16. International trade takes place because of comparative advantage, absolute advantage, the fact that we are not self-sufficient, it provides us with a wider variety of resources, it improves specialization and economies of scale, it improves our links with other countries and so on.

17. A current account deficit means that total exports, including visibles and invisibles, are less than the total imports of visibles and invisibles.

18. Cost–push inflation occurs when rising costs push up prices.
19. The accelerator principle is that when there is a small change in the production of a consumer good, there is a much larger change in investment in capital goods. The construction industry is, therefore, affected much more by recessions and downturns in trade cycles than, say, the supermarket chains.
20. Direct taxes are levied on income or earnings. Indirect taxes are levied on expenditure. Examples of direct taxes include income tax, corporation tax and inheritance tax. Indirect taxes are VAT, licences and customs duties, for example.

Chapter 16

1. An externality is a spillover cost of a business activity. A papermill may, for example, pollute a local river as a result of letting waste chemicals run off.
2. A private benefit is that which gives a return to a particular individual or group, such as the money earned by the ice-cream seller at a football match. A private cost is a cost to an individual or group, such as the cost of buying in the ice-creams from the wholesaler.
3. A pressure group is an organized body of people who try to exert an influence on the activities of others regarding a particular subject or cause.
4. Shelter (action for the homeless), Greenpeace (action for the planet and environment), Save our Schools campaign (a local action group to fight the closure of local schools) are all organized pressure groups.
5. Consumers are an important pressure group because they have the ultimate sanction—not to purchase. Producers must respond to this pressure to stay in business.
6. Wealth is a stock of valuables, money or possessions or combination of these that has been accrued over a period of time. Income is a flow of new earnings in a given time period (such as annual income).
7. Noise, water, air and the food chain are main types of pollution.
8. A boycott occurs when consumers refuse to buy particular items or from particular sellers.
9. A non-renewable resource is one that, once it is used up, cannot be replaced.
10. We describe resources as being non-renewable when they cannot be replaced even over a very long period of time, if ever, such as iron ore, oil and such—even vegetation can be irreparably damaged.
11. Business ethics are generally acceptable rules of conduct, relating to what is right and wrong.
12. Insufficient testing of products may mean that they fail to meet standards when they are put to test properly. Many drugs, for example, have caused terrible side-effects.
13. The duty of care is that, from now on, companies generating waste will have

to dispose of it lawfully or ensure that anyone handling it on their behalf does so. They must also ensure that any third party taking the waste knows exactly what it contains and is equipped to dispose of it according to the law.

14. Integrated Pollution Control means that, instead of organizations dealing with several pollution control bodies, they are now responsible to the Pollution Inspectorate, which is responsible for *all* types of pollution caused at a particular site.

15. Underemployment occurs when people have jobs but the jobs do not engage the talents and skills of a person on a full-time basis. In other words, a lot of hours at work are wasted just filling time. Clearly this leads to low pay and wasted resources.

16. Dereliction leads to wasted resources and to dangerous sites that are a hazard to children among others. It is also unsightly.

17. Taxing companies according to the quantity of pollution they create and the cost of clearing up after them, subsidizing firms to produce less and therefore less pollution, bans and fines on the polluters—these have all been suggested as possible strategies for controlling and reducing pollution.

18. The environment is everything that surrounds a particular individual, group or organization: 'Environment to each must be, all that is, that isn't me!'

19. The absorption of acid-based chemicals into the water cycle, which, when it falls as rain, damages the natural environment because of its acid content.

20. Social costs include all costs to society of a particular course of action (they include all private costs to individuals and groups).

The answers to the integrated case analyses

Case Study 1

1. This is intended to provide a comfortable introduction to the paper. Students can score up to 2 marks for explaining a particular type of risk, such as financial risk (that revenues may not cover outgoings in the short period), selling risk (that demand may not meet expectations), personal risk (that time taken in organizing the venture may detract from home life and so on). Maximum of 4.

2. For the first part, 1 mark for stating that real changes account for inflation, 2 marks for indicating that calculations can be made from a base year, 3 marks for giving appropriate formula and 4–5 marks for a table and/or other appropriate calculation, such as:

Total sales at current prices	45 624	54 706	62 970
Total sales at 1984 prices	53 299	54 706	54 804

For, the second part, that the numbers fell (1 mark).

For the third part, 1 mark for stating that Robin was able to disregard the Newark data, 2–4 marks for showing understanding of *why* Robin felt the off-High Street location could not be compared with a High Street one, 5–6 marks for developing the argument to explore other reasons for Robin's feelings that he was going to be successful.

3. One mark for each component, 1 mark for a brief description and 1 mark for an explanation of its importance, for example:

   - details of the business—name and address of the business, detailed description of the product or service being offered, how and where it will be produced, who is likely to buy it and in what quantities—this provides a thumbnail sketch for outsiders such as banks who then have a clearer, contextual picture of the business;
   - organization of the business—this should state whether the enterprise will take the form of sole trader, partnership, company or cooperative—this gives outsiders a feel for the legal status of the company and who is involved in running it.
   - cash flow—this should give all the expected incomings and outgoings for the first year—cash flow predictions give a picture of whether incomings will exceed outgoings.

4. For the first part, 1 mark for showing understanding that payback shows how quickly the investment cost can be repaid, 2 marks for showing that the initial outlay was £55 000 and that profits are £25 000 a year and 3 marks for showing the above and concluding that payback will be within 3 years.

   For the second part, 2 marks for giving a definition of ROCE:

   $$\frac{\text{Operating profit}}{\text{Net assets}} \times \frac{100}{1}$$

   Also, 3–4 marks for showing that the operating profit was £25 000 and the net assets were £100 000, so that the ROCE was 25 per cent.

   For the third part, 1–2 marks for showing that the ROCE gives an indication of the effectiveness of Robin's applications of his capital, 3–4 marks for the inference of opportunity cost, that Robin should be evaluating this use of capital in terms of alternatives sacrificed, 5–6 for an exploration of at least 1 alternative use of capital and 7–8 marks for all of the above plus an evaluation of the success of the opportunity taken in the light of the opportunities foregone.

5. For the first part, 1 mark for each cost plus an explanation of why cost is thus categorized within the context of a cinema, for example that the fixed costs include council tax paid to the local authority, which is a contribution to local government and is a set annual charge or that the variable costs include tickets supplied to customers, which varies with the number of seats sold and so on.

   For the second part, 1 mark for showing that attention needs to be given to monitoring fixed costs, 2–4 marks for showing how fixed costs can be controlled, such as by minimizing outstanding debts by ploughing back profits to cut interest charges; 1 mark for showing that attention needs also to be given to monitoring variable costs, up to 3 marks for each exploration of how a particular variable cost can be minimized, such as, rather than employing two attendants to supervise two screens, he can adjust his programme schedules so that one attendant can serve *both*, thus cutting labour costs.

For the third part, 2 marks for the answer 250, 1 mark for the provision of the appropriate formula, graph or whatever and 2 marks for accurate working out.

Fourth, up to 5 marks for each appropriate pricing policy described (maximum of 10): for example, Robin could lower his prices, hoping that elastic demand for the product would mean that sales would expand, more than proportionately and more than the price fall, or, alternatively, Robin could raise his prices, hoping that inelastic demand for the product would mean that sales would fall, less than proportionately and less than the price rise.

6. Appropriate definitions of primary and secondary data will receive 1–2 marks and 3–5 marks for arguing effectively for one source rather than another. For example, there is unlikely to have been any specific local research into the demands of cinema consumers, so Robin's needs are more likely to be served by his own enquiries.

In the second part of this question, 1 mark would be given for an appropriate question and a further mark would be given for an explanation of why it is important. An example of a good question would be 'What age group is most likely to attend?' because then Robin could supply appropriate entertainment (maximum of 12 marks).

7. For describing the two indicators, 1–3 marks, plus 4–6 marks for supporting them with valid reasons as to why they are better.

8. There are up to 3 marks for each valid argument. Such a one would be that, by showing films aimed at the 18–24-year-old age range, he is likely to maximize his audiences or that, by providing comfortable conditions, such as leg room, he is likely to get repeat orders (maximum 15).

For the second part of this question, there is 1 mark for showing an understanding of the external environment, 2–4 marks for identifying the major components of the external environment and 5–6 marks for relating these components to the Paragon and showing how they can inhibit success.

Case Study 2

1. This question is designed to enable students to get to grips with the case. They can score up to 2 marks for each function, (maximum 4) and the functions include:

- breaking bulk—buying in volume from organizations and selling in smaller units;
- warehousing—manufacturers do not have to keep finished goods and they can respond quickly to the requirements of the market;
- transport costs—the system is simplified by using wholesalers and costs are cut;
- credit facilities—for business customers either through trade credit or finance facilities.

2. There are 2 marks available for each well-described benefit of the Single Market (maximum 4). Benefits are:

- large market of more than 320 million consumers with few trade impediments;
- standards and safety of all products will be controlled by common policies;
- they can tender for work from public bodies in the Single Market on the basis of fair competition;
- greater freedom to choose financial services from a larger market;
- no permits and restrictions on providing transport facilities overseas.

3. For the first question regarding diversification, 2 marks for indicating that this involves branching out into other activities.

   The second part requires a lengthy, structured answer. Expected answers would include:

- *primary research*—2 marks for a definition and description;
- this would involve some form of sampling of customers or potential customers—1 mark for mentioning sampling and 1 mark for an example of a type of sampling, such as random, quota, systematic or cluster.
- primary research would be to identify needs of customers—1 mark—and see if the location matched the needs—1 mark; (marks could be switched to match any good point that refers to the benefits of collecting primary data);
- *secondary research*—2 marks for a definition and description;
- for saying the type of information that could be collected by means of secondary research, 2 marks—for example, marketing information (from an agency), government statistics (population/economy and so on) and standard industrial classification information—1 mark each, too, for sources of secondary data, such as newspapers DTI or CSO and so on (maximum 2).

4. For the first part, for saying to locate at the lowest cost location, 2 marks.
   For the second part, 1 mark for each factor and 1 mark for each description (maximum 12). Factors likely to appear include transport costs, integration with group, labour, housing, raw materials, communications, amenities, land, regional advantages, government influences and so on.

For the third part, 1 mark for each advantage extracted from the study (maximum 4).

5. For the first part, 2 marks for each suitably described inducement, such as monetary rewards, non-monetary rewards, job satisfaction, commission and so on (maximum 4).

For the second part, 2 marks for each suitable contrast given (maximum 8). Suitable contrasts include that an:

- internal candidate will understand the systems and require a shorter training period;
- organization will not be disrupted by a newcomer who might have unsuitable ideas;
- internal promotion acts as a motivator;
- outside appointment may be a risk.

6. For the first part, 2 marks for each suitable source of finance (maximum 4). These might include, share issue, profit retention, bank loan, membership of USM, venture capital and so on.

For the second part, 2 marks for each correctly calculated appraisal (maximum 6). The correct responses are as follows:

- 46.5 per cent;
- Year 3;
- £355 265.

For the third part, 2 marks for a suitable explanation, which is that overtrading involves an organization financing operational activities without having the working capital to sustain such activities.

For the fourth part, 2 marks for each suitable explanation (maximum of 4). The proposals may:

- involve holding large amounts of stock;
- involve taking on more creditors;
- cause a need to take on short-term debts;
- cause them to deal with new creditors where creditworthiness is not known.

For the fifth part, 2 marks for each action (maximum of 8). These might include:

- improved management of the cash cycle;
- employment of a credit controller;
- constant review of stock levels;
- rent out surplus space at new site;
- use of cash budgeting;
- use of overdraft or factoring services where necessary.

7. There are 2 marks for each well-explained point about high interest rates (maximum 4). These might be along the lines of, with high interest rates, highly geared businesses will suffer, there is little incentive to expand, it is difficult to compete on equal terms with organizations in low-interest markets, changes in rates may upset plans and so on.

    Equally, there are 2 marks for each well-explained point about high exchange rates (maximum 4). For instance, high exchange rates will make goods expensive overseas, they may not then be competitive, they may have to compete simply in parts of the market rather than for volume sales and have to compete on quality.

8. For the first part of the question, there are 2 marks for an appropriate definition of social costs. Such a definition would be that social costs are the undesirable effects of an activity such as pollution, dereliction and so on.

    For the second part, there are 2 marks for each sensible suggestion as to what EPL could do about each social cost (maximum 6). For example, they could do little about congestion on the A1, although massive improvements are soon to begin. They ought to analyse traffic flows to discover which routes might provide minimum inconvenience. Waste requirements would have to be carefully researched. The costs of installing an incinerator might have to be investigated.

9. Answers to this question would vary depending on the prominence of each of these issues at the time of undertaking the study.

    For the first part, 1 mark would be given for the response to each issue (maximum 4) if it is shown that the candidate clearly understands the topicality of each issue.

    For the second part, 1 mark for each response (maximum 4) if they show a brief understanding of the effects of each. For example:

    -   junk mail—if mail-order businesses, due to the abuse of direct mail, lose consumer confidence, setting up a second warehouse might not be a good idea;
    -   accounting standards—these will not affect proposals unless different proposals are introduced for larger businesses;
    -   single currency—this may have a considerable number of benefits for trading in the Single Market;
    -   demographic time bomb—due to hit in 1996, this may affect proposals if EPL then encounter problems recruiting in Darlington.

Index